Closer
to GOD
Each Day

Closer to GOD
Each Day

365 Devotions for Everyday Living

JOYCE MEYER

NEW YORK BOSTON NASHVILLE

Unless otherwise noted, Scriptures are taken from *The Amplified Bible* (AMP). *The Amplified Bible*, copyright © 1965, 1987 by The Zondervan Corporation. *The Amplified New* copyright © 1954, 1958, 1987 by The Lockman Foundation. Used by permission.

Scripture quotations marked (KJV) are taken from the King James Version of the Bible.

Scripture quotations marked (NASB) are taken from *The New American Standard Bible*®, copyright © 1960, 1962, 1963, 1968, 1972, 1975, 1977, 1995 by The Lockman Foundation. Used by permission.

Scripture quotations marked (NIV) are taken from the *Holy Bible: New International Version*®, copyright © 1973, 1978, 1984 by International Bible Society. Used by permission of Zondervan Publishing House. All rights reserved.

Scripture quotations marked (NKJV) are taken from the *New King James Version*. Copyright © 1979, 1980, 1982 by Thomas Nelson, Inc., Publishers.

Scripture quotations marked (NLT) are taken from the *Holy Bible*, New Living Translation, copyright © 1996. Used by permission of Tyndale House Publishers, Inc., Wheaton, Illinois 60189. All rights reserved.

FaithWords
Hachette Book Group
1290 Avenue of the Americas
New York, New York 10104

www.faithwords.com

Printed in the United States of America

RRD-C

First Edition: October 2015
10 9 8 7 6 5 4 3 2 1

FaithWords is a division of Hachette Book Group, Inc.
The FaithWords name and logo are trademarks of Hachette Book Group, Inc.

The Hachette Speakers Bureau provides a wide range of authors for speaking events. To find out more, go to www.hachettespeakersbureau.com or call (866) 376-6591.

The publisher is not responsible for websites (or their content) that are not owned by the publisher.

Library of Congress Cataloging-in-Publication Data

Meyer, Joyce, 1943-
    Closer to God each day : 365 devotions for everyday living / Joyce Meyer.
        pages cm
    ISBN 978-1-4555-1736-7 (hardcover)—ISBN 978-1-4555-3629-0 (hardcover large print)—ISBN 978-1-4789-6035-5 (audio cd)—ISBN 978-1-4789-0832-6 (audio playaway)—ISBN 978-1-4789-6036-2 (audio download)—ISBN 978-1-4555-1735-0 (ebook)   1. Devotional calendars.   I. Title.
    BV4811.M443 2015
    242'.2—dc23
                                        2015028605

Simple, Believing Prayer

And when you pray, do not heap up phrases (multiply words, repeating the same ones over and over) as the Gentiles do, for they think they will be heard for their much speaking.

MATTHEW 6:7

I was dissatisfied with my prayer life for many years. I was committed to praying every morning, but I always felt something was missing. I finally asked God what was wrong, and He responded in my heart by saying, "Joyce, you don't feel that your prayers are good enough." I wasn't enjoying prayer because I had no confidence that my prayers were acceptable.

Too often we get caught up in our own works concerning prayer. Sometimes we try to pray so long, loud, or fancy that we lose sight of the fact that prayer is really just conversation with God. The length or loudness or eloquence of our prayer is not the issue. The only important elements to prayer are the sincerity of our hearts and a confidence that God hears and will answer us.

We can be confident that even if we simply say, "God help me," He hears and will answer. We can depend on God to be faithful to do what we have asked Him to do as long as our request is in accordance with His will.

Simple, believing prayer comes straight out of the heart and goes straight to the heart of God.

I Will Not Quit

I have strength for all things in Christ Who empowers me
[I am ready for anything and equal to anything through Him
Who infuses inner strength into me; I am self-sufficient in
Christ's sufficiency].   PHILIPPIANS 4:13

So often, someone will come to me for advice and prayer, and when I tell them what the Word of God says, or what I think the Holy Spirit is saying, their response is, "I know that's right; God has been showing me the same thing. But, Joyce, it's just too hard." This is one of the most commonly expressed excuses I hear from people.

When I initially started reading in the Word of God about how I could become more like Jesus, and then compared it to where I was, I also said, "I want to do things Your way, God, but it is so hard." God graciously showed me this is a lie the enemy tries to inject into our minds to get us to give up. But God's commandments are never too difficult for us to follow if we do them through Christ's strength.

Walking in obedience to God is not too hard because He has given us His Spirit to work in us powerfully and to help us in all He has asked of us (John 14:16). He is in us and with us all the time to enable us to do what we cannot do, and to do with ease what would be hard without Him!

Things get hard when we try to do them independently without leaning on and relying on God's grace.

Expect to Receive

And therefore the Lord [earnestly] waits [expecting, looking, and longing] to be gracious to you; and therefore He lifts Himself up, that He may have mercy on you and show loving-kindness to you. For the Lord is a God of justice. Blessed (happy, fortunate, to be envied) are all those who [earnestly] wait for Him, who expect and look and long for Him [for His victory, His favor, His love, His peace, His joy, and His matchless, unbroken companionship]!

ISAIAH 30:18

I want you to get this firmly into your heart: You can think about what you think about! So many people's problems are rooted in thinking patterns that end up producing the problems they experience. Remember that your actions are the direct result of your thoughts. And although the enemy offers wrong thinking to everyone, you don't need to accept his offer.

Isaiah 30:18 has become one of my favorite scriptures. If you will meditate on it, it will begin to bring you great hope...and great power. In it, God is saying that He is looking for someone to be gracious (good) to, but it cannot be someone with a sour attitude and a negative mind. It must be someone who is expecting for God to be good to him or her.

The more you change your mind for the better, the more your life will also change for the better. When you begin to see God's plan for you in your thinking, you will begin to walk in it.

The mind is the leader or forerunner of all attitudes and actions. You can always expect good things from God!

By Your Fruit

Even so, every healthy (sound) tree bears good fruit [worthy of admiration], but the sickly (decaying, worthless) tree bears bad (worthless) fruit.   MATTHEW 7:17

The fruit in our lives (our behavior) comes from somewhere. A person who is angry is that way for a reason. His reaction is the bad fruit of a bad tree with bad roots. It is important for us to take a close and honest look at our fruit as well as our roots.

In my own life, there was a lot of bad fruit. I experienced regular bouts of depression, negativity, self-pity, a quick temper, and the chip-on-the-shoulder syndrome. I was harsh, rigid, legalistic, and judgmental. I held grudges and was fearful.

I worked hard at trying to correct it. Yet it seemed that no matter what kind of bad behavior I tried to get rid of, two or three others popped up somewhere else like weeds. I was not getting to the hidden root of the problem, and it would not die.

If this scenario sounds familiar to you, it may be that you have unresolved issues in your life that need to be searched out and removed so that everything can be made fresh and new. Don't run away. If God can change me, He certainly can change you.

Rotten fruit comes from rotten roots; good fruit comes from good roots.

Receive God's Love

. . . God's love has been poured out in our hearts through the Holy Spirit Who has been given to us.   ROMANS 5:5

The Bible teaches us that the love of God has been poured out in our hearts by the Holy Spirit Who has been given to us. That simply means that when the Lord, in the person of the Holy Spirit, comes to dwell in our heart because of our faith in His Son Jesus Christ, He brings love with Him, because God is love (1 John 4:8).

It's important to ask what we are doing with the love of God that has been freely given to us. Are we rejecting it because we don't think we are valuable enough to be loved? Do we believe God is like other people who have rejected and hurt us? Or are we receiving His love by faith, believing that He is greater than our failures and weaknesses?

With God's help, we can love ourselves—not in a selfish, self-centered way that produces a lifestyle of self-indulgence, but in a balanced, godly way, a way that simply affirms God's creation as essentially good and right.

God's plan is this: for us to receive His love, love ourselves in a godly way, generously love Him in return, and then love all the people who come into our lives.

———————

When God reaches out to love us, He is attempting to start a cycle that will bless not only us but also many others.

God Is for You

What then shall we say to [all] this? If God is for us, who [can be]
against us? [Who can be our foe, if God is on our side?]

ROMANS 8:31

God is a big God; nothing is impossible with Him. We have nothing to fear from our enemies because none of them are as great as our God.

God is for us; He is on our side. The devil has one position— he is against us. But God is over us, under us, through us, for us, and He surrounds us. Of whom, then, should we be afraid?

So like Mount Zion, we should never be moved because God is all around us. And if that wasn't enough, I saved the best until last: He is in us, and He said that He will never leave us or forsake us

Salvation is our most awesome blessing from God, and we have been given the Helper, the Holy Spirit Himself, to empower us to be like Jesus. God has blessings and spiritual power in abundance for us. He is powerful and mighty and able to do what we can never do on our own.

God desires that we let the Holy Spirit flow through us in power to show people His love and to help people with His gifts. It all centers in Him.

God chooses the weak and foolish things of this world,
on purpose, so that people may look at them and say,
"It has to be God!"

Putting Your Trust in the Right Place

Some trust in and boast of chariots and some of horses, but we will trust in and boast of the name of the Lord our God.

PSALM 20:7

There are many facets of faith. The most brilliant facet, however, is trust! Trust is something we have, and we decide what to do with it. We decide in whom or in what to put our trust.

Where have you placed your trust? Is your trust in your job, employer, bank account, or friends? Perhaps your trust is in yourself, your past record of successes, education, natural talents, or possessions. All of these are temporal, subject to change. Only the Lord changes not. He alone is the Rock that cannot be moved.

As children of God, we can have the assurance that God will deliver us in current troubles, just as He delivered us in the past. We can then take our trust and put it in the right place, which is in God alone.

Trust is not upset, because it has entered into God's rest. Trust is not confused, because it has no need to lean on its own understanding. Trust does not give up or panic. Trust believes that God is good and that He works all things out for good!

Choose to place your trust in God. It pays marvelous dividends.

The Power of Being Positive

For as he thinks in his heart, so is he.   PROVERBS 23:7

Many years ago, I was an extremely negative person. My whole philosophy was this: "If you don't expect anything good to happen, then you won't be disappointed when it doesn't." So many devastating things had happened to me over the years, I was afraid to believe anything good might happen to me. Since my thoughts were all negative, so was my mouth; therefore, so was my life.

Perhaps you're like I was. You're avoiding hope to protect yourself from being hurt. This type of behavior sets up a negative lifestyle. Everything becomes negative because your thoughts are negative.

When I really began to study the Word and to trust God to restore me, one of the first things I realized was that the negativism had to go. And the longer I serve God, the more I realize the tremendous power in being positive in my thoughts and words.

Our actions are a direct result of our thoughts. A negative mind will result in a negative life. But if we renew our mind according to God's Word, we will, as Romans 12:2 promises, prove in our experience "the good and acceptable and perfect will of God."

It is a life-changing exercise to line up our thoughts with God's thoughts.

How to Pray without Ceasing

*Pray at all times (on every occasion, in every season) in the
Spirit, with all [manner of] prayer and entreaty. To that end
keep alert and watch with strong purpose and perseverance,
interceding in behalf of all the saints (God's consecrated people).*

EPHESIANS 6:18

Most believers are pretty familiar with the King James Version of
1 Thessalonians 5:17. It says, "Pray without ceasing."

I used to wonder, *Lord, how can I ever get to the place that I am able
to pray without ceasing?* To me the phrase "without ceasing" meant
nonstop, without ever quitting. I couldn't see how that was possible.

Now I have a better understanding of what Paul was saying.
He meant that prayer should be like breathing, something we do
continually but often unconsciously. Our physical bodies require
breathing. Likewise, our spiritual life is designed to be nurtured and
sustained by continual prayer.

The problem is that because of legalistic, religious thinking we
have the mistaken idea that if we don't keep up a certain schedule of
prayer we are missing the mark. If we become too "religious" about
prayer, thinking we must do it for a certain amount of time because
that is how someone else does it, we will bring condemnation on
ourselves. The important lesson about prayer is not the posture or
the time or place, but learning to pray your way through the day.
Pray in faith, at all times, in every place.

**It is the Holy Spirit Who will lead you into a life of
consistent prayer.**

Tell Yourself the Truth

Behold, You desire truth in the inner being; make me therefore to know wisdom in my inmost heart.   PSALM 51:6

God wants us to face the truth in our inmost being, then perhaps confess it in an appropriate manner to the right person. And sometimes we're the ones who need to hear the truth the most.

When people come to me for help in this area, I often tell them, "Go and look at yourself in the mirror and confess the problem to yourself." Being honest with yourself sets you free!

If, for instance, your problem is that your parents did not love you as a child and you are resentful and bitter, face the facts as a reality once and for all. Look at yourself in the mirror and say, "My parents did not love me, and perhaps they never will. But God loves me, and that is enough!"

You don't have to be one of those people who spends their life trying to get something they'll never have. If you have let the fact that you were unloved ruin your life thus far, don't let it claim the rest of your life. You can do what David did. Confess to yourself: "Although my father and my mother have forsaken me, yet the Lord will take me up [adopt me as His child]" (Psalm 27:10).

Whatever the problem may be that is bothering you, face it, consider confessing it to a trusted confidant, then admit it to yourself in your inmost being.

Admitting the truth causes the past to lose its grip on us.

Step Out and Take a Chance

But Jesus looked at them and said, With men this is impossible,
but all things are possible with God.   MATTHEW 19:26

Many people I meet want to start at point A in their Christian life,
blink their eyes twice, and be at point Z. Many of them are frustrated
about not knowing what their gifts are or what God has called them
to do with their life. Some of them are so afraid of failing and making
mistakes that it keeps them from stepping out.

We all have undeveloped potential, but we will never see it manifested until we believe that we can do whatever God says we can do
in His Word. Unless we step out in faith, believing that with God
nothing is impossible, He cannot do the work in us that He wants to
do to develop our potential. It takes our cooperation and willingness
through faith, determination, obedience, and hard work to develop
what He has put in us.

Nobody can be determined for us, but we can be determined
for ourselves. If we are not determined, the devil will steal from us
everything we have. I encourage you to give your potential some
form by doing something with it. You will never find what you are
capable of doing if you never try anything. Don't be afraid to step out
into what you believe God is leading you to do. When you step out,
you will find you are capable of great things.

Be bold, be brave, and be all you can be!

Overcoming a Poor Self-Image

*God said, Let Us [Father, Son, and Holy Spirit] make mankind in
Our image, after Our likeness...*   GENESIS 1:26

Second Samuel nine tells the story of Mephibosheth, the grand-
son of King Saul and the son of Jonathan. Crippled as a youth,
Mephibosheth had a poor self-image. Instead of seeing himself as
the rightful heir to his father's and grandfather's legacy, he saw himself as someone who would be rejected.

When David sent for Mephibosheth, he fell down before the king
and displayed fear. David told him not to fear, that he intended to
show Mephibosheth kindness because of David's covenant with Jonathan. Mephibosheth's initial response is an important example of
the kind of poor self-image we all need to overcome.

A poor self-image causes us to operate in fear instead of faith. We
look at what is wrong with us instead of what is right with Jesus. He
has taken our wrongs and given us His righteousness (2 Corinthians
5:21). We can joyfully walk in the reality of that truth.

I love the end of the story. David blessed Mephibosheth for Jonathan's sake. He gave him servants and land and provided for all of
his needs. God will bless us for Jesus' sake!

We can all relate Mephibosheth's lameness to our own weaknesses. We may also fellowship and eat with our King Jesus—
despite our faults and weaknesses.

**We have a covenant with God, sealed and ratified in the
blood of Jesus Christ.**

Winning the Warfare Within

For we are not wrestling with flesh and blood [contending only with physical opponents], but against . . . this present darkness, against the spirit forces of wickedness in the heavenly (supernatural) sphere.   EPHESIANS 6:12

Satan wars against us and one of his tactics is to make us feel bad about ourselves. He reminds us of all our failures and weaknesses, but we need to remember that God knows all about us and He loves us anyway.

We fight many battles, but probably the greatest battle we fight is the one with ourselves. We may struggle with feeling that we should have accomplished more in life than we have; we may feel we've failed in many ways. We can't change anything by being frustrated and struggling within. Only God can change us as we trust in Him. He will fight our battles and win. Our part is to believe, cooperate with Him, and follow the leading of the Holy Spirit.

It is difficult to get to the place where we can be honest with ourselves about our sins and failures, our inabilities and fallibilities, and yet still know that we are seen as being right with God because of what Jesus did for us when He died for us and rose from the dead. If you are at war within yourself, knowing you are the righteousness of God in Christ is a tremendous key to tapping into peace and spiritual power.

———————

We can be changed as we worship and behold God—not as we look at ourselves, adding up our many flaws.

Enjoying the Journey

But Martha [overly occupied and too busy] was distracted with much serving; and she came up to Him and said, Lord, is it nothing to You that my sister has left me to serve alone? ...

LUKE 10:40

I believe that life should be a celebration. Far too many believers don't even enjoy life, let alone celebrate it. Many people truly love Jesus Christ and are on their way to heaven, but very few are enjoying the trip. For many years I was one of those people ... I was like Martha!

Martha was busy doing what I used to do, running around trying to make everything perfect in order to impress God and everyone else. I complicated my relationship with the Lord because I had a legalistic approach to righteousness. I only felt good about myself when I was accomplishing something. And I resented people like Mary, who enjoyed themselves. I thought they should be working like I was working.

My problem was that I was all Martha and no Mary. I loved Jesus, but I had not learned about the simple life He desired me to live. The answer, I discovered, was rooted in faith, discovering what it means to sit at the feet of Jesus, listen to His words, and trust God with all my heart and soul.

———————

If you want to enjoy life, learn to live in balance. Work, worship, play, and rest. All work, with nothing else, produces a person who lives a complicated, complex, joyless life.

Authority Through Prayer

I will give you the keys of the kingdom of heaven; and whatever
you bind (declare to be improper and unlawful) on earth must be
what is already bound in heaven; and whatever you loose (declare
lawful) on earth must be what is already loosed in heaven.

MATTHEW 16:19

Since we are not only physical creatures but spiritual beings as well,
we are able to stand in the physical realm and affect the spiritual
realm. This is a very definite privilege and advantage. We can go
into the spiritual realm through prayer and bring about action that
will cause change in a situation. "God is a Spirit..." (John 4:24), and
every answer we need to every situation is with Him.

Jesus told Peter that He would give him the keys to the kingdom
of heaven. All keys unlock doors, and I believe those keys (at least in
part) can represent various types of prayer. Jesus went on to teach
Peter about the power of binding and loosing, which operates on the
same spiritual principle.

The power of binding and loosing is exercised in prayer. When
you and I pray about deliverance from some bondage in our lives
or in the life of another, we are, in effect, binding that problem and
loosing an answer. The act of prayer binds evil and looses good.

Jesus has given us the power and authority to use
the keys of the kingdom to bring to pass the will of
God on earth.

All Things Work Together for Good

We are assured and know that [God being a partner in their labor] all things work together and are [fitting into a plan] for good to and for those who love God and are called according to [His] design and purpose.   ROMANS 8:28

The apostle Paul does not say that all things are good, but he does say that all things *work together for good.*

Let's say you get in your car, and it won't start. There are two ways you can look at the situation. You can say, "I knew it! It never fails. My plans always flop." Or you can say, "Well, it looks as though I can't leave right now. I'll go later when the car is fixed. In the meantime, I believe this change in plans is going to work out for my good. There is probably some reason I need to be at home today, so I'm going to enjoy my time here."

Paul also tells us in Romans 12:16 to "readily adjust yourself to [people, things]." The idea is that we must learn to become the kind of person who plans things but who doesn't get upset if that plan doesn't work out.

The choice is ours. Any time we don't get what we want, our feelings will rise up and try to get us into self-pity and a negative attitude. Or we can adjust to the situation and go ahead and enjoy what God has for us no matter what happens.

The pathway to freedom from negativity begins when we face the problem and believe God will work good out of it.

Closer
to GOD
Each Day

each day you will be encouraged and strengthened by the truths, promises, and scriptures on each page. No matter what situation you are facing, I pray that each and every day you will be reminded that God loves you, He has a great plan for your life, and He is closer than you think.

—*Joyce Meyer*

Introduction

As I read through the Word of God, one of the most encouraging things I see is that God desires to be in a close relationship with His people. From the very first chapters in the Garden of Eden to the last pages of Revelation, we see God reaching out to His people in order that we might live in intimate fellowship with Him.

Too many people today think of God as distant, uncaring, and out-of-reach. At best, they assume He is uninterested in them; at worst, they fear He is angry with them. But this isn't the God we see in Scripture. The Bible shows us that God is present in our circumstances. God spoke to Moses. He strengthened David. He provided for Ruth. He chose Mary. He walked with the disciples. He wept over Jerusalem. He forgave the thief on the cross. He gave Peter a second chance. He sent the Holy Spirit.

God isn't removed from your daily life. He sees what you're going through, and He wants to help you every step of the way.

That's why I've written this daily devotional. My desire is that

Come close to God and He will come close to you.

JAMES 4:8

The Root of Rejection

May Christ through your faith [actually] dwell (settle down, abide, make His permanent home) in your hearts! May you be rooted deep in love and founded securely on love.

EPHESIANS 3:17

Rejection starts as a seed that is planted in our lives through different things that happen to us. God loves and accepts us, but the devil steals that truth from us by making us think we're rejected so we feel rejected and unloved. When this happens, it affects every area of our lives. It becomes a tree with many branches that all bear bad fruit.

Whatever you are rooted in will determine the fruit in your life—good or bad. If you are rooted in rejection, abuse, shame, guilt, or a poor self-image—if you are rooted in thinking, *Something is wrong with me!*—your "tree" will bear depression, negativism, a lack of confidence, anger, hostility, a controlling spirit, judgmentalism, hatred, and self-pity. If you are rooted in Jesus and in His love, then you can relax and know you are loved and valuable. You can know that God sees you as *right* through your faith in Jesus.

All the areas of your life that are out of order can be reconciled through Jesus and the work that He has done on the cross. It happened to me, and God can do it for you.

Here is the good news—you can be delivered from the power of rejection!

Change Is a Good Thing

But we all, with unveiled face, beholding as in a mirror the glory
of the Lord, are being transformed into the same image from
glory to glory, just as by the Spirit of the Lord.

2 CORINTHIANS 3:18 NKJV

I want to grow and see change, and I am sure you do also. I want to see changes in my behavior. I want to see regular progress. For example, I want more stability; I want to walk in a greater measure of love and all the other fruit of the Spirit. I want to be kind and good to others, even if I don't feel good or am not having a particularly good day. Even when things are coming against me and things aren't working out the way I'd like, I still want to display the character of Jesus Christ.

Through the power of the Holy Spirit within us, we are able to be joyful, nice, and kind, even when things are not going our way. We are able to stay calm when everything around us seems topsy-turvy, when everything seems to be conspiring against us to cause us to lose our patience and get angry and upset.

The key for me has been to finally learn that God changes me through His grace, not through my struggles to change myself. I suffered many years of wrestling with myself before I discovered God's power to change me within—little by little.

**This is how God changes us: He reveals something to us
and then waits until we decide to trust Him with it before
He works His character into that area of our lives.**

Only Jesus

*In [this] freedom Christ has made us free [and completely
liberated us]; stand fast then, and do not be hampered and held
ensnared and submit again to a yoke of slavery [which you have
once put off].*   GALATIANS 5:1

Jesus came to this world and paid for our sins, taking our punishment upon Himself. He became our substitute, paid the debt we owed, at no cost to us. He did all this freely because of His great love, grace, and mercy.

Jesus inherited all the Father has to give and tells us that we are joint heirs with Him by virtue of our faith. He has provided the way for our complete victory both here and hereafter. He has conquered, and we get the reward without paying the price. We are more than conquerors.

How much simpler could it be? The Gospel is wonderfully uncomplicated.

Complication is the work of Satan. He hates simplicity because he knows the power and the joy that our faith brings. Whenever your relationship with God becomes complex, return to the simplicity of believing like a little child. Jesus said, "only believe" and you will see the glory of God (John 11:40).

Return to and celebrate the simplicity of your faith in Jesus alone.

———————

Believing is so much simpler than not believing.

A New Day

*Therefore if any person is [ingrafted] in Christ (the Messiah) he
is a new creation (a new creature altogether); the old [previous
moral and spiritual condition] has passed away. Behold, the fresh
and new has come!*   2 CORINTHIANS 5:17

As "a new creation," you don't have to allow the old things that happened to you to keep affecting your new life in Christ. You are a new creature with a new life in Christ. You can have your mind renewed according to the Word of God. Good things are going to happen to you!

Begin to think positively about your life. That doesn't mean that you can get anything you want by just thinking about it. God has a perfect plan for each of us, and we can't control Him with our thoughts and words. But it's important for us to think and speak in agreement with His will and plan for us.

If you don't have any idea what God's will is for you at this point, you can begin by thinking, *Well, I don't know God's plan, but I know He loves me. Whatever He does will be good, and I'll be blessed.*

God has begun a good work in you and He will bring it to completion (Philippians 1:6). So even when you feel discouraged because you are not making progress quickly, always remember that God is working in you and He will never leave you or forsake you.

**Jesus will set you free to enjoy the good things in life.
Trust God to renew your mind with His Word!**

The Habit of Prayer

Now Peter and John were going up to the temple at the hour of prayer . . .
                                                                 ACTS 3:1

Many people feel vaguely guilty about their prayer life because they compare themselves to others. God is a creative God and wants each person to have his or her own individual prayer life. Your prayer life doesn't have to be just like anyone else's.

Yes, there are proven principles of prayer that you can follow. As we see in Acts 3:1, the early disciples set aside certain hours of the day when they would go to a designated place to pray. That is good self-discipline, but that should be the start of learning to pray and not the finish. We can discipline ourselves to establish a prayer schedule that is individually suited to us, but we can also learn to pray without ceasing. That means to pray at all times, in all places, with all kinds of prayer. I like to say, "Pray your way through the day." Let prayer become like breathing, something you do with ease and without effort.

We never have to "wait" to pray. Each time you see a need or think of anything you need help with, pray right away! Prayer is talking to God, and since He is everywhere, we can talk to Him all the time.

God wants prayer to be a daily, regular part of our lives.

Accepting the Person God Made You to Be

*. . . [Do not merely desire peaceful relations with God, with your fellowmen, **and with yourself,** but pursue, go after them!]*

1 PETER 3:11 (EMPHASIS ADDED)

During my years of ministry, I have discovered that a lot of people really don't like themselves. They reject themselves! This is a much bigger problem than we think. It is certainly not God's will for His children to be against themselves. Rather, it is a part of Satan's attempt to make us miserable and prevent us from loving others.

If we don't get along with ourselves, we won't get along with other people. When we reject ourselves, it may seem to us that others reject us as well. Relationships are a vital part of our lives. How we feel about ourselves is a determining factor in our success in life and in relationships. We need to be totally confident in Christ!

Our self-image is the inner picture we carry of ourselves. If what we see is not healthy, not true to the Scripture, we will suffer from fear, insecurity, and various misconceptions about ourselves.

God loves us and He wants us to accept His love. And because of His love, we can love ourselves in a healthy, balanced way. We are God's children—people who are loved, accepted, and by His grace improving daily!

Jesus came to bring restoration to our lives. One of the things He came to restore is a healthy, balanced self-image.

Hang Tough

And let us not lose heart and grow weary and faint in acting nobly
and doing right, for in due time and at the appointed season we
shall reap, if we do not loosen and relax our courage and faint.

GALATIANS 6:9

In Galatians 6:9, "losing heart" and "fainting" refer to giving up in
the mind. The Holy Spirit tells us not to give up in our mind, because
if we hold on, we will eventually reap good things.

Think about Jesus. Immediately after being baptized and filled
with the Holy Spirit, He was led into the wilderness to be tested
and tried by the devil. He did not complain and become discouraged and depressed. He did not think or speak negatively. He did not
become confused trying to figure out why this had to happen. He
went through each test victoriously (Luke 4:1–13).

Can you imagine Jesus traveling around the country, talking with
His disciples about how hard everything was? Can you picture Him
discussing how difficult the Cross was going to be...or how He
dreaded the things ahead...or how frustrating it was to have no roof
over His head, no bed to sleep in at night?

Jesus drew strength from His heavenly Father and came out in
victory. We have His Spirit dwelling in us and the strength available
to make it through whatever we are facing.

We can handle our situations the same way Jesus did—
by being mentally prepared through "victory thinking"
rather than "give-up thinking."

Be Positive

. . . But we have the mind of Christ (the Messiah) and do hold the thoughts (feelings and purposes) of His heart.

1 CORINTHIANS 2:16

Ever since I started keeping my mind in a positive pattern, I can't stand the feeling of being negative. I've seen so many good changes in my life since I've been delivered from a negative mind that now I'm opposed to anything negative.

Here's what I suggest if you've struggled with staying positive: Ask the Holy Spirit to convict you each time you start to get negative. This is part of His work. John 16:7–8 teaches us that the Holy Spirit will convict us of sin and convince us of righteousness. When the conviction comes, ask God to help you. Don't think you can handle this yourself. Lean on Him.

Being positive does not mean that we don't face reality. The Bible says to do all the crisis demands and then stand firmly in your place (Ephesians 6:13). Our place is "in Christ," and in Him we can always be hopeful and positive because nothing is too hard for Him. Jesus was always positive and full of faith. We have His mind in us, and with His help, we can do the same things.

———————

Think like God thinks, so you can be the person He wants you to be and have all that He wants you to have.

Childlike Trust

... Whoever will humble himself therefore and become like this
little child [trusting, lowly, loving, forgiving] is greatest in the
kingdom of heaven.   MATTHEW 18:4

Children believe what they are told. Some people say children are
gullible, but children are not gullible, they are trusting. It is a child's
nature to trust unless he has experienced something that teaches
him otherwise. And another thing we all know about children is that
they can literally enjoy just about anything. They can even turn work
into a game!

Our heavenly Father desires for us to come to Him as children.
He wants us to know that we are His precious little ones and to put
our complete faith in Him to care for us. He wants us to take His
hand and lean on Him, continually asking for His help. Everything
that God calls us to do, He will help us do. He is ready, waiting, and
more than willing. We can come humbly as little children—sincere,
unpretentious, honest, open—knowing that without Him, we can
do nothing.

As God's children, we were never intended to live in bondage of
any kind. We can experience glorious freedom and liberty—freedom
to enjoy all that God has given us in Christ. He has given us life, and
our goal should be to enjoy it.

Seek to become and remain childlike with all the
simplicity of a child. It will enhance the quality of your
life in the most amazing way.

The Beauty of Dependence

I am the Vine; you are the branches. Whoever lives in Me and
I in him bears much (abundant) fruit. However, apart from Me
[cut off from vital union with Me] you can do nothing.

JOHN 15:5

I was a very independent person, and God began speaking John 15:5 to me early in my walk with Him. When we come into God's power, we get to experience complete dependence upon Him. Faith involves us leaning entirely on God, trusting His power, wisdom, and goodness.

We are to lean on, rely on, and entirely depend on Him, taking all the weight off of ourselves and putting it all on Him. Without God's help, we can't change anything in our lives. We can't change ourselves, our spouse, our family, our friends, or our circumstances. Truly, apart from Him we cannot do anything.

We forfeit peace and joy when we fail to let God be God. We try to figure out things we have no business even touching with our minds. Nothing is too hard or too wonderful for God, but many things are too hard for us. With the help and leading of the Holy Spirit, we can grow to the place where we rest in the truth that we know the One Who knows all the answers, even when we don't... and we can trust Him!

It is so liberating to say, "Lord, I don't know what to do,
and even if I did, I couldn't do it. But my eyes are on You.
I am going to wait and watch You work it all out."

Prayer Produces Peace

Do not be anxious about anything, but in every situation, by prayer and petition, with thanksgiving, present your requests to God. And the peace of God, which transcends all understanding, will guard your hearts and your minds in Christ Jesus.

PHILIPPIANS 4:6–7 NIV

In this passage, the apostle Paul does not say, "Pray and worry." Instead, he is saying "Pray and don't worry." Why are we to pray and not worry? Because prayer is an important way we *cast our care* upon the Lord. Prayer is what opens the door for God to work in our lives and the lives of other people.

When the devil tries to give us something to worry about, we can turn and give that care to God. If we pray about something and then keep on worrying about it, we are mixing a positive and a negative. The two cancel each other out so that we end up right back where we started—at zero.

Prayer is a positive force; worry is a negative force. The Lord has shown me the reason many people operate at zero power spiritually is that they cancel out their positive prayer power by giving in to the negative power of worry.

As long as we are worrying, we are not trusting God. It is only by trusting, by having faith and confidence in the Lord, that we are able to enter into His rest and enjoy the peace that transcends all understanding.

You can make a decision now to cast all your cares on the Lord and begin to trust Him to take care of you.

God Has a Plan

For I know the thoughts and plans that I have for you, says the
Lord, thoughts and plans for welfare and peace and not for evil, to
give you hope in your final outcome.   JEREMIAH 29:11

If you have a poor self-image, it has already adversely affected your past, but you can be healed and not allow the past to repeat itself. I encourage you to let go of what lies behind, including any negative ways you have felt about yourself, and press on toward the things God has in store for you.

God has a good plan and a purpose for each of us and a specific way and perfect time to bring it to pass, but not all of us experience it. Many times we live far below the standard that God intends for us to enjoy.

For years I did not exercise my rights and privileges as a child of God. Although I was a Christian and believed I would go to heaven when I died, I did not know that anything could be done about my past, present, or future. I had a poor self-image, and it affected my day-to-day living, as well as my outlook for the future.

Today, you can accept God's love for you and make His love the basis for your love and acceptance of yourself. Receive His affirmation, knowing that you are changing and becoming all that He desires you to be. Then start enjoying yourself—where you are—on your way to full spiritual maturity.

Let God be God in your life. Put Him in the driver's seat.
He knows what He is doing.

When You Feel Stressed

And the peace of God, which transcends all understanding, will
guard your hearts and your minds in Christ Jesus.

PHILIPPIANS 4:7 NIV

Years ago, I went to a doctor because I was constantly sick. He told
me the symptoms were the result of being under stress. I wasn't getting enough sleep, and I was eating improperly, and pushing myself
too hard.

Stress is a normal part of everyone's life. God has created us to
withstand a certain amount of pressure and tension. The problem
comes when we push beyond our limitations and ignore the warn-
ings our body gives us when it hurts or is exhausted.

I urge you to take good care of yourself, because if you wear out
the body you have, you cannot go to a store and buy a new one. Many
of the things we do that give us stress overload are things we could
change if we would. Be honest with yourself about why you are doing
some of the things you do and let God help you prune off the ones
that are wearing you out and bearing no good fruit.

Peace is meant to be the normal condition for every believer in
Jesus Christ. He is the Prince of Peace, and in Jesus we find our own
inheritance of peace. It is a gift from the Holy Spirit, which He gives
as we live in obedience to His Word.

The peace Jesus gives operates in good times and bad.
His peace operates in the middle of a storm.

What Do You Think of Yourself?

There we saw the Nephilim [or giants], the sons of Anak,
who come from the giants; and we were in our own sight as
grasshoppers, and so we were in their sight.   NUMBERS 13:33

We read in Numbers 13 of how Moses sent twelve men to scout out the Promised Land to see if it was good or bad. Ten of the men came back with what the Bible refers to as "an evil report" (Numbers 13:32). They told Moses, *"The land is good, but there are giants in it!"* They also referred to themselves as "grasshoppers," meaning they believed they were insignificant and incapable of defeating the enemy.

The fear they had of the giants prevented God's people from entering the land that He had promised to give them. It wasn't really the giants that defeated these people; it was their poor self-image. They only saw the giants; they failed to see God, and they failed to believe that with God, they could do anything they needed to do.

Joshua and Caleb were the only ones who had a proper attitude. Caleb said to Moses and the people, *"Let us go up at once and possess it; we are well able to conquer it"* (Numbers 13:30). They had the attitude that God wanted them to have. They believed that with God, all things were possible.

God had a glorious future planned for all of the Israelites, just as He does for us, but only the ones with a proper attitude toward God and themselves will live in it and enjoy it.

God does not have a bad attitude toward you; don't have one toward yourself!

Set Your Mind and Keep It Set

And set your minds and keep them set on what is above
(the higher things), not on the things that are on the earth.

COLOSSIANS 3:2

We can have right and wrong mind-sets. The right ones benefit us, and the wrong ones hurt us and hinder our progress. With God's help we can set our minds in the right direction.

Some people see life negatively because they have experienced unhappy circumstances all their lives and can't imagine anything better. Then there are some people who see everything as negative simply because their personality leans in that direction. Whatever its cause, a negative outlook leaves a person miserable and unlikely to grow spiritually. To enjoy God's good plan for us, we need to be in agreement with Him, and He definitely is not negative!

With God's help and your hard work and determination, you can break negative mind-sets and old habits that are trying to keep you far from God. The devil doesn't want you to break through because he knows that if you do, you will enjoy your life and be a blessing to others. Your life will change, which will cause many other lives to change. If you set your mind in the right direction, it is going to bring you closer to God and allow you to fulfill your God-ordained destiny.

Expect good things to happen to you and through you!

Prayer Produces Rest

Come to Me, all you who labor and are heavy-laden and
overburdened, and I will cause you to rest. [I will ease and
relieve and refresh your souls.]   MATTHEW 11:28

If we are not at rest, we are not truly believing, because the fruit of believing is rest.

For many years of my life I would claim, "Oh, I'm believing God; I'm trusting the Lord." But I was not doing either of those things, because I was anxious, worried, irritable, and on edge most of the time.

Just as we can be involved in outward activity, we can be involved in inward activity. God wants us not only to enter into His rest in our body, He also wants us to enter into His rest in our soul.

To me, finding rest, relief, ease, refreshment, recreation, and blessed quiet for my soul means finding freedom from wrong mental activity. It means not having to live in the torment of reasoning, always trying to come up with an answer I don't have. I don't have to worry; instead, I can remain in a place of quiet peace and rest through prayer.

If we are truly believing God and trusting the Lord, we have entered into His rest. We have prayed and cast our care upon Him and are now abiding in the perfect peace of His daily presence.

You can speak His Word to your anxious mind just as Jesus spoke to the storm and said, "Peace, be still."

Believe

Jesus replied, This is the work (service) that God asks of you: that you believe . . .   JOHN 6:29

Little children usually automatically believe what their parents tell them, and that is how God wants us to be with Him. He wants us to believe what He says in His Word! Christians are often referred to as "believers," and believers should believe!

Are you a believing believer, or a doubtful believer? Simple childlike faith produces a lot of good fruit. For example, joy and peace are found in believing (Romans 15:13). Doubt, reasoning, worry, and fear produce all kinds of misery, but it all can be avoided by making a decision to believe the Word of God. Believe that something good is going to happen to you. Believe that when you repent, your sins are completely forgiven. Believe that God wants to meet all of your needs, that He loves you and is always willing to help you.

When we believe, then we can enter the rest of God and really enjoy each day of our lives. We can take life one day at a time and trust that our future is secure in God.

If you are going to doubt anything, doubt your doubts!

You Are Loved

And we know (understand, recognize, are conscious of, by observation and by experience) and believe (adhere to and put faith in and rely on) the love God cherishes for us. God is love, and he who dwells and continues in love dwells and continues in God, and God dwells and continues in him.   1 JOHN 4:16

We are created by God for love. Loving and being loved are what make life worth living. It gives life purpose and meaning. But if we have allowed sin and unforgiveness and the past to separate us from God's love, it will leave us love-starved and unhappy.

Many people cannot maintain healthy, lasting relationships because either they don't know how to receive love or they place an unbalanced demand on others to give them what only God can give. The resulting frustration can often lead to the ruin of marriages and the suffocation of friendships.

The Bible teaches us that God loves perfectly or unconditionally. His perfect love for us is not based on our perfection. God loves us because He wants to! God is love (1 John 4:8). Love is Who He is. God always loves; all you have to do is receive that love and live with confidence each day knowing that His love gives our lives purpose and meaning.

A revelation of God's perfect love for you can change your life and your walk with Him.

Waiting on God

Wait and hope for and expect the Lord; be brave and of good courage and let your heart be stout and enduring. Yes, wait for and hope for and expect the Lord.   PSALM 27:14

When we "wait" on God, we are not being lazy or passive, but we are actually being very active spiritually. We may not be "doing" anything, but we are trusting God to do what needs to be done. In effect, we are saying, "Lord, I will not try to do this in my own strength. I will wait on You to deliver me. And I'm going to enjoy my life while I wait for You."

Satan wants us to be frustrated from trying to solve our own problems. He hates our joy. He wants to see anything but joy, because the joy of the Lord is our strength (Nehemiah 8:10). Worry robs us of strength, but joy energizes us.

We are tempted to think we are not doing our part if we don't worry or try to figure out an answer to our problems, but this will prevent our deliverance rather than aid it. It is not irresponsible to enjoy life while we wait on God and expect Him to do what we don't know how to do!

Do not fear because the battle is not yours, but the Lord's.

Having a Ready Mind

These were more noble than those in Thessalonica, in that they received the word with all readiness of mind, and searched the scriptures daily, whether those things were so.

ACTS 17:11 KJV

The Bible says that we are to have a ready mind. That means we can have minds that are open to the will of God for us, whatever His will may be.

I once spoke with a young lady who experienced the sorrow of a broken engagement. She wanted the relationship to continue and was thinking, hoping, and believing that her former fiancé would feel the same way.

I advised her to have a "ready mind" in case it didn't work out that way. She asked, "Well, isn't that being negative?"

No, it isn't. Negativism would say, "My life is over. No one will ever want me. I'll be miserable forever."

Having a positive mind says, "I'm really sad this happened, but I'm going to trust God. I'm going to ask and believe for our relationship to be restored; but more than anything, I want God's perfect will. If it doesn't turn out the way I want, I'll survive, because Jesus lives in me. It may be hard, but I trust the Lord. I believe that in the end, everything will work out for the best."

Practice being positive in every situation that arises. God has promised to bring good out of whatever is taking place in your life at the moment.

Combating Fear with Prayer

So we take comfort and are encouraged and confidently and
boldly say, The Lord is my Helper; I will not be seized with
alarm [I will not fear or dread or be terrified]. What can man
do to me?   HEBREWS 13:6

Fear attacks everyone. It is the enemy's way of trying to prevent us
from enjoying the life Jesus died to give us. If we give in to fear and
if we give voice to it, we open the door for the enemy and close the
door to God.

But rather than give in to fear, we can learn to boldly confess that
God is our Helper, our Refuge, and our Stronghold.

The Bible teaches us to watch and pray. Matthew 26:41 says: "All
of you must keep awake (give strict attention, be cautious and active)
and watch and pray, that you may not come into temptation. The
spirit indeed is willing, but the flesh is weak."

The major reference in this passage is to watching ourselves and
the attacks that the enemy launches against our minds and our emotions. When these attacks are detected, we can pray immediately. It
is when we pray that power is released in our lives—not when we
think about praying later.

I encourage you to watch and pray about everything. I believe you
will find this decision to be one that will produce more joy and peace
for your everyday living.

––––––––––––

**In order to live in real victory, it is important that we
dedicate ourselves to prayer.**

Rest for the Weary

Do you not know that your body is the temple (the very sanctuary)
of the Holy Spirit Who lives within you, Whom you have received
[as a Gift] from God?   1 CORINTHIANS 6:19

The first key to overcoming stress is to recognize or admit we are
experiencing it, and look for the source of it. There was a time in my
life when I was constantly having headaches, backaches, stomach-
aches, neck aches, and all the other symptoms of stress, but I found
it very difficult to admit I was pushing too hard physically, mentally,
emotionally, and spiritually. I wanted to do all of the things I was
doing and wasn't willing to ask God what He wanted me to do. I was
afraid that He would lead me to give up something I wasn't ready to
give up yet.

Although the Lord gives power to the faint and weary, if you are
worn-out from continually exceeding your physical limitations, you
will have stress. Our bodies are the sanctuary (home) of God, and
we are in disobedience when we push ourselves past God-ordained
limitations and live in continual stress. We all have limits and we
need to recognize what they are and eliminate excess stress from
our lives.

If you wear out your body, you can't go to a department store and
purchase another one, so take care of the one you have!

Getting regular rest is one of the wisest things
you can do.

It's Your Choice

For we are God's [own] handiwork (His workmanship), recreated in Christ Jesus, [born anew] that we may do those good works which God predestined (planned beforehand) for us [taking paths which He prepared ahead of time], that we should walk in them [living the good life which He prearranged and made ready for us to live].   EPHESIANS 2:10

God has given you a wonderful gift: *free will.* God is offering you the opportunity to accept yourself as He created you to be, but you have a free will and can refuse to do so if you choose. To accept something means to view it as usual, proper, or right.

People who reject themselves do so because they cannot see themselves as proper or right. They only see their flaws and weaknesses, not their beauty and strength. This is an unbalanced attitude often instilled by authority figures in the past who focused on what was weak and wrong rather than what was strong and right.

In Amos 3:3, we read, *"Do two walk together except they make an appointment and have agreed?"* You can walk with God—you can be close to Him—when you decide to agree with Him. He says He loves you and accepts you; therefore, if you agree with Him, you no longer have to dislike or reject yourself.

When God created you, He created something wonderful.

Keep On Keeping On

Therefore, since Christ suffered in his body, arm yourselves also with the same attitude, because whoever suffers in the body is done with sin. As a result, they do not live the rest of their earthly lives for evil human desires, but rather for the will of God.

1 PETER 4:1–2 NIV

Peter's beautiful passage teaches us a secret concerning how to make it through difficult times and situations. Here is my rendition of these verses:

"Think about everything Jesus went through and how He endured suffering in order to do God's will, and it will help you make it through your difficulties. Arm yourselves for battle; prepare yourselves for it by thinking as Jesus did... 'I will patiently suffer rather than fail to please God.' For if you suffer, having the mind of Christ toward it, you will no longer be living just to please yourself, doing whatever is easy and running from all that is hard. But you will be able to live for what God wills and not by your feelings and carnal thoughts."

There are difficulties that we go through in life, but we also experience the joy of victory. Trials and tests will come, and God uses them to develop the potential He has put in you. Your part is to decide that you are never going to quit, no matter what, until you see the promises of God revealed in your life. There is one kind of person the devil can never defeat—one who is not a quitter.

———————

Keep on keeping on, and you'll get there.

Prayer Produces Patience and Hope

Moreover [let us also be full of joy now!] let us exult and
triumph in our troubles and rejoice in our sufferings, knowing
that pressure and affliction and hardship produce patient and
unswerving endurance. And endurance (fortitude) develops
maturity of character (approved faith and tried integrity).
And character [of this sort] produces [the habit of] joyful and
confident hope of eternal salvation.   ROMANS 5:3–4

It is easy to say, "Don't worry." But to actually do that requires experience with the faithfulness of God. When we trust God and then see and experience His faithfulness in our lives, it gives us great confidence to live without worry, fear, and anxiety.

That's why it is so important to continue to have faith and trust in God in the very midst of trials and tribulations. With God's help, we can steadfastly resist the temptation to give up and quit when the going gets rough. God uses those hard, trying times to build in us patience, endurance, and character that will eventually produce the habit of joyful and confident hope.

Always remember that when you are in a battle, you are gaining valuable experience that will benefit you in the future. You will more easily trust God when difficulty comes, and you will be able to testify to others regarding the goodness and faithfulness of God. If you are in a battle right now, you can let it defeat you or make you stronger! Make the right decision and let it help bring you into a deeper level of spiritual maturity.

We serve a God Who is so marvelous that He can work out things for our good that Satan intends for harm.

Faith and Grace

For by grace you have been saved through faith, and that not of yourselves; it is the gift of God, not of works, lest anyone should boast.   EPHESIANS 2:8–9 NKJV

It is wonderful to realize that salvation comes by the free grace of God and can be easily received through simple childlike faith. Thankfully, we don't have to work for our salvation because Jesus has already done all the work. We receive by faith alone! I believe the same way that we receive forgiveness of our sins and eternal life (salvation) is the same way that we should live out our daily lives. We should mix our faith with everything we do.

Faith is the leaning of the entire human personality on God in absolute trust and confidence in His power, wisdom, and goodness. When we go through life leaning on Him in absolutely everything, He will always guide us and give us the strength and ability to do whatever we need to do. The good news is that you never have to try to do things on your own! God has sent the Holy Spirit Who is your helper, so ask for and receive the help you need today and every day, and relax in God's love, mercy, and grace.

Trade all your fears, anxieties, and worries for simple faith and enjoy your day!

Forgiving Others

And become useful and helpful and kind to one another,
tenderhearted (compassionate, understanding, loving-hearted),
forgiving one another [readily and freely], as God in Christ
forgave you.   EPHESIANS 4:32

I once heard that medical studies indicate 75 percent of physical sickness is caused by emotional problems. And one of the greatest emotional problems people experience is guilt. They are refusing to relax and enjoy life because, after all, they feel they don't *deserve* to have a good time. So they live in a perpetual strain of regret and remorse. This kind of stress often makes people sick.

Two of the things that cause us to get all knotted up inside are meditating on all the negative things done to us by others, and the sinful and wrong things we have done. We have a hard time getting over what others have done to us, and we find it difficult to forget the mistakes we have made.

In my own life I had a choice to remain bitter, full of hatred and self-pity, resenting the people who had hurt me, or I could choose to follow God's path of forgiveness. This is the same choice you have today. I pray that you will forgive others and receive God's forgiveness for yourself. You will be healthier and happier if you do!

God's way is forgiveness.

Take Your Position

And Jehoshaphat bowed his head with his face to the ground, and all Judah and the inhabitants of Jerusalem fell down before the Lord, worshiping Him. 2 CHRONICLES 20:18

In 2 Chronicles 20:18, the king and the people of Judah bowed with their faces to the ground and worshipped when they heard the Lord's instruction. The position of worshipping God was helping them prepare for battle. If you are in a battle right now, I strongly urge you to trade all worry for worship. Kneeling in reverence before God, or other types of worship, is a battle position and a key to spiritual power.

To "praise" God has been defined as to ascribe to Him the glory due to His name. It is to talk about and sing out about the goodness, grace, and greatness of God. To "worship" has been defined as to give reverence to and to serve. Broadly, it may be regarded as the direct acknowledgment of God, of His nature, attributes, ways, and claims, whether by expressing your heart in praise and thanksgiving or by deed done in such an acknowledgment.

With God's help, we can learn to fight His way, not the world's way. Our battle position is one of worship, and this is a position that brings us closer to God. We fight every battle with a heart of praise and worship, believing that God will work in our life and circumstances.

As we worship the Lord, we release the emotional or mental burden that is weighing us down. It is swallowed up in the awesomeness of God.

The Power of Hope

[For Abraham, human reason for] hope being gone, hoped in faith that he should become the father of many nations, as he had been promised . . .

No unbelief or distrust made him waver (doubtingly question) concerning the promise of God, but he grew strong and was empowered by faith as he gave praise and glory to God.

ROMANS 4:18–20

In our ministry we want to help more people every year, and we believe God wants us to grow. But we also realize that if God has a different plan, and if we end our year with no growth, we cannot let that situation control our joy.

We believe *for* many things, but beyond them all, we believe *in* Someone. That Someone is Jesus. We don't always know what is going to happen. We just know it will always work out for our good!

It is reported that Abraham, after sizing up his situation (he didn't ignore the facts), considered the utter impotence of his own body and the barrenness of Sarah's womb. Although all human reason for hope was gone, he hoped in faith. *Abraham was very positive about a very negative situation!*

Hebrews 6:19 tells us that hope is the anchor of the soul. Hope is the force that keeps us steady in a time of trial. Don't ever stop hoping. Don't be afraid to hope. No one can promise that you'll never be disappointed. But you can always have hope and be positive.

Have hopeful expectation every day of your life.

Prudence

I, Wisdom [from God], make prudence my dwelling, and I find
out knowledge and discretion.   PROVERBS 8:12

A word you don't hear very much teaching about is "prudence." In the Scriptures "prudence" or "prudent" means being good stewards of the gifts God has given us to use. Those gifts include abilities, time, energy, strength, and health as well as material possessions. They include our bodies as well as our minds and spirits.

God has given each of us different gifts and grace according to how He wants us to use them. One person may be gifted to sing and does so in their local area, while another person's singing ability is known in most of the world. The Bible tells us to use our gifts according to the grace given to us (Romans 12:6).

Each of us would be wise to know how much we are able to handle, to be able to recognize when we are reaching "full capacity" or "overload." Instead of pushing ourselves into overload to please others, satisfy our own desires, or reach our personal goals, we can learn to listen to the Lord and obey Him. If we follow the Lord's leading, we will enjoy blessed lives.

We all experience stress and at times we feel the effects of it, but we should learn to manage it well. Ask God to show you areas in your life that could be changed to help you eliminate excess stress better.

―――――――――――

God is good, and He wants you to enjoy a peaceful life.

Self-Acceptance

For whom the Lord loves He corrects, even as a father corrects the son in whom he delights.   PROVERBS 3:12

Perhaps you have been struggling with accepting yourself. You see the areas in yourself where change is necessary. You desire to be like Jesus. Yet it is very difficult for you to think or say, "I accept myself." You feel that to do so would be to accept all that is wrong with you, but that is not the case. We can accept and embrace ourselves as God's unique creation, and still not like everything we do.

God will change us, but we cannot even begin the process of change until this issue of self-acceptance is settled in our individual lives. When we truly believe that God loves us unconditionally just as we are, then we will have a closeness to Him, and we will be willing to receive His correction, which is necessary for true change.

Change requires corrections—people who do not know they are loved have a very difficult time receiving correction. Correction is merely God giving us divine direction for our lives. He is guiding us to better things, but if we are insecure we will always feel condemned by correction instead of joyfully embracing it.

God does not approve of all of our actions, but He does love and approve of us as His beloved children.

Be patient with yourself. Keep pressing on and believe that you are changing every day.

Run Your Race

Wherefore seeing we also are compassed about with so great a cloud of witnesses, let us lay aside every weight, and the sin which doth so easily beset us, and let us run with patience the race that is set before us.   HEBREWS 12:1 KJV

If we are going to run our race in life, if we want to fulfill our destiny and do God's will, it is important that we lay aside every weight and sin and run the race with patience. In the days this verse was written, runners conditioned their bodies for a race just as we do today. But at the time of the race, they stripped off their clothing except for a loincloth, so that when they ran there would be nothing to hinder them. They also oiled their bodies with fine oils.

In our Christian life, we are called to remove anything that hinders us from running the race that God has set before us. It is essential to be well oiled, or anointed, with the Holy Spirit (often symbolized by oil) if we are going to win our race.

The devil has many ways to entangle us and prevent us from living in obedience to God's Word, developing an intimate relationship with Him. There are many distractions and requirements on our time. But with God's guidance, we can strip away the things that will hinder us. Keep your eyes on your goal and learn to say "no" to things that distract you and keep you from fulfilling your full potential.

Be determined that nothing is going to hinder you from fulfilling God's plan and purpose for your life.

Freedom from Self-Pity

There was a certain man there who had suffered with a deep-seated and lingering disorder for thirty-eight years.

When Jesus noticed him lying there [helpless], knowing that he had already been a long time in that condition, He said to him, Do you want to become well? [Are you really in earnest about getting well?]   JOHN 5:5–6

For many, many years, "Why me, God?" was the cry of my heart, and it filled my thoughts and affected my attitude daily. I lived in the wilderness of self-pity, and it was a problem for me, my family, and the plan of God for my life. I felt as though I was due something for the way I had been mistreated as a child, but I was looking to people to pay me back when I should have been looking to God.

When Jesus met the man who had been lying by the pool of Bethesda for thirty-eight years waiting for a miracle, He asked if he was serious about getting well. Many people would like a miracle, but like the man in our story, they are not willing to give up their blame and self-pity.

God wants to give us beauty for ashes, but we must be willing to let go of the ashes! That means giving up the self-pity, blame, and bitter attitudes. This day can be a new beginning for anyone who is willing to forget the past and truly follow Jesus!

We can be pitiful or powerful, but we can't be both.
Choose to give up self-pity to be free.

God's Way Is Not Too Hard

*When Pharaoh let the people go, God led them not by way of the
land of the Philistines, although that was nearer; for God said,
Lest the people change their purpose when they see war and
return to Egypt.*   EXODUS 13:17

God led the Children of Israel on a longer, harder route in the wilderness because He knew they were not ready for the battles they would face in order to possess the Promised Land. He needed to do a work in their lives first, teaching them Who He was and that they could not depend on themselves.

You can be assured that anywhere God leads you, He is able to keep you. He never allows more to come against us than we can bear. We do not have to live in a constant struggle if we learn to lean on Him continually for the strength we need.

If you know God has asked you to do something, don't back down because it gets hard. When things get hard, spend more time with Him, lean more on Him, and receive more grace from Him (Hebrews 4:16). Grace is the power of God coming to you at no cost, to do through you what you cannot do by yourself.

God knows that the easy way is not always the best way for us. That's why it is so important that we don't lose heart, grow weary, and faint.

———————

**Satan knows that if he can defeat us in our mind, he can
defeat us in our experience.**

The Power of Agreement

All of these with their minds in full agreement devoted themselves
steadfastly to prayer.   ACTS 1:14

Whenever believers are united in prayer, there is great power present. Jesus Himself said, "For wherever two or three are gathered (drawn together as My followers) in (into) My name, there I AM in the midst of them" (Matthew 18:20).

Throughout the book of Acts, we read that the people of God came together "with one accord" (Acts 2:1, 46; 4:24; 5:12; 15:25 KJV). And it was their united faith, their corporate agreement, and love that made their prayers so effective. They saw God move in mighty ways to confirm the truth of His Word as they gave testimony to their faith.

Living in agreement doesn't necessarily mean that we feel the exact same way about everything, but it does mean that we are committed to walking in love. We can respect someone's opinion even if we don't share it! Dave and I don't share the same opinions about many things, but we do live in peace and harmony and it gives us power in prayer.

In Philippians 2:2 we are told by the apostle Paul, "Fill up and complete my joy by living in harmony and being of the same mind and one in purpose..."

Prayer is a wonderful privilege, and one that we should exercise often. But in order to have good results, we should also strive to remove all disharmony and disunity from our lives.

Being in agreement is often more important than
being right!

Courage and Obedience

After these things, the word of the Lord came to Abram in a
vision, saying, Fear not, Abram, I am your Shield, your abundant
compensation, and your reward shall be exceedingly great.

GENESIS 15:1

In Genesis 12:1, God gave Abram a tall order. In so many words He
said, "Pack up and leave everyone you know and everything you are
comfortable with and go to a place I will show you."

If Abram had bowed his knee to doubt and uncertainty, the rest
of the story would never have come to pass. He would never have
experienced God as his Shield, his great compensation, and he
would never have received his exceedingly great reward.

In the same way, if Joshua had not overcome his fear and been
obedient to God's command to lead His people into the Promised
Land, neither he nor they would ever have enjoyed all that God had
planned and prepared for them.

There is power in God's Word to equip us to stop bowing our
knee in fearful uncertainty. We can do what God wants us to do,
even if we have to do it afraid. When we're intimidated by an obstacle, we can say: "Lord, strengthen me. This is what You have told
me to do, and with Your help I am going to do it, because it is Your
revealed will for me. I am determined that my life is not going to be
ruled by fear but by Your Word."

**God doesn't always deliver us "from" things; often He
walks us "through" them.**

The Purpose of Faith

... Be vigilant and cautious at all times; for that enemy of yours, the devil, roams around like a lion roaring [in fierce hunger], seeking someone to seize upon and devour.

Withstand him; be firm in faith [against his onset—rooted, established, strong, immovable, and determined] ...

I PETER 5:8–9

Oftentimes we make the mistake of trying to use faith to get to the place where there is total freedom from trouble. But the purpose of faith is not always to keep us from having trouble; it is often to carry us through trouble. If we never had any trouble, we wouldn't need any faith.

The temptation exists to run away from our problems, but the Lord says that we are to go through them. The good news is that He has promised that we will never have to go through them alone. He will always be there to help us in every way. He has said to us, "Fear not, for I am with you" (Isaiah 41:10).

In our daily experience, we can learn to stand our ground and effectively resist the devil. Learning to be stable in hard times is one of the best ways to get close to God and to press through any difficulty we may face. God is with you to help you, so don't give up!

The devil will give up when he sees that you are not going to give in.

Receive Your Forgiveness

I, even I, am He Who blots out and cancels your transgressions,
for My own sake, and I will not remember your sins.

ISAIAH 43:25

No matter what your problem or how bad you feel about yourself as a result of it, take this truth into your heart: God loves you. Jesus Christ gave His life that you might be forgiven, and He has given you a new life. God has given you a new family and new friends to love and accept and appreciate and support you. You are going to make it because of the One Who lives inside you and cares for you.

Repent of whatever sin it is that stands between you and Him and receive forgiveness. No matter what you may have done, say, "Lord, I did it, and it is a marvel to me to realize that You love me unconditionally, and that You forgive me. You have put my sins as far away from me as the east is from the west, and You remember them no more!" (Psalm 103:12.)

Once you have repented of your sins and received God's forgiveness, if you continue to drag them up to Him every time you go to Him in prayer, you are reminding Him of something He has not only *forgiven* but also actually *forgotten*.

———————

From this moment, stop punishing yourself for something that no longer exists.

How Long, Lord?

But those who wait for the Lord [who expect, look for, and hope in Him] shall change and renew their strength and power; they shall lift their wings and mount up [close to God] as eagles [mount up to the sun]; they shall run and not be weary, they shall walk and not faint or become tired.   ISAIAH 40:31

Waiting on God does not mean that we do nothing, while expecting God to do everything for us. To me it means that I wait, expecting God to give me direction if there is something He wants me to do, while also trusting Him to do what only He can do. Often as I have waited on God and put my trust in Him, He has shown me things that need to be adjusted in my behavior or attitude. You see, God doesn't merely want to change our circumstances, but He also wants to change us.

As we spend quiet time with God, He reveals things to us, and we are refreshed in His presence. Closeness and intimacy with God is one of our greatest privileges as His children. The more time we spend with Him, the more we are transformed into His image. Study God's Word and receive it as a personal letter from Him to you. It will both comfort and correct you. Wait on God with a trusting, expectant heart, and look forward to all the good things He has planned for you.

God will change you little by little each day, as you trust Him.

A Glad Heart

All the days of the desponding and afflicted are made evil [by anxious thoughts and forebodings], but he who has a glad heart has a continual feast [regardless of circumstances].

PROVERBS 15:15

An "evil foreboding" is a vague, threatening feeling that something bad is going to happen. There was a point when I realized that I had actually carried these feelings with me most of my life. In fact, I had been made miserable by evil thoughts and forebodings.

Perhaps you have these feelings as well. You have circumstances that are very difficult, but even when you don't you are still miserable because your thoughts are poisoning your outlook and robbing you of the ability to enjoy life and see good days.

Proverbs 15:15 promises you that these feelings need not remain. Faith's attitude is one of leaning on God, trusting and being confident in Him—it is joyful feasting on the expectancy of good. Rather than dreading something by anticipating that it will make you miserable, you can have faith that God will give you the power to enjoy it.

Your joy, peace, righteousness, and power are on the inside of you through the presence of the Holy Spirit. Don't let worry and anxiety rule in your life any longer. Expect God's help, blessing, and power in all that you do.

With the proper attitude, you can be energized to do mundane, everyday tasks with great joy.

Victory over Stress

...Now we serve not under [obedience to] the old code of written regulations, but [under obedience to the promptings] of the Spirit in newness [of life]. ROMANS 7:6

There are times in life when we have to deal with stress, but we can be on *top* of it, not *under* it. Through the Holy Spirit's guidance and power, we can handle our work and responsibilities with ease instead of stress. As we follow the promptings of the Spirit we will know how to handle each situation we encounter.

All of us have situations that come our way that we don't like. But with the power of God, we can go through those circumstances while also avoiding stress. The more we lean on, and trust in, God, the easier life is. Every situation in life is not "easy," but we can handle them with what I call "Holy Spirit Ease." In other words, God empowers us to do whatever we need to do through Him. He energizes us and helps us.

God will guide us, but we need to trust Him enough to follow His directions. He never gives us any advice that is not for our benefit and progress in life. God is leading you into a place of victory and triumph, not into a place of defeat. As you follow His lead, I believe you will experience less stress than ever before. He may prompt you not to do something you want to do, or to do something you don't want to do, but obedience to His leadership keeps us from taking wrong roads in life and wasting time and energy!

Simply obeying the promptings of the Holy Spirit will often relieve stress quickly.

How Can I Change?

Do not be conformed to this world (this age), [fashioned after and adapted to its external, superficial customs], but be transformed (changed) by the [entire] renewal of your mind . . .

ROMANS 12:2

Change does not come through struggle, human effort without God, frustration, self-hatred, self-rejection, guilt, worry, or works of the flesh. We are new creatures in Christ (2 Corinthians 5:17), and as such we all want to please God. We want to be what He wants us to be, and behave the way He wants us to behave, but in order for that to happen, we need to learn how to think like He thinks.

Change in your life comes as a result of having your mind renewed by the Word of God. As you agree with God and really believe that what He says is true, it gradually begins to manifest itself in you. You begin to think differently, then you begin to talk differently, and finally you begin to act differently. This is a process that develops in stages, but while it is taking place you can still have the attitude, "I'm okay, and I'm on my way!"

Enjoy yourself while you are changing. Enjoy where you are on the way to where you are going. Enjoy the journey! Don't waste all of your "now time" trying to rush into the future. Relax. Let God be God. Stop being so hard on yourself. Change comes little by little, but in that process you're getting closer to Him each day.

We can come to Jesus just as we are. He takes us "as is" and makes us what we ought to be.

Be Patient

But let endurance and steadfastness and patience have full play
and do a thorough work, so that you may be [people] perfectly and
fully developed [with no defects], lacking in nothing.

JAMES 1:4

James teaches us that we can rejoice when we find ourselves involved in difficult situations, knowing that God is trying our faith
to bring out patience. I have found that trials did eventually bring
out patience in me, but first they brought a lot of other junk to the
surface—such as pride, anger, rebellion, self-pity, complaining, and
many other things. It seems that these ungodly traits, with God's
help, need to be faced and dealt with because they hinder patience
as well as other good fruit like kindness, love, humility, and other
things.

The Bible talks about purification, sanctification, and sacrifice.
These are not popular words; nevertheless, these are things we go
through in order to become like Jesus in our character. God's desire
is to make us perfect, lacking in nothing. He wants us to ultimately
be filled with the fruits of righteousness, which usually requires us
to go through some difficulties that, although are unpleasant, do
eventually help us mature.

I struggled with the difficulties in my life for a long time until I
finally learned that God would work them out for good and use them
to help me in many ways. He simply wants you and me to surrender
and say, "I trust You, God. I believe when this difficulty is over, I will
be a better person than I was before it began!"

No matter what you are going through, trust God that
you are growing closer to Him each day!

God Changes People Through Prayer

First of all, then, I admonish and urge that petitions, prayers,
intercessions, and thanksgivings be offered on behalf of all men.
1 TIMOTHY 2:1

In Exodus 32, Moses interceded for the children of Israel so that the wrath of God would not destroy them. It's a stirring example that depicts how sincere prayer can change situations.

There are times when I find myself being led to pray for God to be merciful to a person, or to continue working with them and making the changes in them that are needed.

As Jesus told His disciples at Gethsemane, we can "watch and pray" (Matthew 26:41 KJV). We have the opportunity to pray for one another, not judge and criticize each other. God allows us to discern people's needs in order to be part of the answer, not part of the problem. Remember we are not the potter. God is, and we certainly don't know how to "fix" people. We cannot change people, but we can pray and watch Him work.

When people are hurting, even from their own poor choices, they often are blinded to the truth. We can pray for their eyes to be opened and for them to truly see the truth so it will set them free. People who are hurting need God to intervene in their lives, but if they don't know how to call on Him, we can stand in the gap between them and God as intercessors and see breakthrough as we pray.

We can do the praying and let God do the work.

Faith and Contentment

*. . . I have learned how to be content (satisfied to the point where
I am not disturbed or disquieted) in whatever state I am.*

PHILIPPIANS 4:11

The Bible teaches us to be content no matter what our circumstances
may be (Hebrews 13:5). We don't have to be upset about anything,
no matter what is happening. Instead, we can pray about it and tell
God our need. While we are waiting for Him to move, we can be
thankful for all that God has done for us already (Philippians 4:6).

I have discovered that the secret of being content is to ask God for
what we want, knowing that if it is right, He will bring it to pass at
the right time. And if it is not right, He will do something much better than what we asked for.

It is important that we learn to trust God completely if we ever
intend to enjoy peaceful living. We have the opportunity to meditate
on what God has done in our life instead of what we are still waiting
on Him to do.

God loves you. He is a good God Who wants to be close to you.
Be content knowing that His way is perfect, and He brings with Him
a great reward for those who trust in Him (Hebrews 10:35).

**God is working in secret, behind the scenes, even when it
looks as though nothing will ever change.**

Purchased by Jesus' Blood

In Him we have redemption (deliverance and salvation)
through His blood, the remission (forgiveness) of our offenses
(shortcomings and trespasses), in accordance with the riches and
the generosity of His gracious favor.

EPHESIANS 1:7

Say aloud to yourself, "I was bought and cleansed from sin with a price; purchased with a preciousness; paid for and made God's own."

You are delivered from sin and all the "death" it brings with it. Worry, anxiety, and fear are forms of death. Strife, bitterness, resentment, and unforgiveness are forms of death. The blood of Jesus is the only antidote for death.

Jesus' blood is precious before the Father and should be precious to us. A precious thing is something we protect, something we are careful with, and something we don't want to part with. The blood of Jesus is precious and it allows us to be close to our heavenly Father. His sacrifice lifted the veil between God and man, and now we have free access and an opportunity for closeness and intimacy with God (Hebrews 10:18–22).

The blood of Jesus cleanses us from sin and will continuously cleanse us (1 John 1:9). His blood is like a powerful cleansing agent. Just as our blood works to keep our bodies cleansed of all poison, the blood of Jesus continuously cleanses us from sin in all its forms and manifestations.

Have faith in the power of Jesus' blood to keep you continually cleansed from sin in all its forms and manifestations.

The Words You Speak

Death and life are in the power of the tongue, and they who
indulge in it shall eat the fruit of it [for death or life].

PROVERBS 18:21

The apostle Peter plainly tells us that enjoying life and seeing good days, and having a positive mind and mouth, are linked together. If we change our words, we can change our life!

Our mouth gives expression to what we think, feel, and want. Our minds tell us what to think, not necessarily what God thinks. Our wills tell us what we want, not what God wants. Our emotions tell us what we feel, not what God feels. As our soul is purified, it is trained to carry God's thoughts, desires, and feelings; then we will begin to speak life instead of death.

Your words, as reflections of your thoughts, have the power to bring blessing or destruction not only to your life but also to the lives of many others. In 1 Corinthians 2:16, the Word of God teaches us that we have the mind of Christ and that we hold the thoughts, feelings, and purposes of His heart. We don't manifest them all the time, but we are daily growing and being transformed into Christ's image. He that has begun a good work in us will complete it and bring it to its finish (Philippians 1:6). The closer we come to God, the quicker we will experience victory in our mind, mouth, moods, and bad attitudes.

No matter how far you have to go, I know you can change because I did. It took time and "heaping helpings" of the Holy Spirit, but it was worth it.

God Blesses Obedience

Now therefore, if you will obey My voice in truth and keep
My covenant, then you shall be My own peculiar possession and
treasure from among and above all peoples; for all the earth is
Mine.   EXODUS 19:5

God's grace and power are available for us to use. God enables us
or gives us an anointing of the Holy Spirit to do what *He* tells us to
do. Sometimes after He has prompted us to go another direction, we
still keep pressing on with our original plan. If we are doing something He has not approved, He is under no obligation to give us the
energy to do it. We are functioning in our own strength rather than
under the guidance of the Holy Spirit. Then we get so frustrated,
stressed, or burned out, we lose our self-control, simply by ignoring
the promptings of the Spirit.

Many people are stressed and burned out from going their own
way instead of God's way. They end up in stressful situations when
they go a different direction from the one God prompted. Then they
burn out in the midst of the disobedience and end up struggling to
finish what they started outside of God's direction, all the while beg-
ging God to bless them.

Thankfully, God is merciful, and He helps us in the midst of our
mistakes. But He is not going to give us strength and energy to dis-
obey Him. We can avoid many stressful situations simply by obeying
the Holy Spirit's promptings at all times.

More obedience always equals less stress!

Healing for Damaged Emotions

The Spirit of the Lord God is upon me, because the Lord has anointed and qualified me to preach the Gospel of good tidings to the meek, the poor, and afflicted; He has sent me to bind up and heal the brokenhearted, to proclaim liberty to the [physical and spiritual] captives and the opening of the prison and of the eyes to those who are bound.

ISAIAH 61:1

Emotional healing is an important topic, because our inner life is much more important than our outer life. Romans 14:17 lets us know that the kingdom of God is not meat and drink (not outward things), but it is righteousness, peace, and joy in the Holy Spirit (inner things). Also, Luke 17:21 says the kingdom of God is within you.

Because of the abuse I suffered as a child, I was an "emotional prisoner" for a long time, but God has healed and transformed me with His love. And He will do the same for you!

In Isaiah 61 the Lord said that He came to heal the brokenhearted. I believe that means those broken inside, those crushed and wounded inwardly. Jesus wants to lead you out of emotional devastation and into a place of health, wholeness, and closeness to God. Invite Him into every area of your heart and soul and let the healing work begin!

God will meet you wherever you are and help you get to where you need to be.

Wait on the Lord

For you have need of steadfast patience and endurance, so that you may perform and fully accomplish the will of God, and thus receive and carry away [and enjoy to the full] what is promised.

HEBREWS 10:36

There are multitudes of unhappy, unfulfilled Christians in the world simply because they are busy trying to make something happen, instead of waiting patiently for God to bring things to pass in His own time and His own way. We are in a hurry, but God isn't.

Humility says, "God knows best, and He will not be late!" Pride says, "I'm ready now. I'll make things happen my own way." A humble man waits patiently; he actually has a "reverential fear" of moving in the strength of his own flesh. Patience is the ability to keep a good attitude while waiting. But a proud man tries one thing after another, all to no avail. Pride is at the root of impatience.

Patience is a fruit of the Holy Spirit that manifests itself in a calm, positive attitude despite our life circumstances. Don't think you can solve all your problems or overcome difficulties on your own. As we humble ourselves under God's mighty hand, we begin to die to our own way and our own timing, and we become alive to God's will and way for us.

It is only through patience and endurance in faith that we receive the promises of God.

You Are the Place of Prayer

For we are fellow workmen (joint promoters, laborers together)
with and for God; you are God's garden and vineyard and field
under cultivation, [you are] God's building.

1 CORINTHIANS 3:9

Under the Old Covenant, the temple was the house of God, the place of prayer for His people, the children of Israel. The temple had three compartments, one of which was the Holy of Holies, and it held the presence of God! Amazingly, now our renewed and sanctified spirit is the place where His presence dwells!

Under the New Covenant, the apostle Paul tells us that God's presence is now a mystery revealed, which is of Christ in us, "the Hope of glory" (Colossians 1:27). Because of the union you now have with Christ, you can be close to God because you are God's living temple. You are indwelt by the Holy Spirit, a building still under construction, but nonetheless His house, His tabernacle. Paul goes to great length in encouraging us to live a holy life because we are the temple of God.

Whereas the children of Israel had to go to a specific place to offer their worship with detailed instructions, we have the incredible privilege of worshipping God anywhere and at any time. Therefore, we can be called a house of prayer.

We are always close to God because He dwells in us!

God Cares for You

Casting the whole of your care [all your anxieties, all your worries, all your concerns, once and for all] on Him, for He cares for you affectionately and cares about you watchfully.

1 PETER 5:7

Worry, anxiety, and care have no positive effect on our lives. They do not bring a solution to problems. They do not help us achieve good health, and they prevent our growth in the Word of God.

One of the ways that Satan steals the Word of God from our heart is through cares. The Bible says we are to cast our cares onto God, which is done by prayer. We cannot handle our own problems; we are not built for it. We are created by God to be dependent upon Him, to bring Him our challenges, and to allow Him to help us with them.

It is not wise to take the cares of life upon ourselves. Keeping our cares is a manifestation of pride. It shows that we think we can solve our own problems and that we don't need the Lord.

We show our humility by leaning on God. Worry, anxiety, and care are not manifestations of leaning on God, but they state by their mere existence that we are attempting to take care of ourselves.

Pray about everything and worry about nothing. You will enjoy life much more.

Worry is like rocking in a rocking chair: it keeps you busy and gets you nowhere!

Christlikeness

*For those whom He foreknew [of whom He was aware
and loved beforehand], He also destined from the beginning
[foreordaining them] to be molded into the image of His Son [and
share inwardly His likeness], that He might become the firstborn
among many brethren.*

ROMANS 8:29

The best goal a Christian can have is Christlikeness. Jesus is the
express image of the Father, and we are called to follow in His footsteps. He came as the Pioneer of our faith to show us by example
how we can live. We have the chance to behave with people the way
Jesus did. Our goal is not to see how successful we can be in business or how famous we can be. It is not prosperity, popularity, or
even building a big ministry, but to be transformed into the image of
Jesus Christ.

Spiritual maturity or Christlikeness cannot be obtained without
"dying to self." That simply means saying *yes* to God and *no* to ourselves when our will and God's are in opposition. Jesus told His disciples that if they wanted to follow Him, they would need to take up
their cross daily.

To follow Christ and become like Him, we choose to forget about
what we want—our plans, having our own way—and instead trust
Him to show us what His will is for us. His will always leads to deep
joy and satisfaction.

You are God's Ambassador—represent Him well!

The Battle for the Mind

For we are not wrestling with flesh and blood [contending only with physical opponents], but against the despotisms, against the powers, against [the master spirits who are] the world rulers of this present darkness, against the spirit forces of wickedness in the heavenly (supernatural) sphere.

EPHESIANS 6:12

A careful study of Ephesians 6 informs us that we are in a war, and that our warfare is not with other human beings but with the wicked one. Our enemy, Satan, attempts to defeat us with lies and deceit, through well-laid plans and deliberate deception.

Jesus called the devil "the father of lies and of all that is false" (John 8:44). He lies to you and me. He tells us things about ourselves, about other people, and about circumstances that are just not true. He usually does not, however, tell us the entire lie all at one time.

He begins by bombarding our mind with a cleverly devised pattern of little nagging thoughts, suspicions, doubts, fears, wonderings, reasonings, and theories. He moves slowly and cautiously. Remember, he has a strategy for his warfare.

Satan has studied us for a long time and knows what we like and what we don't like. He knows our insecurities, weaknesses, and fears. He knows what bothers us most and is willing to invest any amount of time it takes to defeat us. But we can outlast the enemy through the power of the Holy Spirit and through learning the truth of God's Word!

You are more than a conqueror through Christ Who loves you!

Be Still and Know God

Let be and be still, and know (recognize and understand) that
I am God. I will be exalted among the nations! I will be exalted
in the earth!

PSALM 46:10

Many people today run from one thing to the next. They are addicted to activity, and I used to be one of those people!

For a long time, I felt I had to find something to do all the time. I had to be involved and a part of whatever was going on. I thought I couldn't afford to miss anything because I didn't want anything to go on that I didn't know about. I couldn't be still. I had to be up doing something. I was not a human being—I was a human doing.

Thankfully, I discovered that if we will be still and not take matters into our own hands, we will see the amazing power of God working in our lives. We are often stressed to the maximum degree simply because we keep trying to do things that only God can do. God wants to guide us, but to sense His direction we need to be still! Take time daily to listen. We have two ears and only one mouth, so God must have intended that we listen more than we talk.

When we have plans and ideas, we can submit them to God (acknowledge Him), and make sure we have peace as well as a plan!

God gives His highest and best to those whose trust is in Him. Be still and let Him show Himself strong in your life.

One Step at a Time

. . . He Who began a good work in you will continue until the day of Jesus Christ . . . developing [that good work] and perfecting and bringing it to full completion in you.

PHILIPPIANS 1:6

When I speak on the healing of emotional wounds, I like to hold up several different-colored shoestrings tied together in a knot. I tell the audience, "This is you when you first start the process of transformation with God. You're all knotted up. Each knot represents a different problem in your life that has developed from the things you have gone through. Untangling those knots and straightening out those problems may take a bit of time and effort, so don't get discouraged if it doesn't happen all at once."

If you want to receive healing and come into an area of wholeness, you must realize that healing is a process. Allow the Lord to deal with you and your problems in His way and in His time. Your part is to cooperate with Him in whatever area He chooses to start dealing with you first.

In our modern, instantaneous society, we expect everything to be quick and easy. The Lord never gets in a hurry, and He never quits. Sometimes it may seem that you are not making any progress. That's because the Lord is untying your knots one at a time. During the process, we are learning to trust God, and we are developing a close and intimate relationship with Him. God always finishes what He starts, and you will see freedom and victory in your life!

Don't give up!

Choosing to Persevere

That is why I would remind you to stir up (rekindle the embers of, fan the flame of, and keep burning) the [gracious] gift of God...

For God did not give us a spirit of timidity... but [He has given us a spirit] of power and of love and of calm and well-balanced mind...
2 TIMOTHY 1:6–7

On difficult days it is helpful to be reminded to persevere in order to fulfill the call of God on our lives. On those days when you feel like giving up, just remember that God has given you the power to hold on!

In the scripture for today we learn that Timothy was a young minister who simply felt like giving up. The fire that had once burned within him was beginning to grow cold. The church in those days was experiencing a great deal of persecution, and Timothy had some fears. Perhaps he felt worn-out and that everything was crashing down upon him. He had reached a place where he needed to be encouraged to stir himself up in faith.

Paul was saying, "Timothy, you may feel like quitting, but I am reminding you of the call on your life. Remember the power of the Holy Spirit that changed your life. He gives you a spirit of power, love, discipline, and self-control." Paul encouraged Timothy to be stable.

If we have stability, we do what is right even when it is difficult and does not feel good. Be encouraged today that you can do whatever you need to do. In Christ, you've got what it takes!

Giving up is only an option for those who plan to fail in life.

How to Pray Effectively

[Yes] I will grant [I Myself will do for you] whatever you shall ask in My Name [as presenting all that I Am].

JOHN 14:14

I reached a point in my prayer life where I felt frustrated, so I began to seek God about it. I wanted the assurance that my prayers were being effective. I wanted to have confidence that when I prayed, power was released to work in the situation I had prayed about. I wanted those things, but to be honest, I didn't have that assurance or confidence.

Satan definitely wants to steal our confidence concerning prayer. Many people express the same frustrations that I felt. They pray, but all the while they're wondering if they are being effective. What is wrong? I believe that we mistakenly think that we need to be perfect in order to have power in prayer, but we don't. That is why we have been given the name of Jesus in which to pray!

When we pray in Jesus' name, we are presenting to God the Father all that Jesus is, not what we are. Thankfully, I don't pray in Joyce's name; if I did I would never accomplish anything! The Holy Spirit helps us pray as we ought to, and the name of Jesus guarantees the answer! Be bold in prayer because you have the name above every other name and at the mention of that name, every knee must bow (Philippians 2:10).

Pray boldly, expecting results!

The Simplicity of Grace

But by the grace (the unmerited favor and blessing) of God
I am what I am, and His grace toward me was not [found to
be] for nothing (fruitless and without effect). In fact, I worked
harder than all of them [the apostles], though it was not really I,
but the grace (the unmerited favor and blessing) of God which
was with me.   1 CORINTHIANS 15:10

There is nothing more powerful than the grace of God. Everything
in the Bible—salvation, the infilling of the Holy Spirit, closeness to
God, and all victory in our daily lives—is based upon it. Without
grace, we are nothing, we have nothing, we can do nothing.

The grace of God is not complicated or confusing. In fact, it is so
simple that many of us miss its true meaning and end up making our
lives incredibly complex. I know I did.

Reading God's Word, I constantly saw the need for change in my
life. But I didn't know that the grace of God could bring about those
changes. I didn't know how to allow the Holy Spirit to fill my life and
cause those things to happen. So I tried to change myself and everything else in my life in my own strength. The results went beyond
frustration and became emotionally destructive.

It was when I discovered the grace of God that I realized His
power would enable me to do with ease what I could never do on my
own. It changed my life, and it can change yours too.

Let everything you do in life be "by grace through faith,"
and you will live with peace and joy!

No More Guilt or Condemnation

Therefore, [there is] now no condemnation (no adjudging guilty of wrong) for those who are in Christ Jesus, who live [and] walk not after the dictates of the flesh, but after the dictates of the Spirit.

ROMANS 8:1

One of the major problems for many believers is the recurrence of feeling guilty and condemned for past sins that they have received forgiveness for. Satan's great delight is to make us feel bad about ourselves, and one way to do that is by making us feel guilty. Even though it is a false guilt, if we accept it, we are affected adversely by it.

The Bible teaches that through the blood of Jesus, we have complete forgiveness and total freedom from condemnation. We don't need to add our guilt to His sacrifice upon the cross. He is more than enough.

If the devil tries to bring that sin to your mind again in the form of guilt and condemnation, declare to him: "I was forgiven for that sin! It has been taken care of; therefore, I take no care for it." You will find that speaking aloud is often helpful to you because by doing so, you are declaring your stand on the Word of God. Declare to the enemy that Christ has set you free.

Don't just sit and listen to the devil's accusations and lies. Learn to talk back to him with the truth.

Supernatural Favor

For You, Lord, will bless the [uncompromisingly] righteous [him who is upright and in right standing with You]; as with a shield You will surround him with goodwill (pleasure and favor).

PSALM 5:12

When I first started ministering, I was scared. I was afraid of being rejected. In those days, for a woman to do what I was doing was even less popular than it is today when women preachers are more widely accepted. So I bent over backward to speak and behave the way I thought was expected of me.

The problem was that I was trying to have favor with people through my own works, and it didn't work. Trying to get favor on your own is not only hard work, it is often pointless. The harder you try, the less people are attracted to you.

At the time, I knew nothing about supernatural favor. I didn't know that favor is a part of grace. In fact, in the English New Testament the words *grace* and *favor* are both translated from the same Greek word *charis*. So the grace of God is the favor of God. And the grace of God causes things to happen in our lives that need to happen. Grace is the power of God coming through our faith to do what we cannot do on our own. It is not by human power, or by human might, but by the Holy Spirit that we receive favor. It is by God's Spirit of grace that we find favor with God and with man.

Every day declare out loud that you believe you have favor with God and that He gives you favor with man! (Proverbs 3:4)

Tearing Down Strongholds

For the weapons of our warfare are not physical [weapons of flesh and blood], but they are mighty before God for the overthrow and destruction of strongholds.   2 CORINTHIANS 10:4

Through careful strategy and cunning deceit, Satan attempts to set up "strongholds" in our minds. A stronghold is an area in which we are held in bondage (in prison) due to a certain way of thinking. Strongholds are lies that are believed.

The apostle Paul tells us that we have the spiritual weapons we need in order to overcome Satan's strongholds. Using our weapons, we refute the enemy's lies, arguments, theories, reasonings, and every other thing that tries to exalt itself against the truth of God's Word. We must take our thoughts captive and refuse to indulge in the fleshly luxury of receiving and meditating on every thought that falls into our heads (2 Corinthians 10:5).

The primary weapon with which we do battle is the Word of God used in various ways—preached, taught, sung, confessed, meditated upon, written, and read. The knowledge of God's Word will renew our minds and teach us to think in a brand-new way. It will tear down old strongholds that have kept us in bondage!

No one will ever live a truly victorious life without being a sincere student of God's Word.

Jesus, Your Prince of Peace

Peace I leave with you; My [own] peace I now give and
bequeath to you. Not as the world gives do I give to you. Do not
let your hearts be troubled, neither let them be afraid. [Stop
allowing yourselves to be agitated and disturbed; and do not
permit yourselves to be fearful and intimidated and cowardly
and unsettled.]   JOHN 14:27

When we are all stressed out, we usually try to eliminate the things
that are causing our problems. But the source of stress is not really
our difficulties, circumstances, and situations. Stress comes when
we approach problems with the world's perspective rather than faith
in Jesus Christ, the Prince of Peace.

It was Jesus' blood that bought our peace. Peace is ours as a gift
from Him, but we need to be willing to change our approach to life.
We cannot have anxiety, frustration, bitterness, strife and offense, or
rigid, legalistic attitudes and enjoy the peace of God.

Even though we will have disturbing issues to deal with, we can
have Jesus' peace because He has overcome the world and deprived
the world of its power to harm us (John 16:33). He left us with the
power to "stop allowing" ourselves "to be agitated and disturbed"!
Peace is available; all you have to do is choose it!

The Prince of Peace, Jesus, Who lives inside those who have
received Him, knows and will reveal to us the specific actions for us
to take in every situation to lead us into peace.

It is absolutely amazing what we can accomplish in
Christ if we live one day at a time in His peace.

Jesus and Emotions

*For we do not have a High Priest Who is unable to understand
and sympathize and have a shared feeling with our weaknesses
and infirmities and liability to the assaults of temptation, but
One Who has been tempted in every respect as we are, yet
without sinning.*   HEBREWS 4:15

According to the writer of Hebrews, Jesus experienced every emotion and suffered every feeling you and I do, yet without sinning. He did not sin because He did not give in to His wrong feelings. He knew the Word of God in every area of life because He spent years studying it before He began His ministry. You and I will never be able to say no to our feelings if we don't have a strong knowledge of God's Word.

When someone hurts me and I feel angry or upset, I pray, "Jesus, I am so glad that You understand what I am feeling right now and that You don't condemn me for feeling this way. I don't want to give vent to my emotions. Help me to forgive those who have wronged me and not slight them, avoid them, or seek to pay them back for the harm they have done me."

No matter when or how temptation comes, God has enabled us to resist it. But we need to know His Word and lean on Him for help. We cannot do it in our own strength; it is His Word and Spirit that enable us to resist temptation! It is not wrong to feel tempted, but it is wrong if we give in to the temptation.

———————

Manage your emotions—don't let them manage you!

Stopping the Emotional Yo-Yo

But the fruit of the [Holy] Spirit . . . is love, joy (gladness), peace,
patience (an even temper, forbearance), kindness, goodness
(benevolence), faithfulness, gentleness (meekness, humility), self-
control . . .   GALATIANS 5:22–23

I remember the years when I was what I call a "yo-yo Christian." I
was continually up and down emotionally. If my husband, Dave, did
what I liked, I was happy. If he didn't do what I liked, I would get
mad. I had not yet learned how to be led by the Holy Spirit and was
letting my feelings control my behavior.

More than anything else, believers tell me how they feel. "I feel
nobody loves me." "I feel my spouse doesn't treat me right." "I feel
that I'll never be happy." "I feel . . . I don't feel . . ." and on and on it
goes.

God wants us to realize that our emotions are never going to go
away, so we must learn to manage them rather than let them manage us. We can choose to exercise self-control and not let our flesh
rule us. Not one of us will, or even should, get everything we want.
A spiritually mature believer can be peaceful and happy even when
they don't get what they want. We can choose to tell ourselves that
we are not going to be able to say everything we want to say, eat
everything we want to eat, and always do what we feel like doing.
Choose to let the Holy Spirit help you do what is right no matter how
you feel!

———————

**As Christians, instead of concentrating on how we
feel, we can focus on what we know is true in the
Word of God.**

The Prayers of a Righteous Man

*Elijah was a man with a nature like ours, and he prayed earnestly
that it would not rain; and it did not rain on the land for three
years and six months.*   JAMES 5:17 NKJV

James tells us that the fervent prayer of a "righteous" man is powerful
(James 5:16). This person has placed his faith in Jesus for salvation
and the forgiveness of sins and is not under condemnation—one
who has confidence in God and in the power of prayer. It does not
mean a person without any imperfection in his life.

Elijah was a man of God who did not always behave perfectly,
but he did not allow his imperfections to steal his confidence in
God. Elijah had faith, but at times we also see fear in his life. He was
obedient, but at times he was also disobedient. He loved God and
wanted to fulfill His will and calling upon his life. But sometimes he
gave in to human weaknesses and tried to avoid the consequences.

In 1 Kings 18 we see him moving in tremendous power, calling down fire from heaven and slaying 450 prophets of Baal. Then
immediately after that we see him fearfully running from Jezebel,
becoming negative and depressed, and even wanting to die.

Like many of us, Elijah let his emotions get the upper hand sometimes. He was a human being just like us, and yet he prayed powerful prayers. His example should give us enough "scriptural power"
to defeat condemnation when it rises up to tell us we cannot pray
powerfully because of our weaknesses and faults.

**Never underestimate the power of confident, effective,
fervent prayer.**

More and More Grace

But He gives us more and more grace (power of the Holy Spirit, to meet this evil tendency and all others fully). That is why He says, God sets Himself against the proud and haughty, but gives grace [continually] to the lowly (those who are humble enough to receive it).
JAMES 4:6

All human beings have evil tendencies, but James teaches us that God will give us more and more grace to meet these tendencies.

I spent much of my Christian life trying to overcome my own wrong motives and intentions. But all my trying just brought much frustration. I had to come to a place of humility and learn that God gives grace to the humble—not the proud. He gives help to those who are humble enough to ask for it.

We have our own ideas about what we can accomplish, but often we think more highly of ourselves than we ought. We should have a humble attitude, knowing that apart from God, we can do nothing.

If you are planning your own way, trying to make things happen in the strength of your own flesh, then you are frustrated. You probably have said, "No matter what I do, nothing seems to work!" Nothing will ever work until you learn to trust in God's grace.

Relax. Let God be God. Stop being so hard on yourself. Change is a process that brings you closer to Him little by little. You're on your way, so enjoy the trip.

———————

If you desire to be free, be willing to exchange human effort for trusting in God.

Doorways of Pain

They who sow in tears shall reap in joy and singing.

PSALM 126:5

For many of us, forgiving someone who has hurt us is the most difficult part of emotional healing. It can even be the stumbling block that prevents it. Those who have been badly wounded by others know that it is much easier to say the word *forgive* than it is to do it.

First, let me say that it is not possible to have good emotional health while harboring bitterness, resentment, and unforgiveness toward someone. It's poison to your system. And it is impossible to get better if it's there.

When I finally allowed the Lord to begin to work in my life, He revealed to me I had been hiding behind "doorways of pain"—the painful events and situations of my past. To pass back through the same, or similar, doorways and to be delivered and healed meant facing the issues, people, and truths I found so difficult, if not impossible, to face on my own.

Don't be afraid of the pain of healing. The temptation is to run away, but the Lord is close to you, and He wants to bring you through your problems. Going through is always better than running from a thing. Endure whatever you need to, knowing that there is joy on the other side.

God does not bring hurts and wounds upon us. But if they are inflicted upon us, He is able to make miracles out of mistakes.

Different Kinds of Favor

And let the beauty and delightfulness and favor of the Lord our
God be upon us; confirm and establish the work of our hands—
yes, the work of our hands, confirm and establish it.

PSALM 90:17

There is a distinction between natural favor and supernatural favor. Natural favor can be earned, whereas supernatural favor can't.

If you work hard enough and long enough, you can get people to like and accept you most of the time. But that acceptance must be maintained the same way it was gained. Having to say and do all the right things all the time in order to stay in favor with people is a form of bondage.

If we will choose to follow God instead of people, He will grant us His favor. It is a gift of His grace and cannot be earned. God doesn't want us to waste our time and energy trying to earn favor; He wants us to trust Him for it. When God gives us His favor, amazing things begin to take place. Doors of opportunity will open for you. You will end up with benefits and blessings that you have not earned or deserved.

We can pray daily for God's supernatural favor. It is a gift of God that comes by grace through our faith. Go ahead and ask, and keep on asking and you will receive!

When we know that everything we have and enjoy is a gift from God, a result of His supernatural favor upon us, then there is nothing left to do but say, "Thank You, Lord."

The Sword of the Spirit

And take the helmet of salvation and the sword that the Spirit wields, which is the Word of God.   EPHESIANS 6:17

The attacks of Satan against the church are more intense than ever before. So many people are experiencing tremendous attacks against their minds and enduring great attacks of fear.

A person who learns to abide in the Word of God and let the Word abide in him will have a two-edged sword with which to do battle. To abide means to remain, to continue in, or to dwell in. If you make God's Word a small part of your life, you will know only a partial truth and will experience only limited freedom. But those who *abide* in it will know the full truth and will experience complete freedom.

My life used to be a mess because I was ignorant of the Word. For many years I was a Christian who loved God and was active in church work, but I had zero victory because I did not know the Word. Thankfully, I can now testify that the Word of God has caused me to be victorious and to recognize the attacks of Satan.

Learn the Word and allow the Holy Spirit to wield it by speaking, singing, or meditating on the portions of Scripture that you feel He is placing on your heart.

If you keep your sword drawn, the enemy won't be so quick to approach you. Speak the Word!

Works Versus Grace

Even when we were dead (slain) by [our own] shortcomings and trespasses, He made us alive together in fellowship and in union with Christ; [He gave us the very life of Christ Himself, the same new life with which He quickened Him, for] it is by grace (His favor and mercy which you did not deserve) that you are saved (delivered from judgment and made partakers of Christ's salvation).   EPHESIANS 2:5

We often get frustrated because we are trying to live by our own *works*, when our lives were brought into being and designed by God to be lived by *grace*. The more we try to figure out what to do to solve our dilemmas, the more confused, upset, and frustrated we will become.

When you get into a frustrating situation, just stop and say, "O Lord, give me grace (Your power and ability)." Then believe that God has heard your prayer and is answering that prayer and working out the situation.

Faith is the channel through which you and I receive the grace of God. If we try to do things on our own, without being open to receive the grace of God, then no matter how much faith we think we have, we will still not receive what we are asking of God.

We can trust in and rely on the grace of God. He is close to us, He knows what we are facing in every situation of life, and He will work out things for the best if we will trust Him enough to allow Him to do so.

———

Remember, it is not by power or by might, but by the Spirit that we win the victory over our enemy.

No Pain, No Gain

> ...[The Lord] has sent me to comfort the brokenhearted and to
> proclaim that captives will be released and prisoners will be freed.
> He has sent me to tell those who mourn that the time of the Lord's
> favor has come... To all who mourn... he will give a crown of
> beauty for ashes, a joyous blessing instead of mourning, festive
> praise instead of despair....   ISAIAH 61:1–3 NLT

When moving to emotional wholeness, even with the Holy Spirit
leading us, the pain of the healing process from emotional wounds
can be more traumatic than experiencing physical pain. Because I
experienced so much emotional pain early in my life, I grew weary of
hurting. I was attempting to find healing by following the leadership
of the Holy Spirit, yet I could not understand why the process had to
be so painful.

The Lord revealed to me that I had been hiding behind many
"doorways of pain." I was deep in bondage, taking refuge behind
false personalities, pretenses, and facades. I began to understand
that when people are led out of bondage into freedom, they must
pass back through similar doorways of pain to get on the other side
of those doors. They pass through the emotional responses to their
initial pain as the Lord leads them to face issues, people, and truths
that are difficult. The good news is that we don't have to face them
on our own. He is always near to you, and He will bring you to a
place of healing if you will let Him.

**Thank God, He heals the brokenhearted, opens prison
doors, and sets the captives free! You don't have to live
in the pain of your past!**

God Is Unchanging

Jesus Christ (the Messiah) is [always] the same, yesterday, today, [yes] and forever (to the ages).   HEBREWS 13:8

What is the main thing that we love so much about Jesus? There are many answers to that question, of course, such as the fact that He died for us on the cross so we wouldn't have to be punished for our sins; then He rose again on the third day. But in our daily relationship with Him, one of the things we appreciate the most about Him is the fact that we can count on His unchanging nature. He can change anything else that needs to be changed, but He Himself always remains the same.

That is the kind of person we can aspire to be, but it will never happen if we cannot control our emotions. Being emotionally mature means making decisions based on the leading of the Holy Spirit, not on our feelings. But it doesn't come naturally.

Our emotions will never go away, but we can learn to manage them. God is able to bring us into balance. It doesn't mean we become emotionless or dull. God gave us emotions so we could enjoy life. But it does mean we take control in the strength and power of the Holy Spirit as we're led by Him.

God does not want us to change every time our circumstances change. He wants us to always be the same, just as He is.

Short and Simple

And when you pray, do not keep on babbling like pagans, for
they think they will be heard because of their many words. Do not
be like them, for your Father knows what you need before you
ask him.   MATTHEW 6:7–8 NIV

I believe if I can keep my request very simple and not confuse the issue by trying to come up with too many words, my prayer actually seems to be more clear and powerful.

We can choose to spend our energy releasing our faith, not repeating phrases over and over that only serve to make the prayer long and involved.

I remember a time when it was difficult for me to keep my prayers short and simple. I began to realize that my problem in praying was that I didn't have faith that my prayer would get through if it was short, simple, and to the point. I had fallen into the same trap that many people do—"the-longer-the-better" mentality. I'm not advocating that we should only pray for short periods of time, but I am suggesting that each prayer be simple, direct, to the point, and filled with faith.

Now as I follow God's direction to keep it simple and make my request without repeating myself over and over, I experience a much greater release of my faith. And I know that God has heard me and will answer.

If your prayers are complicated, simplify them.
Remember, you are heard because of your faith, not
your amount of speaking!

Quick to Forgive

*And become useful and helpful and kind to one another,
tenderhearted . . . forgiving one another [readily and freely], as
God in Christ forgave you.*   EPHESIANS 4:32

The Bible teaches us to forgive "readily and freely." That is God's
standard for us, no matter how we feel about it. We are to be quick
to forgive.

According to 1 Peter 5:5, we can clothe ourselves with the character of Jesus Christ, meaning that we can choose to be long-suffering,
patient, not easily offended, slow to anger, quick to forgive, and filled
with mercy. My definition of "mercy" is to look beyond what is done
to me that hurts and discover the reason why it was done. Many
times people do things even they don't understand themselves, but
there is always a reason why people behave as they do. Perhaps they
are hurting and in their own pain they don't even realize they are
hurting someone else.

God forgives! We are to be merciful and forgiving, just as God
in Christ forgives us our wrongdoing. He not only sees what we do
that is wrong, but He understands why we did it, and is merciful
and long-suffering. The choice to forgive others is ours. God will not
force anyone to do it. Even if you don't understand it, believe that
God's way is the best. It works. He can take what Satan meant to
destroy you and turn it for your good.

**We are to forgive in order to keep Satan from getting
the advantage over us.**

Get Plugged In

I am the Vine; you are the branches. Whoever lives in Me and
I in him bears much (abundant) fruit . . .   JOHN 15:5

In our Christian walk, many times we end up with a lot of principles, formulas, and methods, but no real power. That may be true for teachings on faith, prayer, praise, meditation, Bible study, confession, spiritual warfare, and all the other precepts we have been hearing about and engaging in. They are all good, and we need to know about them, but they alone cannot solve our problems.

It's important to remember that, as good as these disciplines are, they are only channels to receiving from the Lord. They are of no help unless we are plugged in to the divine power source.

We get plugged in through a personal relationship with God, which requires time. We will never have any real lasting victory in our Christian life without spending time in personal, private fellowship with the Lord. He has an individual plan for you. If you ask Him, He will come into your heart and commune with you. He will teach and guide you in the way you should go.

Learn to respond quickly to the promptings of the Holy Spirit for an intimate relationship with God. Come apart with Him privately, and you will be rewarded in abundance.

It is only in the presence of the Lord that we receive the power of the Lord.

Closer to God in Prayer

Watch and pray so that you will not fall into temptation. The
spirit is willing, but the flesh is weak.   MATTHEW 26:41 NIV

Prayer is a spiritual weapon God has given us to wage warfare.
Prayer is relationship with the Godhead. It is coming and asking for
help or talking to God about something that bothers us. Prayer inter-
rupts Satan's plan for evil!

If you want to have an effective prayer life, develop a good personal relationship with the Father. Know that He loves you, that He
is full of mercy, that He will help you. Get to know Jesus. He is your
Friend. He died for you. Get to know the Holy Spirit. He is with you
all the time as your Helper. Let Him help you.

All kinds of prayer are to be used in our walk with God. There
is the prayer of agreement between two people and also the united
prayer of a group of people. There are prayers of thanksgiving, praise
and worship, petition, intercession, commitment, and consecration.

Whatever kind of prayer you bring, learn to fill your prayers with
the Word of God and offer them with the assurance that God keeps
His Word.

**We tend to put off praying, but I recommend that you
pray right away any time you see or think of a need!**

The Faith Attitude

But the Lord was with Joseph, and showed him mercy and loving-kindness and gave him favor in the sight of the warden of the prison.   GENESIS 39:21

Although Joseph was being punished unfairly because he was jailed for something he didn't do, the Lord was still with him, giving him supernatural favor and taking care of him. He proved that a person is really not in too bad a shape, even if he ends up in prison, if God gives him favor.

No matter what happens to us in life, we can have favor with God and with other people (Luke 2:52). But like so many good things in life, just because something is available to us does not mean that we will partake of it. The Lord makes many things available to us that we never receive and enjoy because we never activate our faith.

For example, if we go to a job interview confessing fear and failure, we will almost be assured not to get the job. On the other hand, even if we apply for a job that we know we aren't fully qualified for, we can still go in confidence, believing that God will give us favor in every situation that is His will.

God doesn't want us to be afraid of the hardships we face in life. He is in control, and He will work all things out for our good if we love and trust Him.

Joseph maintained a good attitude in a bad situation. He had a "faith attitude," and God gave him favor.

God Is Able

Now unto him that is able to do exceeding abundantly above all
that we ask or think, according to the power that worketh in us.
EPHESIANS 3:20 KJV

Ephesians 3:20 is a powerful scripture that tells us that our God
is able—able to do far above and beyond anything that you and
I can ever dare to hope, ask, or even think. We can pray, do the
asking in faith and trust. But it is God Who does the work, not us.
How does He do it? *According to [or by] the power [or grace of God]*
that worketh in us. Whatever you and I receive from the Lord is
directly related to the amount of grace we learn to receive.

I was putting unbelievable stress on myself trying to change. I
was under tremendous condemnation because every message I
heard seemed to be telling me to change; yet I couldn't change no
matter how hard I tried. I was in terrible torment because I saw all
the things about me that needed to be changed, but I was powerless
to bring about those changes.

The closer you get to the Lord, the more you see that He has to
be your Source in all things. He is the only One who can bring about
changes in your life. Learn to say, "God, I cannot do anything without You, but You can do all things through me!"

God promises to strengthen us in our weaknesses if we
trust Him and turn to Him. God's grace will be sufficient
to meet our needs.

Walking Free

*For God did not send the Son into the world in order to judge
(to reject, to condemn, to pass sentence on) the world, but that
the world might find salvation and be made safe and sound
through Him.*   JOHN 3:17

One of the biggest tools the enemy uses to try to make us feel bad is
condemnation, which certainly can be a cause of discouragement.
According to the Word of God, we who are in Christ Jesus are no
longer condemned, no longer judged guilty or wrong. Yet so often we
judge and condemn ourselves.

Until I learned and understood the Word of God, I lived a large
part of my life feeling guilty. If someone asked me what I felt guilty
about, I could not answer. All I knew was that there was a vague feeling of guilt that followed me around all the time.

From that experience, God gave me a real revelation about walking free from guilt and condemnation. He showed me that you and
I must not only receive forgiveness from Him, we must also forgive
ourselves. We must stop beating ourselves over the head for something that He has forgiven and forgotten (Jeremiah 31:34; Acts
10:15).

I believe it is nearly impossible to get discouraged if the mind is
kept under strict control. That is why we are told in Isaiah 26:3 that
God will guard and keep us in perfect and constant peace—if we
will keep our mind stayed on Him.

———————

**God has new things on the horizon of your life, but you
will never see them if you live in and relive the past.**

Do You Want to Get Well?

There was a certain man there who had suffered with a deep-
seated and lingering disorder for thirty-eight years. When Jesus
noticed him lying there [helpless], knowing that he had already
been a long time in that condition, He said to him, Do you want to
become well? [Are you really in earnest about getting well?]

JOHN 5:5–6

Isn't this an amazing question for Jesus to ask this poor man who
had been sick for thirty-eight long years: "Do you really want to
become well?" That is the Lord's question to each of us as well.

Do you know there are people who don't really want to get well?
They only want to talk about their problem. We should all ask ourselves if we truly want to get well, or if our problem has become
our identity. Sometimes people get addicted to having a problem.
It becomes their identity, their life. It defines everything they think
and say and do. All their being is centered around that particular
problem.

If you have a "deep-seated and lingering disorder," the Lord
wants you to know that it does not have to be the focal point of your
entire existence. He wants you to trust Him and cooperate with Him
as He leads you to victory over that problem one step at a time.

Whatever our problem may be, God has promised to meet our
need and to repay us for our past hurts. Facing truth is the key to
unlocking prison doors that may have held us in bondage.

God yearns to see you become all that He has planned
for you to be.

God Is Always Good

Every good gift and every perfect (free, large, full) gift is from
above; it comes down from the Father of all [that gives] light,
in [the shining of] Whom there can be no variation [rising or
setting] or shadow cast by His turning [as in an eclipse].

JAMES 1:17

James tells us that God is good, period. He is not good sometimes;
He is always good.

Isn't it wonderful to have a God Who is always the same? With
God there is no turning, no variation. We can depend on Him to be
faithful all the time, to be merciful and forgiving all the time, to only
do us good as long as we live.

If we are having a hard time, if we feel like giving up, God is
still good. He is not the Author of our problems. If something bad
happens to us, God is still good. He doesn't do good things for us
because we are good and we deserve them; He does good things for
us because He is good and He loves us. We can depend on God's
goodness in our lives!

The key to happiness and fulfillment is not in changing
our situation or circumstances, but in trusting God to be
God in our life.

How Many Times Should I Pray?

Keep on asking and it will be given you; keep on seeking and you
will find; keep on knocking [reverently] and [the door] will be
opened to you. For everyone who keeps on asking receives; and he
who keeps on seeking finds; and to him who keeps on knocking,
[the door] will be opened.   MATTHEW 7:7-8

I don't believe we can make any strict rules on the subject of how often to pray about the same thing. But I do think there are some guidelines that may apply to help us have even more confidence in the power of prayer.

If my children need something, I want them to trust me to do what they have asked me to do. I wouldn't mind, and might even like it, if they occasionally said, "Boy, Mom, I'm sure looking forward to those new shoes." That statement would declare to me that they believed I was going to do what I promised. They would actually be reminding me of my promise, but in a way that would not question my integrity.

I believe sometimes when we ask God the same thing over and over, it is a sign of doubt and unbelief, not of faith and persistence.

When I ask the Lord for something in prayer and that request comes to my mind later, I talk to Him about it again. But when I do, I refrain from asking Him the same thing as if I think He didn't hear me the first time. I thank the Lord that He is working on the situation I prayed about previously and expect Him to do what is best.

Faithful, persistent prayer builds even more faith and confidence in us as we continue to pray.

Grace Is Not for Sale

Through Him also we have [our] access (entrance, introduction)
by faith into this grace (state of God's favor) in which we [firmly
and safely] stand. And let us rejoice and exult in our hope of
experiencing and enjoying the glory of God.   ROMANS 5:2

The devil wants you and me to think that we can buy the grace (favor)
of God with our works. But God's grace is not for sale, because by its
very definition—*unmerited favor*—it is a gift.

Grace cannot be earned by prayer, good works, reading the
Bible, confessing scriptures, or church attendance. It cannot even
be bought by faith. The grace of God is receivable, but it is not
"buyable."

Even when we do all the right things, it is important that our
motives are pure. When we are fellowshipping with the Lord, if our
motive is to get something from Him, we have moved from grace
to works. Let us not fall into the trap of thinking that we *deserve*
anything good from the Lord. God's goodness is a gift and all we
can do is thank Him and be filled with gratitude. Anything we do
for God should be done because we love Him, and never to get anything from Him.

We can seek the Lord and fellowship with Him for no other reason than the fact that we love Him and want to be closer to Him
each day.

———————

Salvation and every good thing from God is a gift and is
received by faith alone, so that man cannot boast.

When You Feel Discouraged

[What, what would have become of me] had I not believed that
I would see the Lord's goodness in the land of the living!

PSALM 27:13

We have all been disappointed at some time. It would be surprising if we went through the week without encountering some kind of disappointment. We are "appointed" (set in a certain direction) for something to happen a certain way, and when it doesn't happen that way, we become "dis-appointed."

Disappointment not dealt with turns into discouragement. If we stay discouraged very long, we are liable to become devastated, and devastation leaves us unable to handle anything.

Many devastated Christians live defeated lives because they have not learned how to handle disappointment. The devastation they are experiencing most likely began with a minor disappointment that was not dealt with properly.

It is not God's will for us to live disappointed, devastated, or oppressed. When we become "disappointed," we can choose to become "re-appointed" to keep from becoming discouraged, then devastated.

When we learn to place our hope and confidence in Jesus the Rock (1 Corinthians 10:4) and resist the devil at his onset (1 Peter 5:8–9), we can live in the joy and peace of the Lord, free from discouragement.

Choose to aggressively withstand the devil so you can live in the fullness of life God has provided for you through His Son Jesus Christ.

High Praises of God

Let the saints be joyful in the glory and beauty [which God confers upon them]; let them sing for joy upon their beds. Let the high praises of God be in their throats and a two-edged sword in their hands.   PSALM 149:5–6

We should form a habit of thanking and praising God as soon as we wake up each morning. While we are still lying in bed, let's give thanks and fill our minds with Scripture.

Praise defeats the devil quicker than any other battle plan. Praise is an invisible garment that we put on and it protects us from defeat and negativity in our minds. But it must be genuine, heartfelt praise, not just lip service or a method being tried to see if it works. We praise God for the promises in His Word and for His goodness.

Worship is a battle position! As we worship God for Who He is and for His attributes, for His ability and might, we draw closer to Him and the enemy is defeated.

We can never be too thankful! Thank God all day long and remember the many things He has done for you.

God never loses a battle. He has a definite battle plan, and when we follow Him, we will always win.

Under God's Control

... [The Lord] brings low and He lifts up.

1 SAMUEL 2:7

It is important to remember that the Lord can bring one person down and lift up another. One instance is in the life of Esther. God raised her up from obscurity to become the queen of the entire land. He gave her favor with everyone she met, including the king, because she had found favor with God.

Esther drew upon that favor to save herself and her people, the Jews, from being murdered by the evil Haman, who was out to destroy them. She may have been afraid to go to the king and ask him to intervene, because doing so could have cost her very life, but she did it because she trusted her life to God.

Whatever situation comes into your life, even if you are being harassed, persecuted, or discriminated against, or someone is trying to take something from you that rightfully belongs to you—whether it is your job, your home, your reputation, or anything in life—believe God for supernatural favor. Despite how hopeless things may look, God can lift up and He can bring down. If your life is in His hands, believe that the light of the Lord shines upon you to give you favor.

Don't go through life being afraid; God loves you and will always help you!

Face the Truth

... If you abide in My word [hold fast to My teachings and live in accordance with them], you are truly My disciples. And you will know the Truth, and the Truth will set you free.

JOHN 8:31–32

Anyone who needs emotional healing and restoration from past hurts must learn to face truth. We cannot be set free while living in denial. If you are hurt, talk to God about it openly because He cares about everything that concerns you.

Many times people who have suffered abuse or some other tragedy in their lives try to act as though it never happened. Early traumatic experiences can cause us to be emotionally damaged and wounded later in life because we develop opinions and attitudes about ourselves based on what happened to us.

From my own experience, as well as my years of ministry to others, I have come to realize that we human beings are marvelously adept at building walls and hiding things in dark corners, pretending they never happened. We do this because it may seem easier. But avoiding issues will keep us in bondage; facing them with God's help will set us free.

It is so wonderful to be in relationship with Jesus, because we don't have to hide anything from Him. He already knows everything about us anyway. We can always come to Him and know we will be loved and accepted no matter what we have suffered or how we have reacted to it.

Even though it may be hard to face the truth, Jesus promises to be with us and set us free.

The Lord Is Our Rock

He is the Rock, His work is perfect, for all His ways are law and justice. A God of faithfulness without breach or deviation, just and right is He.   DEUTERONOMY 32:4

God always loves us unconditionally. He doesn't love us if we are good and then stop loving us if we are bad. He always loves us. He is always kind, always slow to anger, always full of grace and mercy, always ready to forgive.

God is a Rock, unchanging and without deviation. He is great and unfailing, faithful and just, perfect and right in all His doing. He will never leave us or forsake us.

What would happen in our lives and in the lives of those around us if we were more like God? What would happen if we were always loving, always slow to anger, always filled with grace and mercy, always ready to forgive? What would happen if we, like our God, were always positive, peaceful, and generous? He is our Rock, but He is also our Example. We are to strive to be the way He is.

We can all grow spiritually and be changed into the image of Christ. God does not expect us to become perfect overnight, but He wants to help us to become more and more like Him day by day.

God helps us daily to become more and more like Him. Don't be discouraged by how far you have to go—rejoice that you are growing!

Believe God Hears You

And this is the confidence (the assurance, the privilege of boldness) which we have in Him: [we are sure] that if we ask anything (make any request) according to His will (in agreement with His own plan), He listens to and hears us.

And if (since) we [positively] know that He listens to us in whatever we ask, we also know [with settled and absolute knowledge] that we have [granted us as our present possessions] the requests made of Him.   1 JOHN 5:14–15

In John 11:41–42, just before Jesus called Lazarus forth from the tomb, He prayed: "Father, I thank You that You have heard Me." What a confident prayer!

Satan does not want you to have that kind of confidence. But I encourage you to be confident when you pray. Make a decision that you are a believer, not a beggar. Go to the throne in Jesus' name—His name will get attention!

As human beings, we often enjoy knowing someone important and being able to mention their name, hoping it will give us favor and open doors. If that works for us as human beings, just think how well it must work in the heavenly realm—especially when we use the name that is above all other names—the blessed name of Jesus!

When we pray in Jesus' name, we are offering to God all that Jesus is. That can give us great confidence that God hears and answers our prayers.

Go to God in prayer—boldly. With confidence. In the name of Jesus.

Forgiving God

*Therefore I will not restrain my mouth; I will speak in the anguish
of my spirit, I will complain in the bitterness of my soul [O Lord]!*

JOB 7:11

Like Job, many people have problems with blaming God for their
troubles. They are angry with God! Those who have never experienced that feeling may not understand it. But those who have know
what it is to feel animosity toward God because they blame Him for
not providing them with something important in their lives. Things
have not worked out the way they had planned. They believe that
God could have changed things if He had wanted to, but since He
didn't, they feel disappointed and blame Him for their situation.

If you are holding on to an attitude like this, you must realize that
it is impossible to have close fellowship with someone you are mad
at. God is the One Who can help you, so the only answer is to let go
of anger. When you are disappointed with life, run *to* God, not away
from Him.

Often we think if we just knew why certain things happened to
us, we would be satisfied. I believe God tells us only what we really
need to know, what we are prepared to handle, and what will not
harm us but will, in fact, help us. With God's help, we can learn to
let go and not try to figure out everything in life.

**There must come a time when we stop living in the past
and asking why. Instead, we can learn to let God turn
our scars into stars.**

The Divine Enabler

Behold, I am the Lord, the God of all flesh; is there anything too hard for Me?   JEREMIAH 32:27

Our God is able to do far above and beyond anything we can ever dare to hope, ask, or even think (Ephesians 3:20). When we pray in faith, it opens the door for God to work in our lives. Nothing is too hard for Him.

If you are struggling with changes that need to be made in your own personality, this word is especially for you. You can't change yourself. But thanks be to God, He can! He knows what is wrong with you, and He's ready and able to bring about the changes that you need if you just ask.

You and I don't have a problem that is too big for the grace of God. If our problem gets bigger, God's grace gets bigger. If our problems multiply, the grace of God also multiplies so that we are able to handle them.

It isn't any harder for God to deliver us from three problems than it is for Him to deliver us from one or two. Our biggest problem is still small to Him. God is able to do anything, so ask in faith and relax and let Him work.

God knew all of our faults when He accepted us, and He will never reject us because of them.

God Chooses the Unlikely

*God selected (deliberately chose) what in the world is foolish
to put the wise to shame, and what the world calls weak to put
the strong to shame.*   1 CORINTHIANS 1:27

When you feel discouraged, remember that God chose you for His
very own purpose, however unlikely a candidate you feel that you
are. By doing so, He has placed before you a wide open door to show
you His boundless grace, mercy, and power to change your life.

When God uses any one of us, though we may all feel inadequate
and unworthy, we realize that our source is not in ourselves but in
Him alone: "[This is] because the foolish thing [that has its source
in] God is wiser than men, and the weak thing [that springs] from
God is stronger than men" (1 Corinthians 1:25).

Each of us has a destiny, and there is absolutely no excuse not to
fulfill it. We cannot use our weakness as an excuse, because God
says that His strength is made perfect in weakness (2 Corinthians
12:9). We cannot use the past as an excuse, because God tells us
through the apostle Paul that if any person is in Christ, he is a new
creature; old things have passed away, and all things have become
new (2 Corinthians 5:17).

Spend some time with yourself and take an inventory of how you
feel about yourself. What is your image of yourself? Do you see yourself re-created in God's image, resurrected to a brand-new life that is
just waiting for you to claim it?

———————

**Each of us can succeed at being everything God intends
for us to be.**

Never an Excuse

*The Lord will fight for you, and you shall hold your peace and
remain at rest.*   EXODUS 14:14

Sadly, many people do not always accept the truth that God reveals
to them. It is painful to face our faults and deal with them. We tend
to justify misbehavior. We allow our past and how we were raised to
negatively affect the rest of our lives.

Our past may explain why we're suffering, but we don't have to
use it as an excuse to stay in bondage.

Everyone is without excuse because Jesus always stands ready to
fulfill His promise to set us free. He is close to us, and He will walk
us across the finish line in any area if we are willing to go all the way
through it with Him.

God doesn't abandon us and leave us helpless. He promises us
that He will not allow us to be tempted beyond what we can bear,
but with every temptation He will also provide the way out, the
escape (1 Corinthians 10:13).

You may have some major strongholds in your life that need to be
broken. Let me encourage you by saying, "God is on your side." In
the spiritual battle going on in your mind, God is fighting on your
side.

**No matter how great the temptation before us, God has
promised us everything we need to walk in victory.**

Over and Above

Now God made Daniel to find favor, compassion, and loving-
kindness . . .   DANIEL 1:9

The story of Daniel and the Hebrew children finding favor with the
Babylonian king may be a familiar story, but we must not miss the
lesson of how God's supernatural favor was with them after being
taken far from their homes and families.

Because of their sins against the Lord, the nation of Judah was
carried away into captivity in Babylon. There, some of the most
promising of them, including Daniel and three of his friends, were
chosen to become attendants to the Babylonian king. As part of their
three-year period of training, these young men were to follow a diet
of rich meat and wine provided from the king's table. However, Daniel and his friends determined not to defile themselves with this diet
and asked to be allowed to follow their own Hebrew diet.

They refused to compromise their convictions, and we are told
that the Lord gave Daniel "favor, compassion, and loving-kindness"
with their overseers. They had permission to follow their own diet
as long as it didn't harm them. Of course, not only did it not harm
them, it made them stronger and healthier and led them to be chosen as trusted counselors.

––––––––––

Always stand firm in your convictions and don't compro-
mise. You will be rewarded in the end!

Obey the Word

But be doers of the Word [obey the message], and not merely listeners to it, betraying yourselves [into deception by reasoning contrary to the Truth].   JAMES 1:22

I recall a woman who attended one of my seminars. She desperately wanted to be free of the emotional wounds that had left her insecure and fearful, but nothing seemed to work for her. At the conclusion of the seminar, she told me that she now understood why she had never experienced any progress.

She said, "Joyce, I sat with a group of ladies who had a lot of the same problems that I did. Step by step God had been delivering them. As I listened, I heard them say, 'God led me to do this, and I did it. Then He led me to another thing, and I did it.' I realized that God had also told me to do the same things. The only difference was they did what He said to do, and I didn't."

To live in a close relationship with God and to receive what He promises, we must obey the Word. We should become doers of the Word and not hearers only. Obeying the Word requires consistency and diligence. Let us be dedicated and committed to following God's lead.

God's way works! And there is no other way that does. Make a determined decision to obey His Word step-by-step, every day.

A Rock-Solid Foundation

[Jesus] said to them, But who do you [yourselves] say that I am?
Simon Peter replied, You are the Christ, the Son of the living God.

MATTHEW 16:15–16

When Peter said that Jesus was the Christ, the Son of the living God, it was a statement of faith. In making this statement, Peter was displaying faith.

I don't think Peter just casually or nonchalantly made that statement. I think he did it with a surety and a certainty that impressed Jesus because He immediately turned to Peter and told him that he was blessed. Then He went on to say that it was upon this rock-solid foundation of faith that He would build His church.

Jesus was saying to Peter, "If you maintain this faith, it will be a rocklike substance in your life upon which I will be able to build My kingdom in you, and through you. Your faith will be developed to the place that even the gates of hell will not be able to prevail against you."

There have been many times in my life when I have been discouraged and not known what to do, or felt that nothing was working and that everybody was against me. The words I have heard over and over again are, "Only believe."

This promise was not just for Peter alone. Jesus is saying the same thing to you and me. Only believe!

Know God as Your Father

And He said to them, When you pray, say: Our Father Who is in
heaven, hallowed be Your name ...   LUKE 11:2

For many years I prayed the "Lord's Prayer," and I didn't really know
God as my Father. I didn't have any kind of a close personal relationship with God. I was just repeating something I had learned.

If you want to be closer to the Lord and effective in your prayer
life, it is important to know God as your Father. When the disciples
asked Jesus to teach them to pray, He taught them what we call the
"Lord's Prayer," which is a spiritual treasure house of principles
for prayer. But foremost, Jesus started it by instructing them to say,
"Our Father Who is in heaven, hallowed be Your name."

Jesus was showing them the privileged relationship He came to
bring to every believer. He told them they could have a relationship
with God as their Father if they expected to go to Him in prayer.
Don't go to God as someone that you're afraid of, but develop a
Father-child relationship with Him. That intimate relationship will
give you liberty to ask Him for things you would not have asked for if
you had a distant, stiff relationship with Him.

Our heavenly Father loves us and has His eye on us at all times.
Learn to enjoy God!

———————

When you pray, remember you have a loving Father
Who is listening.

Decide to Go On

And as for you, brethren, do not become weary or lose heart in
doing right [but continue in well-doing without weakening].

2 THESSALONIANS 3:13

All of us must face and deal with disappointment at different times.
No person alive has everything happen in life the way they want it
to, in the way they expect.

When things don't prosper or succeed according to our plan, the
first emotion we feel is disappointment. This is normal. There is
nothing wrong with feeling disappointed. But we must know what
to do with that feeling, or it will move into something more serious.

In the world we cannot live without experiencing disappointment, but in Jesus we can always be given re-appointment!

The apostle Paul stated that one important lesson he had learned
in life was to let go of what lay behind and press toward all that lay
ahead! (Philippians 3:13–14.)

When we get disappointed, then immediately get re-appointed,
that's exactly what we're doing. We're letting go of the causes for the
disappointment and pressing toward what God has for us. We get
a new vision, plan, idea, a fresh outlook, a new mind-set, and we
change our focus to that. *We decide to go on!*

Every day is a brand-new start! We can let go of
yesterday's disappointments and give God a chance
to do something wonderful for us today!

His Grace Is Sufficient

For sin shall not [any longer] exert dominion over you, since now you are not under Law [as slaves], but under grace [as subjects of God's favor and mercy].   ROMANS 6:14

The grace of God is greater than our sin or any other problem that we may have. You might be feeling guilty and tempted to shrink from God's presence, but He wants you to run *to* Him, not away from Him.

We have all sinned and come short of God's perfection, but God has provided the solution to our dilemma through Jesus. He ransomed us from all the misery of sin and offers us His grace that is received by simple faith.

We all have many challenges, struggles, and temptations in life, but God is always available to help us. No problem is too big for Him. You might have what seems to be a mountain of problems, but God has a mountain of grace that is bigger. Even when we don't deserve God's help, it is still available if we will ask in childlike faith and believe!

God never leads us where He cannot keep us. His grace is always sufficient for us—in any and every circumstance of life.

A Work in Progress

... The Word of God ... is effectually at work in you who believe [exercising its superhuman power in those who adhere to and trust in and rely on it].   1 THESSALONIANS 2:13

I encourage you to say every day, "*God is working in me right now—He is changing me!*" Speak out of your mouth what the Word says, not what you feel. When we talk only about how we feel, it is difficult for the Word of God to work in us effectively.

As we step out to be all we can be in Christ, we will make some mistakes—everyone does. But it takes the pressure off of us when we realize that God is only expecting us to do the best we can. He is not expecting us to be perfect. If we were perfect, we would not need a Savior. I believe God will always leave a certain number of defects in us, just so we will know how much we need Jesus every single day.

I am not a perfect preacher. There are times when I say things the wrong way, times when I believe I have heard from God and find out I was hearing from myself. There are many times when I fall short of perfection. I don't have perfect faith, a perfect attitude, perfect thoughts, and perfect ways.

Jesus knew that would happen to all of us. That is why He stands in the gap between God's perfection and our imperfection. He continually intercedes for us because we continually need it (Hebrews 7:25).

We do not have to believe that God accepts us only if we perform perfectly. We can believe the truth that He accepts us "in the Beloved" (Ephesians 1:6).

You Have the Power

Behold! I have given you authority and power to trample upon
serpents and scorpions, and [physical and mental strength and
ability] over all the power that the enemy [possesses]; and nothing
shall in any way harm you.   LUKE 10:19

Far too many believers are fainthearted, weak in determination, and diseased with an "I can't" attitude. They are plagued with a lack of spiritual power.

You and I don't have to beg God to give us power. We just need to realize and accept that we have been given power and then walk in what is already ours. We can develop and maintain a "power consciousness"—an aggressive, power-packed attitude.

God has given us spiritual power for spiritual warfare. Spiritual power is released when our faith is firm. When we walk in faith in God, we can approach every situation with an enemy-conquering attitude.

An attitude of confidence will exude from us when we know who we are in Christ, how close He wants to be to us, and the power that the Bible says is ours through faith.

Do you desire to be a powerful believer? Try approaching every situation in your life with a simple, childlike faith—believing that God is good, that He has a good plan for your life, and that He is working in your situation.

You have the power and authority of the name of Jesus.
Walk in the strength of His conquering name!

Favored of the Lord

And Jesus increased in wisdom (in broad and full understanding)
and in stature and years, and in favor with God and man.

LUKE 2:52

From childhood, Jesus walked in the supernatural favor of God and men. In fact, once He began His public ministry, He was so popular that He could hardly find time to get alone to pray and fellowship with His heavenly Father. Even those who did not believe in Him recognized that He enjoyed the favor of God. When the Pharisees sent guards to arrest Jesus, they went back saying, "Never has a man talked as this Man talks!" (John 7:46). Right up until the very end of His life, even on the cross, that special favor and power were recognized (Luke 23:47–48).

That is the way we need to see ourselves: as the favored of the Lord. He doesn't see us as weak, helpless, sinful creatures. He sees us robed in righteousness, shod with the shoes of peace, adorned with the full armor of God, and wielding the sword of the Spirit, which is the Word of the Lord (Ephesians 6:13–17). That is how we ought to see ourselves.

Our children have favor with us, and anytime we can, we help them. Just think of how much more this must be true for us as God's children. No matter how we may appear to ourselves or to others, we must never forget that God can cause the light of His favor to shine upon us—just as He did for Jesus!

See yourself as God does and get excited about your inheritance in Him.

Grace to Be His Ambassadors

So we are Christ's ambassadors, God making His appeal as it were through us. We [as Christ's personal representatives] beg you for His sake to lay hold of the divine favor [now offered you] and be reconciled to God.   2 CORINTHIANS 5:20

One time while I was reading about a famous minister and his great faith, I was deeply impressed by all the wonderful things he did in his ministry. I thought, *Lord, I know I'm called, but I could never do anything like that.* Just that quickly, I sensed the Lord speak to my heart, "Why not? Aren't you as big a mess as anybody else?"

You see, we often have it backward. We think God is looking for people who "have it all together." But that is not true. The Word of God says that God in His grace and favor chooses the weak and foolish things of the world in order to confound the wise (1 Corinthians 1:27). He is looking for those who will humble themselves and allow Him to work His will through them.

If you will be careful not to get prideful, the Lord can use you just as mightily as any of the other great men and women of God. He doesn't choose us because we are able, but simply because we are available. That too is part of God's grace and favor that He pours out upon us when He chooses us to be Christ's personal ambassadors.

God wants you to have a dream for your life. And He wants you to walk it out by His grace as you put your faith in Him.

Be a Fighter

Fight the good fight of the faith; lay hold of the eternal life to which you were summoned and [for which] you confessed the good confession [of faith] before many witnesses.

1 TIMOTHY 6:12

Just as the apostle Paul said that he had fought the good fight of faith (2 Timothy 4:7), so he instructed his young disciple Timothy to fight the good fight of faith. That means that we should trust God at all times and never give up!

One part of fighting the good fight of faith is being able to recognize the enemy. As long as we are passive, Satan will torment us. Nothing is going to change about our situation if all we do is just sit and wish things were different. We can choose to take action. Too often we don't move against the enemy when he comes against us with discouragement or fear or doubt or guilt. We listen to his lies, but we should tell him to get lost!

You and I don't have to be punching bags for the devil; instead, we can be fighters. We can stand firm in faith and know that God is good and that good things are going to happen to us.

God is faithful, and we will see His blessing manifested in our lives if we don't give up. Stand firm! Fight! Lift up your shield of faith! God is on your side and it is impossible for you to lose your battles if you follow Him.

Come against Satan when he is trying to get a foothold, and he will never get a stronghold.

God's Work in Your Life

And all of us, as with unveiled face, [because we] continued to behold [in the Word of God] as in a mirror the glory of the Lord, are constantly being transfigured into His very own image in ever increasing splendor and from one degree of glory to another; [for this comes] from the Lord [Who is] the Spirit.

2 CORINTHIANS 3:18

God changes us from one degree of glory to another, but don't forget to enjoy the glory you are in right now while you are headed for the next one. Don't compare yourself with other people, or examine what God is doing for you compared to what He is doing for them. Each of us is an individual, and God deals with us differently, according to what He knows we need.

You may not notice changes on a daily basis, but I want to stir your faith up so you will believe that God is at work, just as He said He would be. Remember, we see *after* we believe, not *before*. We struggle with ourselves because of all that we are not, when we could be praising and worshipping God for all that we are. As we worship Him for Who He is, we see things released into our lives that we could have never made happen ourselves.

As we worship God, we are released from frustration. We enter God's rest and begin to enjoy life more than ever. The flaws that we have begin to vanish and God's character is released in our lives.

We release God to work in our lives as we release our faith in Him.

No More Pretending

For we are God's [own] handiwork (His workmanship), recreated
in Christ Jesus, [born anew] that we may do those good works
which God predestined (planned beforehand) for us [taking paths
which He prepared ahead of time], that we should walk in them
[living the good life which He prearranged and made ready for us
to live].   EPHESIANS 2:10

For many years I was miserable and unhappy. Yet, like so many people, I pretended that everything was fine. We human beings pretend
for the benefit of others, not wanting them to know about our misery, but we also pretend for ourselves so that we do not have to face
and deal with difficult issues.

Perhaps this describes you. Maybe you know what it's like to be
one person on the inside and another on the outside. In my life, I
pretended to be confident, and in some ways I was. Still, I had very
low self-esteem, and my so-called confidence was not really based
on who I was in Christ. It was based on the approval of others, on
my appearance and accomplishments, and on other external factors.
Strip away the superficial exterior, and I was scared stiff.

The day came for me when I realized I had to face the truth and
stop pretending. When we truly open our hearts and let God work
in our lives, we can stop pretending to be something we are not. We
can be happy and free, enjoying the person God made each of us
to be.

We are never truly free until we can live without pretense
and be comfortable being who we are!

The Help of the Holy Spirit

For they that are after the flesh do mind the things of the flesh;
but they that are after the Spirit the things of the Spirit.

ROMANS 8:5 KJV

Romans 8:5 teaches us that if we "mind" the flesh, we will walk in the flesh. But if we "mind" the things of the Spirit, we will walk in the Spirit. Our actions follow our thoughts!

Let me put it another way: If we think fleshly thoughts, wrong thoughts, and negative thoughts, we cannot walk in the Spirit. It seems as if renewed, godlike thinking is a vital necessity to a successful Christian life.

Your life may be in a state of chaos because of years of wrong thinking. If so, it is important for you to come to grips with the fact that *your life will not get straightened out until your mind does*. You should consider this area one of *vital necessity*.

Ask God to help you learn to think thoughts that He would have you think. You cannot overcome any problem by determination alone. It is important to be determined, but determined in the Holy Spirit, not in the effort of your own flesh. The Holy Spirit is close to you. He is your Helper—seek His help. Lean on Him. You can make it with His help.

Give the Holy Spirit control of your life. He will lead
you into the perfect will of God for you, which includes
exceeding, abundant blessings, peace, and joy.

The Missing Link

*And I will pour out upon the house of David and upon the
inhabitants of Jerusalem the Spirit of grace or unmerited favor
and supplication . . .*   ZECHARIAH 12:10

The message of God's grace has been the single most important message that the Holy Spirit has ministered to me. My entire Christian experience was a struggle before I learned about the spiritual power of grace. To teach people faith and not teach them grace is, in my opinion, "the missing link" in many people's faith walk.

Grace is the power of the Holy Spirit that is available to do whatever needs to be done in our lives, and power to bring and sustain change. It is the ability of God that comes to us free for the asking. Through faith the grace of God is received. Faith is not the price that buys the blessings of God, but it is the hand that receives them.

Just hearing the word *grace* is soothing to me. Always remember that when you feel frustrated, it is because you have entered into your own effort and need to get back into God's power. Grace leaves you strong and calm; works of the flesh render you weak and powerless, frustrated and frantic. Lean on God in all that you do today and every day, for apart from Him, you can do nothing (John 15:5).

**Receive not only the grace that saves, but receive grace,
grace, and more grace so you may live victoriously and
glorify Jesus in your daily life.**

Receive Forgiveness and Forget Your Sin

... For I will forgive their iniquity, and I will [seriously] remember their sin no more.   JEREMIAH 31:34

No matter what your problem or how bad you feel about yourself as a result of it, God loves you and He wants to be in close relationship with you. In Jesus Christ He has given you a new life. He will give you a new family of Christian friends to love and accept and appreciate and support you. You are going to enjoy a victorious life because of Jesus, the One Who lives on the inside of you and cares for you.

When you sin, you can repent and receive forgiveness. When God shows you any sin in your life, just agree with Him and be amazed by His goodness. God not only forgives us, but He promises to forget our sin.

God's mercy is wonderful and as we receive His love, forgiveness, and mercy, we can also learn how to give it to people in our lives who hurt and disappoint us. If you are angry with anyone, I recommend that you extend the same mercy to that person that God has given you. The more you let love flow to you from God and through you to others, the happier you will be.

God's mercy is new every morning. Each day we can find a fresh place to begin.

From Faith to Faith

For therein is the righteousness of God revealed from faith to faith: as it is written, The just shall live by faith.

ROMANS 1:17 KJV

It is always my goal to live from faith to faith. A number of years ago the Lord revealed to me, "Joyce, you often go from faith to faith to doubt to unbelief, and then back to faith to doubt to unbelief."

Sometimes we have too much mixture in life. We are confident at times, and then we are fearful at other times; we are positive and then we are negative, or we have faith, but then we have doubt. That mixture is even evident in our speech, as we see in James 3:10: "Out of the same mouth come forth blessing and cursing. These things, my brethren, ought not to be so."

I am sure that it sounds almost impossible to always have faith and to never doubt, but even though it is impossible with man, with God all things are possible. Let's trust God to help us go from faith to faith, and to be confident in Him at all times.

————————

Let each thing that you do, be done by faith, trusting that God is with you and that He is ready to help you!

Be Bold

Let us then fearlessly and confidently and boldly draw near to the throne of grace (the throne of God's unmerited favor to us sinners), that we may receive mercy [for our failures] and find grace to help in good time for every need [appropriate help and well-timed help, coming just when we need it].   HEBREWS 4:16

When you and I pray, we are to approach God as believers, not as beggars. Remember, according to Hebrews 4:16, we can come boldly to the throne: not beggarly, but boldly; not belligerently, but boldly.

Be sure to keep the balance. Stay respectful, but be bold. Approach God with confidence. Believe He delights in your prayers and is ready to answer any request that is in accordance with His will.

As believers, we should know the Word of God, which is His will. The more we study God's Word, the more confident we become in our asking.

As you and I come boldly before the throne of God's grace, asking in faith according to His Word and in the name of His Son Jesus Christ, we can know that we have the petitions that we ask of Him. Not because we are perfect or worthy in ourselves, or because God owes us anything, but because He loves us and wants to give us what we need in life.

Jesus has purchased a glorious inheritance for us by the shedding of His blood. As joint-heirs with Him, we can pray boldly.

A Root of Bitterness

Exercise foresight and be on the watch to look [after one another],
to see that no one falls back from and fails to secure God's grace
(His unmerited favor and spiritual blessing), in order that no
root of resentment (rancor, bitterness, or hatred) shoots forth and
causes trouble and bitter torment . . .   HEBREWS 12:15

When we allow unforgiveness in our lives, we are filled with resentment and bitterness. *Bitterness* refers to something that is pungent or sharp to the taste.

We remember that when the children of Israel were about to be led out of Egypt, they were told by the Lord to prepare a Passover meal that included bitter herbs. Why? God wanted them to eat those bitter herbs as a reminder of the bitterness they had experienced in bondage. Bitterness always goes hand in hand with bondage.

How does bitterness get started? It grows from a root, which *The King James Version* speaks of as a *root of bitterness*. A root of bitterness from the seed of unforgiveness always produces the fruit of bitterness.

Bitterness results from the offenses people commit against us that we don't let go of, the things we rehearse over and over until they have become blown way out of proportion. The longer we allow them to grow and fester, the more deeply rooted they become. Learn to be quick to repent because the sooner you do it, the easier it is!

A root of bitterness will infect our entire being—
our attitude and behavior, our perspective, and our
relationships, especially our relationship with God.

Let It Go

*Do not be quick in spirit to be angry or vexed, for anger and
vexation lodge in the bosom of fools.* ECCLESIASTES 7:9

There are certain things in life in which you have a measure of
control—you can control who you spend time with, what you eat,
and when you go to bed, for example. But there are many other
things you can't control, such as what others say about you or the
flat tire you got while running errands. The way you respond to the
things you can't control—no matter how big or how small—often
determines your stress level and your quality of life and health.

I have two suggestions about dealing with things you can't control. First, if you can't control them, don't take responsibility for
them. And second, I like to say, "Do your best, pray, and let God do
the rest."

People who regularly get upset over things beyond their control
suffer in many ways. People who let them go do much better. Letting
go of certain things doesn't mean you don't care; it simply means
you've accepted the fact that you can't do anything to change them at
that time. The flat tire has already happened. Calmly repairing it or
changing it makes sense; throwing a tantrum and kicking the tire do
not. If we appropriately deal with each stressor when it happens, we
won't end up exploding in frustration over the unavoidable bumps
on the road of life.

**God can even use an inconvenience or frustration for
your good. He is right there with you, and He is in
control. If you trust Him to work things out, you'll be
able to ride the ups and downs of life with peace, joy,
and strength.**

Don't Lose Yourself

Whoever finds his [lower] life will lose it [the higher life],
and whoever loses his [lower] life on My account will find it
[the higher life].   MATTHEW 10:39

Life is like a maze sometimes, and it is easy to get lost. Everyone, it seems, expects something different from us. There is pressure coming at us from every direction to keep others happy and meet their needs.

When we attempt to become what others want us to be, in the process, we may lose ourselves. We may fail to discover what God's intention is for us because we are trying so hard to please everyone else and yet are not pleased ourselves.

For years I tried to be so many things that I wasn't, and I got myself totally confused. I had to get off the merry-go-round and ask myself: "Who am I living for? Why am I doing all these things? Have I become a people-pleaser? Am I really in God's will for my life?"

Have you also lost yourself? Are you frustrated from trying to meet all the demands of other people while feeling unfulfilled yourself? If so, you can choose to take a stand and be determined to know your identity, your direction, and your calling—God's will for your life. You will find yourself by drawing close to God, finding His will for your life, and doing it.

———— ————

If you give your heart to doing God's will, you'll find your true self.

Jesus Is Your Rock

For as many as are the promises of God, they all find their Yes
[answer] in Him [Christ]. For this reason we also utter the Amen
(so be it) to God through Him [in His Person and by His agency]
to the glory of God.   2 CORINTHIANS 1:20

In several places in the Bible, for example in 1 Corinthians 10:4, Jesus is referred to as the Rock. The apostle Paul goes on to tell us in Colossians 2:7 that we are to be rooted and grounded in Jesus.

If we get our roots wrapped around Jesus Christ, we are in good shape. But if we get them wrapped around anything or anyone else, we are in trouble.

No person or thing is going to be as solid and dependable as Jesus. That's why it is important to point people to Jesus. Humans are always liable to failure. But Jesus Christ isn't. Put your hope wholly and unchangeably in Him. Not in man, not in circumstances, not in anything or anyone else.

If you don't put your hope and faith in the Rock of your salvation, you are headed for disappointment, which leads to discouragement and devastation. We should have so much confidence in God's love for us that no matter what comes against us, we know deep inside that He is with us and He will never let us down.

———————————

We are bankrupt in our own ability apart from Christ.
Without God, we are helpless; with Him nothing is
impossible to us.

A Vital Necessity

Either make the tree sound (healthy and good), and its fruit
sound (healthy and good), or make the tree rotten (diseased and
bad), and its fruit rotten (diseased and bad); for the tree is known
and recognized and judged by its fruit.   MATTHEW 12:33

For the believer, right thinking is something that is so important that one simply cannot live without it—like a heartbeat is vital or blood pressure is vital. There are things without which there is no life. Our life source, our source for right thinking, is regular, personal fellowship with God in prayer and in the Word.

The Bible says that a tree is known by its fruit. The same is true of our lives. Thoughts bear fruit. Think good thoughts, and the fruit in your life will be good. Think bad thoughts, and the fruit in your life will be bad.

Actually, you can look at a person's attitude and know what kind of thinking is prevalent in his life. A sweet, kind person does not have mean, vindictive thoughts. By the same token, a truly evil person does not have good, loving thoughts.

As you go through your day today, I encourage you to think healthy, positive, godly thoughts and allow them to set the course for your life, because as a man thinks in his heart, so is he (Proverbs 23:7).

The more time you spend in the Word of God, the easier
it is to reject wrong thoughts and choose right thoughts.

Special Favor

. . . How much more will your Father Who is in heaven [perfect as He is] give good and advantageous things to those who keep on asking Him!   MATTHEW 7:11

Each of us would like to be favored or featured. Is that pride? No, not if that position comes from God and not from mere personal ambitions or our own selfish efforts to call attention to ourselves.

To be totally honest, I find it delightful to watch God feature a person. It is fun to watch Him single out someone for special attention or preferential treatment. To see Him work powerfully in someone's life provokes genuine praise and thanksgiving.

It is always enjoyable to have favor with God. It just seems that it doesn't happen as often as we would like. Part of the problem is us. There are so many things that God would love to do for us, but He cannot because we won't ask. One reason we won't ask is because we don't feel worthy. None of us are worthy in ourselves, but God will give us favor if we ask!

It is time we believe that God wants to bless us. He loves to give us His favor. As a redeemed, forgiven, loved child of God, get this down in your heart today: You are the apple of God's eye. He loves you!

———

Our heavenly Father wants His children to stand up and be everything for which His Son, Jesus, gave His life that they might become.

At All Times

I will bless the Lord at all times; His praise shall continually be in my mouth.   PSALM 34:1

Faith and trust in God is meant to be exercised more than once in a while or from time to time; we can live in faith at all times. With God's help we can learn to live from faith to faith, trusting the Lord when things are good, and when things are difficult. It is easy to trust God when things are good, but when things are challenging and we decide to trust God, then we really develop character.

Psalm 34:1 encourages us to bless the Lord at all times. There are several other scriptures that tell us things to do at all times—resist the devil at all times, believe God at all times, love others at all times—not just when it's convenient or it feels good.

Temptation is a frequent visitor in our lives and as long as we are here on earth, we will have to discipline our emotions, our moods, and our mouths, so that we remain stable and calm, and peaceful—whatever our situation or circumstances. That enables us to be in close fellowship with God and walk in the joy of His Spirit.

Since you can choose your own thoughts, when doubt comes, you can learn to recognize it for what it is, say, "No, thank you," and keep on believing!

Led by the Holy Spirit to Pray

But you, beloved, build yourselves up [founded] on your most
holy faith [make progress, rise like an edifice higher and higher],
praying in the Holy Spirit.   JUDE 20

Just as Ephesians 6:18 tells us that we are to pray at all times with
all manner of prayers, we are also told by Jude that our prayers are to
be "in the Holy Spirit." The apostle Paul tells us in Romans 8:26 that
when we don't know how to pray, the Holy Spirit knows how to pray
in our weakness.

It is the Holy Spirit of God within us Who provokes us and leads
us to pray. Rather than delaying, we can learn to yield to the leading
of the Spirit as soon as we sense it. That is part of learning to pray all
manner of prayers at all times, wherever we may be, and whatever we
may be doing.

Our motto can be like the old spiritual song, "Every time I feel
the Spirit moving in my heart, I will pray." If we know we can pray
anytime and anywhere, we won't feel far from God, and we won't
feel we have to wait until just the right moment or place to pray.

When we are being led by the Holy Spirit, we can know that our
prayers are reaching the throne of God and will be answered.

Ask the Holy Spirit to get involved in everything you do.
He is the Helper, and He is waiting for you to ask.

The Simplicity of Joy and Peace

[After all] the kingdom of God is not a matter of [getting the]
food and drink [one likes], but instead it is righteousness
(that state which makes a person acceptable to God) and [heart]
peace and joy in the Holy Spirit.   ROMANS 14:17

Many years ago, I had this thought: *Life should never be this compli-cated.* Something was lurking inside, constantly draining the joy out of me. It began to dawn on me that I was doubting instead of believing. I was doubting God's call on my life, wondering if He would meet our needs, questioning my decisions and actions.

I had become negative instead of positive. I was doubting instead of believing.

Doubt complicates everything. It creeps in through the door of your heart, filling your mind with reasoning that leads to negativity. It rotates around and around the circumstances or situations of your life, attempting to find answers for them.

The Word of God does not instruct us to search for our own answers. We are, however, instructed to trust God with all of our heart and soul (Proverbs 3:5). When we follow the simple guidelines the Lord has laid out for us, they will unerringly bring us closer to Him, causing us to live in joy and peace.

When doubt knocks at your door, answer with a believing heart, and you'll always maintain the victory.

**Joy is never released through unbelief but is always
present where there is belief.**

Quitting Is Not an Option

*Looking away [from all that will distract] to Jesus, Who is the
Leader and the Source of our faith . . .*   HEBREWS 12:2

It does not take any special talent to give up and lie down on the
side of the road of life and say, "I quit." Anybody, whether they are a
believer or not, can do that.

Quitting is a temptation we all face at one time or another, but
when you get close to Jesus, or better yet, when He gets close to you,
He begins to pump strength and energy and courage into you. And
something wonderful begins to happen—He causes you to *want* to
press forward!

I used to want to give up and quit. But now I get out of bed and
start each day fresh and new. I begin my day by praying and reading
the Bible and speaking the Word, seeking after God. It's amazing
what a difference it makes when you begin your day drawing closer
to God.

When you feel the urge or the temptation to quit, don't give in.
Look to Jesus and follow His example. He pressed forward even in
the most difficult circumstances, and He will give you the strength
to do the same. He is your Leader; He is the Source and the Finisher
of your faith.

**Let's make a decision today that, come what may, we
are going to keep pressing on, looking to Jesus, no
matter what.**

Matters of the Heart

Keep thy heart with all diligence; for out of it are the issues of life.
PROVERBS 4:23 KJV

Our hearts represent our minds and the deepest parts of us. It is important that we serve God with a pure heart. A person can do the right thing, and yet not do it with a right heart. King Amaziah was such a man. We are told that he did all the right things, but his heart was not right; and therefore, God was not pleased (2 Chronicles 25:2).

Taking the time to truthfully examine our motives can be a painful exercise, but it is very valuable. Serving God wholeheartedly is what brings us closer to Him.

The Bible says that we are not to do good works to be seen of men, or pray in order to impress people. If we do what we do unto the Lord, then our reward will come from Him.

Take the time to prayerfully look at all the things you do and ask God to reveal to you if any of your motives are impure. If they are, then you can make a change with God's help. Do what you do because you truly believe it is God's will for you and do it to glorify Him. When you do this, your intimacy and closeness with God will increase.

——— — ———

God is more concerned with *why* we do things, than what we do. People see our actions, but God sees our heart!

You Are Not a Failure

*[God] disarmed the principalities and powers that were ranged
against us and made a bold display and public example of them,
in triumphing over them in Him and in it [the cross].*

COLOSSIANS 2:15

People who have been abused, rejected, or abandoned usually lack
confidence. Such individuals are shame-based and guilt-ridden and
have a very poor self-image. The devil knows that and begins his
assault on personal confidence whenever and wherever he can find
an opening. His goal is to make people believe they are failures.

The devil knows that an individual without confidence will never
step out to do the things they truly want to do. He does not want
you to fulfill God's plan for your life. If he can make you believe that
you are incapable, then you won't even try to accomplish anything
worthwhile. Even if you do make an effort, your fear of failure will
seal your defeat, which, because of a lack of confidence, you probably expected from the beginning. This is often what is referred to
as the "Failure Syndrome." People fail because of wrong beliefs, and
they continue to have wrong beliefs because they fail. It is hard to
know which came first, but they find themselves in a trap they cannot seem to get out of.

Jesus defeated Satan and triumphed over him on the cross, and
His victory is our victory. You can defeat failure syndrome because
you are more than a conqueror through Christ (Romans 8:37).

**God's victory purchased on the cross is total and
complete.**

Keep on Walking

And Peter answered Him, Lord, if it is You, command me to come to You on the water. He said, Come! So Peter got out of the boat and walked on the water, and he came toward Jesus.

MATTHEW 14:28–29

When Peter stepped out of the boat at the command of Jesus, he was doing something he had never done before. As long as he remained in faith he was successful, but when fear gripped his heart, he began to sink!

Peter's mistake was that he became preoccupied with the storm. When he focused on the circumstance around him, rather than the Savior close to him, he lost his faith and began to doubt.

Romans 4:18–21 tells us that Abraham did not waver in his faith when faced with difficult circumstances. He was aware of his situation, but unlike Peter, he was not preoccupied with it. It was this determined and focused faith that propelled Abraham forward.

I believe that you and I can learn from Peter's mistake and Abraham's example. We can be aware of our circumstances but not preoccupied with them. We can purposely keep our mind on Jesus, trusting in faith that He will provide the miracle we need.

When the storms come in your life, keep your eyes on Jesus and be determined to walk with Him no matter how high the waves are.

Pray and Fear Not

For God did not give us a spirit of timidity (of cowardice, of craven and cringing and fawning fear), but [He has given us a spirit] of power and of love and of calm and well-balanced mind and discipline and self-control.   2 TIMOTHY 1:7

God wants us to pray about everything and fear nothing. We would find ourselves in a closer, deeper personal relationship with the Lord if we would pray more, worry less, and fear less. Timothy says that God has not given us a spirit of fear. So when we feel fear, it is not from God. It's from the devil. The devil will try to intimidate us with all kinds of fear, and we can become so preoccupied with how we feel that we forget to pray.

If Abraham or Joshua or David had bowed their knee to fear when the task before them seemed overwhelming, they never would have experienced God as their abundant provision.

Talking to God and spending time in His Word gives you the power to resist fear when it comes. When you put the Word into your heart, it will come out when you need it. I believe we should confess God's Word out loud and fill our prayers with the Word of God. Satan may not be afraid of you, but he is afraid of God's Word spoken in faith from a believer's mouth.

Fear cannot be wished away, it must be confronted. Prayer and the Word of God are our two most powerful weapons, so let's use them!

Put on the armor of God through prayer and stand against all the enemy's fiery darts of fear.

Bless, Not Curse

*Bless those who persecute you [who are cruel in their attitude
toward you]; bless and do not curse them.*   ROMANS 12:14

God in His Word instructs us to *forgive* others and then to *bless*
them. In Romans 12:14, the word *bless* means "to speak well of."
It is extending mercy to people who do not necessarily deserve it.
And we are to pray for them to be blessed. We are to ask God to
bring truth and revelation to them about any changes that need to
be made in their attitude and behavior, and to help them come to a
place of repentance so they can be set free from their sins.

Revenge says, "You mistreated me, so I will mistreat you." Mercy
says, "You mistreated me, so I'm going to forgive you, restore you,
and treat you as if you never hurt me." What a blessing to be able to
give and receive mercy. Give mercy, and you will receive mercy.

Mercy is an attribute of God that is seen in how He deals with
His people. Mercy comes near to us when we deserve to be cast out.
Mercy is good to us when we deserve judgment. Mercy accepts and
blesses us when we deserve to be totally rejected. Mercy understands
our weaknesses and does not judge us.

When we really appreciate the mercy God has shown us, we will
be quick to give that same mercy to other people.

**The power of forgiveness will never work if we say we
forgive but then turn around and curse the offender with
our tongues or rehash the offense with others.**

More Joy

A cheerful heart is good medicine, but a crushed spirit dries up the bones. PROVERBS 17:22 NIV

My understanding of *joy* is that it covers a wide range of emotions, from calm delight to extreme hilarity. The hilarious times are fun, and we all need those moments of laughing until our sides hurt. We probably won't live our daily lives that way, but we need those times. Why else would God give us the ability to laugh?

As Christians, we can grow in our ability to enjoy life and be able to say, "I live my life in a state of calm delight." I think calm delight is a mixture of peace and joy.

Some of the Greek words relating to joy in the Bible mean *delight, gladness, exceeding joyful, exuberant joy, to exult, rejoice greatly...with exceeding joy.* I've also heard it defined as *great pleasure or happiness, a source of pleasure or satisfaction, to fill with joy, or to enjoy.*

Whichever definition you prefer, the sad reality is that so few believers know the joy of the Lord. Don't let another day pass by without experiencing the kingdom of God at its center—righteousness, peace, and joy in the Holy Spirit (Romans 14:17).

There is nothing as tragic as being alive and not enjoying life.

Meditate on the Things of God

. . . Whatever is true, whatever is worthy of reverence and is honorable and seemly, whatever is just, whatever is pure, whatever is lovely and lovable, whatever is kind and winsome and gracious, if there is any virtue and excellence, if there is anything worthy of praise, think on . . . these things [fix your minds on them].   PHILIPPIANS 4:8

Did you know that your feelings are hooked up to your thinking? If you don't think that is true, just take about twenty minutes or so and think about nothing but your problems. I can assure you that by the end of that time your feelings, and maybe even your countenance, will have changed.

I got up one day thinking about a problem I had. Suddenly the Spirit of the Lord spoke to me. He said to me, "Joyce, are you going to fellowship with your problem or with Me?"

When you get disappointed, don't sit around and feel sorry for yourself. As difficult as things may seem, we do have a choice. We can choose to be in close fellowship with our problems or to be in close fellowship with God. We can allow our thoughts to dwell on our problems until we become totally discouraged and devastated, or we can focus our attention on all the good things that have happened to us in our life—and on all the blessings that God still has in store for us in the days ahead.

———————

Our thoughts are silent words that only the Lord and we hear, but those words affect our inner man, our health, our joy, and our attitude.

Be a Believing Believer

Therefore, as the Holy Spirit says: Today, if you will hear His voice, do not harden your hearts, as [happened] in the rebellion [of Israel] and their provocation and embitterment [of Me] in the day of testing in the wilderness.　　　　HEBREWS 3:7–8

In Hebrews 3 we see two wrong conditions of the heart—a hard heart and an unbelieving heart. In the wilderness, a hard heart caused the Israelites to rebel. A person with a hard heart cannot believe God easily, which is a major problem because everything we receive from God comes through believing. To receive from Him, all we have to do is come to Him in simple, childlike faith and just believe.

We call ourselves believers, but the truth is, there are a lot of "unbelieving believers." For a long time, I was one of them. I had been hurt so much during my childhood, I developed a hardness of heart that God had to break through in my life.

Even Moses got to the place in the wilderness where he was slow of heart to believe God. That's why it's important for us to stay sharp spiritually so we can be quick to believe and to walk in faith day by day. We can choose to be careful to go from faith to faith and not begin to mix in any doubt and unbelief. A believing heart is essential if we want to live in close relationship with God.

———————

Jesus wants to restore your soul, including your emotions. Let Jesus into those areas of your life that no one else could ever reach. Ask Him to change you into a person who has the same kind of heart that He has.

Pursuing God

My whole being follows hard after You and clings closely to You;
Your right hand upholds me.   PSALM 63:8

I remember the emptiness I felt years ago when I realized that I sometimes had temporary happiness but not deep, satisfying joy. My relationship with God was much like the Israelites', who could only see God from a distance while Moses talked with God face-to-face. I wanted a closer walk with God, but had no idea how to do it.

Perhaps you are experiencing what I went through. I lived by the law, doing the things my church taught, and expecting my routine of good works to bring the peace and joy and spiritual power the Scripture promises. Instead, I found myself deeply disheartened that nothing seemed to be working. It wasn't until I learned to stop trying to "do" so much for God and just "be" in relationship with Him that I began to live with a peace and contentment from the Lord.

If you want the blessings and power of God, crave and pursue Him. Lay aside other things and go after Him. Do what David spoke about in Psalm 27:4: Commit yourself to one thing—the manifest presence of God.

The only thing that truly satisfies the longing within is to know God more intimately today than we did yesterday.

Confidence in God Alone

*Some trust in and boast of chariots and some of horses, but we
will trust in and boast of the name of the Lord our God.*

PSALM 20:7

In order to succeed at anything, it is essential to have confidence,
but first and foremost it must be confidence in God and His promises, not confidence in anything else. As believers, we can be confident in God's love, goodness, and mercy. This confidence assures us
that our heavenly Father wants us to succeed.

God did not create us for failure. We may fail at some things on
our way to success, but if we trust Him, He will take even our mistakes and work them out for our good (Romans 8:28).

Hebrews 3:6 tells us to "...hold fast and firm to the end our joyful and exultant confidence and sense of triumph in our hope [in
Christ]." It is important to realize that a mistake is not the end of
things if we hold on to our confidence.

We all have a destiny, but just because we are destined to do
something does not mean that it will automatically happen. I went
through many things while God was developing me and my ministry. There were times I nearly lost my confidence concerning the
call on my life. Each time I had to rely on the Lord and put my confidence in Him before I could go forward again. The same is true for
you. When you're tempted to lose your confidence, draw closer to
God and place your trust in Him.

**Put your confidence in God alone, and He will cause
you to truly succeed.**

The Prayer of Thanksgiving

Thank [God] in everything [no matter what the circumstances may be, be thankful and give thanks], for this is the will of God for you [who are] in Christ Jesus [the Revealer and Mediator of that will].   1 THESSALONIANS 5.18

After instructing us to pray without ceasing in 1 Thessalonians 5:17, the apostle Paul spends verse 18 directing us to give thanks to God in everything, no matter what our circumstances may be, stating that this is the will of God for us.

Just as prayer is a lifestyle that brings us closer to God, thanksgiving is the same thing. Giving thanks to God isn't just something we do once a day as we sit down somewhere and try to think of all the good things He has done for us and merely say, "Thanks, Lord." It is not just something we do at mealtime. That can be empty religion, something we do simply because we think God requires it.

True thanksgiving flows continually out of a heart that is full of gratitude and praise to God for Who He is as much as for what He does. It is not something that is done to meet a requirement, win favor, gain a victory, or qualify for a blessing.

The type of thanksgiving that God the Father desires is heartfelt and it flows from us regularly because we are continually seeing and recognizing how good God is to us at all times. Let us be thankful and say so!

Be thankful always, continually acknowledging, confessing, and glorifying His name in prayerful praise and worship.

Every Good Gift

For out of His fullness (abundance) we have all received [all had a share and we were all supplied with] one grace after another and spiritual blessing upon spiritual blessing and even favor upon favor and gift [heaped] upon gift.   JOHN 1:16

You and I can live in victory today because the Holy Spirit is empowering our lives and teaching us to pray. He helps us ask God for what we need rather than trying to make things happen on our own.

The Holy Spirit is the One Who brings every good gift into your life, everything you need. His multiple roles as Comforter, Counselor, Helper, Intercessor, Advocate, Strengthener, and Standby can be summarized by saying that His purpose is to get as close to us as possible and cause our lives to work out for the glory of God.

God is interested in every detail of your life. He wants to help with everything in your life. He stands by us at all times waiting for the first available opportunity to enter in and give us the help and strength we need. Ask for help as often as you need it. We have not because we ask not (James 4:2), so ask and ask and ask. Keep on asking so that you may receive and your joy may be full (John 16:24).

God's part is to give us His grace and Spirit; our part is to ask for His help and offer ourselves to Him as vessels for Him to work through.

Forgiveness Versus Feelings

Be still and rest in the Lord; wait for Him and patiently lean yourself upon Him; fret not yourself because of him who prospers in his way, because of the man who brings wicked devices to pass. Cease from anger and forsake wrath; fret not yourself—it tends only to evildoing.   PSALM 37:7–8

Perhaps the greatest misconception about forgiveness is the idea that if a person's feelings have not changed, he has not forgiven. Many people have this false idea. They decide to forgive someone who has harmed them, but if they continue to have angry and hurt feelings, they feel like they have not fully forgiven that individual.

You can be obedient to the Lord and make sound biblical decisions and still go a long time without "feeling" any different from the way you felt before you decided to forgive. This is where faith can carry you through. You have done your part and now you are waiting for God to do His. His part is to heal your emotions, to make you feel well and not wounded. You have the power to make the decision to forgive, but only God has the power to change your feelings toward the person who hurt you.

Healing takes time. So don't get impatient and discouraged if you don't "feel" everything right at once. God is in control, and He is doing a wonderful work in you and your life.

Make the decision to obey God, and trust Him to change your heart. Eventually, your feelings will follow and line up with your decisions.

Pass Your Tests

But, O Lord of hosts, Who judges rightly and justly, Who tests the heart and the mind . . . to You I have revealed and committed my cause [rolling it upon You].   JEREMIAH 11:20

All of our life is filled with challenges that test our resolve and determination and the quality of our character—tests that can strengthen us and bring us into deeper relationship with God. They help us truly know ourselves, and they are helpful in locating weak areas in our character.

How is something tested? Pressure is applied to see if it can perform in the proper way. God allows tests to come into our lives to reveal both our strengths and weaknesses, and our goal should always be to pass our tests, not avoid them. Tests always come before promotion! If you want promotion, you will have to take and pass your tests from God.

The apostle James stated that tests bring out the things that are in us (James 1:2–4), and I have certainly found that to be true. They show us the areas where we have grown in God, and the areas in which we still need help. This is a good thing, because we cannot improve in any area if we don't know where our weaknesses are.

Character is truly revealed when pressure is applied.

Celebrate Life

There is nothing better for a man than that he should eat and
drink and make himself enjoy good in his labor. Even this, I have
seen, is from the hand of God.   ECCLESIASTES 2:24

It is possible to live life blandly—going through the motions of working, accomplishing, doing, but never truly enjoying life. This is true of people who have not learned to really embrace and love the life God has given them.

Enjoying life is a decision that is based on more than just enjoyable circumstances. It is an attitude of the heart, a decision to enjoy everything, because everything—even little, seemingly insignificant things—has a part in God's overall "big picture" for our lives.

Our joy is found in Jesus, and if we do all that we do with and for Him, then we can truly enjoy it all. Even when we have problems that we are waiting for God to solve, we can still enjoy our lives. Doubt and unbelief are thieves of joy, but simple, childlike believing releases the joy that is resident in our spirit because the Holy Spirit lives there. Trust God at all times and enjoy His presence! Your life is a gift from Him, so celebrate it!

You can choose to celebrate in God's joy and enjoy every day of your life with Him!

Catch the Foxes

*Catch the foxes for us, the little foxes that are ruining the
vineyards* . . .

SONG OF SOLOMON 2:15 NASB

Little disappointments can create frustration, which in turn may
lead to bigger problems that can produce a great deal of damage.

Besides the huge disappointments that occur when we fail to
get the job promotion or house we wanted, we can become just as
upset by minor annoyances. For example, suppose you are expecting someone to meet you for lunch and they arrive late. Or suppose
you make a special trip to the mall to buy something at a discount,
but it's sold out.

These kinds of frustrations are minor, but they can add up to
cause a lot of grief. That's why we have to know how to handle them
and keep them in perspective. Otherwise, they can get out of hand
and be blown out of proportion.

We would be wise to be on our guard against the little foxes that
steal our peace.

With God's help, we can learn to do as Paul did in the book of
Acts when the serpent attached itself to his hand—he simply shook
it off (Acts 28:1–5)! If we practice dealing quickly with disappointments as they come, they will not pile up and become a mountain of
devastation.

**Victory is not the absence of problems; it is the presence
of God's power.**

Secret Prayer

But when you pray, go into your [most] private room, and, closing the door, pray to your Father, Who is in secret; and your Father, Who sees in secret, will reward you in the open.

MATTHEW 6:6

Although some prayers are public prayers or group prayers, most of our prayer life is made up of secret prayers made in the secret place.

"Secret prayer" means that we don't tell everyone we know about our personal experiences in prayer and how much we pray. We pray about the concerns and people God places on our heart, and we keep our prayers between us and Him unless we have a really good reason to do otherwise. We refuse to make a display of our prayers to impress others.

For prayer to be properly called "secret prayer," it must come from a humble heart as demonstrated in the prayer of the despised tax collector in Luke 18:10–14. He humbled himself, bowed his head, and quietly, with humility, asked God to forgive him. In response to his sincerity, a lifetime of sin was wiped away in a moment.

God has not given us a bunch of complicated, hard-to-follow guidelines for prayer. Talking with God is a simple and powerful way to draw closer to Him.

Build your relationship with God by spending time with Him on a daily basis.

A Proud Heart

... That is why He says, God sets Himself against the proud and haughty, but gives grace [continually] to the lowly (those who are humble enough to receive it).   JAMES 4:6

Has God ever had to deal with you about pride? Here are some ways you can tell if you have an issue with pride: If you have an opinion about everything, if you are judgmental, if you can't be corrected, if you rebel against authority, if you want to take all the credit for yourself, or if you say "I" too often. These are signs of pride.

It is hard to let God replace our pride with His humility, but it is vital. If we want to live in close relationship with God, we must come to Him with an attitude of humility. Pride relies on self, but humility relies on God. It is only in the place of humility that God can bless us.

The humble get the help! If we humble ourselves under God's hand, He will exalt us in due time (James 4:10). Proud people think they deserve everything they want "now," but humility says, "My times are in Your hands, Lord."

———————

Pride says "I can," but humility says, "Christ can through me."

True Satisfaction

But He replied, It has been written, Man shall not live and be upheld and sustained by bread alone, but by every word that comes forth from the mouth of God.

MATTHEW 4:4

I don't think there is anything better than just to be satisfied. To wake up in the morning and think, *Life is good; praise God, I'm satisfied*, and to go to bed at night still satisfied is truly living abundantly. On the other hand, I don't think there is anything much worse than living in a low level state of dissatisfaction all the time.

Here is a spiritual reality check: No matter what you own, where you go, or what you do, nothing can give you true gratification besides the close, personal, intimate presence of God. Money, trips, vacations, clothes, new opportunities, new furniture and new houses, and getting married and having children are all things that can give us a degree of happiness. But we will never be permanently, consistently satisfied if we seek things to own or do in order to quench the empty void inside us.

There are many unhappy believers who live unfulfilled lives because they are seeking the wrong thing! Don't miss out on a close, intimate relationship with God because you're seeking the gift instead of the Giver.

The things of the world cannot truly satisfy. Always look to God first and He will satisfy the desires of your heart.

God's Good Plan

Your eyes saw my unformed substance, and in Your book all the
days [of my life] were written before ever they took shape, when as
yet there was none of them.   PSALM 139:16

God had a good plan laid out for each of us before we made our appearance on this planet. And His unique plan for each of us is not a plan of failure and every type of misery.

In John 10:10, Jesus said, "The thief comes only in order to steal and kill and destroy. I came that they may have and enjoy life, and have it in abundance." The devil comes to destroy the good thing God has in mind for us, and we need to steadfastly resist him.

God's good plan may have been disrupted in your life, but it is not too late! God is reaching out to you right now and offering to restore to you anything the enemy has stolen, and to give you double blessing for your former trouble (Zechariah 9:12). Ask Him to do it, and watch Him work in your life.

God will do for you what you cannot do for yourself.

Determined to Love

Iron sharpens iron; so a man sharpens the countenance of his friend [to show rage or worthy purpose].   PROVERBS 27:17

We all have a few people in our lives who are like sandpaper to us. Some are like an entire package of sandpaper. Believe it or not, God places them in our lives to smooth off our rough edges. We are all like diamonds in the rough. We have something beautiful and valuable underneath the hard crusty surface of our flesh.

When God began to work spiritual maturity in me, He placed several people in my life who were very difficult for me to deal with. I thought they needed to change, but God wanted to use them to change me. We must learn to deal with all kinds of people and appreciate the ways in which they are different from us.

Dave can wait a long time for things and never get frustrated, but I want things to happen quickly. He is quiet and I talk a lot; he likes to play music in the morning and I like it quiet. I am sure you have people in your life who are very different than you are also. Instead of being irritated, or proudly thinking we are right and they are wrong, we should seek to accept them in love, just as Christ accepts us.

We can be determined to love and to get along with each other no matter how different our personalities or situations may be. Because when we love the people around us—even the most difficult people—we are opening ourselves up to learn something God may be trying to teach us.

Choose to walk in the love of Christ and let Him shape you through the other people He brings into your life.

Become a *Now* Person

*. . . One thing I do [it is my one aspiration]: forgetting what
lies behind and straining forward to what lies ahead, I press
on toward the goal to win the [supreme and heavenly] prize to
which God in Christ Jesus is calling us upward.*

PHILIPPIANS 3:13–14

Regret over the past is a primary thief of joy and peace. Whether a
mistake was made twenty years ago or twenty minutes ago, there is
nothing you can do about it except repent, receive forgiveness, forget
the past, and go on. If there is something you can do to undo the
results of your mistakes, then by all means, do it. But the bottom line
is that you still must let go of the past in order to grasp the future.

Like Paul, we are all pressing toward the mark of perfection, but
none of us have arrived. Even though he endured difficulty, I believe
Paul enjoyed his life journey and ministry, and this "one aspiration"
of his was part of the reason why. He had learned to forget his mistakes and refused to live in regret of the past.

Always remember that regret steals *now*! God has called us to be
closer to Him in the *now*. When we cling to the past, we lay aside our
faith and stop believing, then lose our peace and joy.

Let this be a day of decision for you—a day when you decide to no
longer operate in regret. Become a now person. Live in the present.
God has a plan for you now. Trust Him today.

––––––––––

**God gives grace and joy and peace for today, but He does
not give grace today for yesterday or tomorrow. Live life
one day at a time.**

Christ in You, the Hope of Glory

To whom God was pleased to make known how great for the
Gentiles are the riches of the glory of this mystery, which is
Christ within and among you, the Hope of [realizing the] glory.
                                    COLOSSIANS 1:27

You and I can realize and experience the glory of God in our lives because of Christ in us. He is our hope of seeing better things.

The glory of God is His manifested excellence. As the children of God, we have an inheritance in Christ, a right to experience that manifested excellence. Satan furiously fights to deceive us. He wants us to believe we are incapable, unworthy, and disqualified from God's best. That is why many look at themselves and feel defeated.

But if you'll remember that because of Christ in you, you can experience the glory of God—the manifested excellence of God— you'll live full of hope. You'll press on toward better things each day of your life. Look past what you can do and focus on what God can do through you.

Are you ready to believe for an outpouring of God's goodness and excellence in your life? God is looking for someone to be good to, so let it be you!

God's best for you is on its way, so get excited and expect good things!

Life Under the New Covenant

*But as it now is, He [Christ] has acquired a [priestly] ministry
which is as much superior and more excellent [than the old] as
the covenant (the agreement) of which He is the Mediator (the
Arbiter, Agent) is superior and more excellent, [because] it is
enacted and rests upon more important (sublimer, higher, and
nobler) promises.*   HEBREWS 8:6

The Old Covenant was a covenant of works, based on doing everything ourselves—struggling, striving, and laboring to be acceptable
to God. It leaves us trapped in the works of the flesh. That kind of
covenant steals our joy and keeps us at a distance from God.

But the New Covenant is a covenant of grace, which is not based
on what we can do, but what Christ has already done for us. Therefore, we are justified by our faith, not our works. That is so wonderful because it takes the pressure off of us to perform. We can give up
struggle and frustration, and allow God to work through us by the
power of His Holy Spirit within us.

The bottom line is this: The Old Covenant brings us bondage; the
New Covenant brings us liberty. That's why a relationship with God,
made possible by the work of Christ Jesus, is better than anything
else we may experience. It frees us to be who we were created to be
and then do what we are supposed to do for God.

**Life in the New Covenant is an awesome journey of living
in the presence of God and enjoying victory through
Christ.**

More Than Conquerors

Yet amid all these things we are more than conquerors and gain a
surpassing victory through Him Who loved us.   ROMANS 8:37

As believers we can live with a sense of triumph because Paul assures us that through Christ Jesus we are more than conquerors. Believing that truth gives us boldness for daily living.

Sometimes our confidence is shaken when trials come, especially if they are lengthy. But when we have an assurance of God's love for us, no matter what comes against us, we know deep inside that we are more than conquerors. If we are truly confident, we have no need to fear trouble or trying times, because we know they will pass.

Whenever a trial of any kind comes against you, always remember: *This too shall pass!* Be confident that during the trial you will learn something that will help you in the future.

The closer we are to God, the more steps of faith we take, deciding to be confident in all things in Him. Confident people get the job done. They are fulfilled because they are succeeding at being themselves.

We will not succeed at being ourselves until our confidence is in God.

The Importance of Intercession

And I sought a man among them who should build up the wall and stand in the gap before Me for the land . . .   EZEKIEL 22:30

To intercede means to *stand in the gap* for someone else, to plead his case before the throne of God. If there is a breach in people's relationship with God for any reason, we have the privilege of placing ourselves in that breach and praying for them. We can intercede for them and expect to see them comforted and encouraged while they wait. We can also expect a timely breakthrough for them concerning their need being met.

I don't know what I would do if people did not intercede for me. I petition God to give me people to intercede for me and for the fulfillment of the ministry to which He has called me. We need each other's prayers of intercession.

Praying for others is equivalent to sowing seed. We must sow seed if we are to reap a harvest (Galatians 6:7). Sowing seed into the lives of other people through intercession is one sure way to reap a harvest in our own life. Each time we pray for someone else, we are inviting God to not only work in that person's life but also in our own.

Intercession is one of the most important ways we carry on the ministry of Jesus Christ that He began in this earth.

We can release God's power in the lives of others by praying for them.

Do It Afraid

Now [in Haran] the Lord said to Abram, Go for yourself [for your own advantage] away from your country, from your relatives and your father's house, to the land that I will show you.

GENESIS 12:1

How would you feel if God told you to leave your home, your family, and everything familiar and comfortable to you and head out to who knows where? Would you be afraid? That is precisely the challenge Abram faced, and it frightened him. That's why God kept saying to him again and again, "Fear not."

Elisabeth Elliot, whose husband was killed along with four other missionaries in Ecuador, tells how her life was controlled completely by fear. Every time she started to step out, fear stopped her, until a friend told her something that set her free. She said, "Why don't you do it afraid?" Elisabeth Elliot and Rachel Saint, sister of one of the murdered missionaries, went on to evangelize the Indian tribes, including the people who had killed their husband and brother.

If we wait to do something until we are not afraid, we will probably accomplish very little for God, for others, or even for ourselves. Both Abram and Joshua had to step out in faith and obedience to God to do what He had commanded them to do—even while they felt afraid. We can do the same!

Be determined that your life is not going to be ruled by fear but by God's Word.

Secure in Jesus

*I am the Vine; you are the branches. Whoever lives in Me and I
in him bears much (abundant) fruit. However, apart from Me
[cut off from vital union with Me] you can do nothing.*

JOHN 15:5

God wants us to be as totally dependent and reliant upon Him as a
branch is on a vine. We would be unwise to put confidence in the
flesh—ours or anybody else's.

How many times have you trusted in your own strength and
failed miserably? How many times have other people let you down
after you put your trust in them? How many times have you been
disappointed when others rejected you or failed to do what you
expected? God will allow us to be disappointed time after time until
we learn to lean on Him and put our confidence in Him alone.

I am not suggesting that we shouldn't have any confidence in people, but we do need to realize they are imperfect and it is impossible
for them to never let us down. Jesus, however, does not disappoint
us! He is always with us, always for us, and is the only one we can
put our total trust in.

**Have great relationships with people, but don't give them
the trust that belongs only to God!**

A Prayer of Commitment

Commit your way to the Lord [roll and repose each care of your load on Him]; trust (lean on, rely on, and be confident) also in Him and He will bring it to pass.   PSALM 37:5

When we are tempted to worry or take on the care of some situation in life, we can pray a "prayer of commitment." God intervenes in our situations when we commit them to Him.

In my own life, I found that the more I tried to take care of things myself, the bigger mess my life became. I was quite independent and found it difficult to humble myself and admit that I needed help. However, when I finally submitted to God in these areas and found the joy of casting all my care on Him, I could not believe I had lived so long under such huge amounts of pressure.

Commit to the Lord your children, your marriage, your personal relationships, and especially anything you may be tempted to be concerned about. Only God really knows what needs to be done, and He is the only One Who is qualified to do it. The more we sincerely commit ourselves to God, the closer we will be to Him and the happier we will be.

A believer who can trust the Father when things do not seem to make sense is a mature believer.

From the Pit to the Palace

And Pharaoh said to Joseph, Forasmuch as [your] God has
shown you all this, there is nobody as intelligent and discreet and
understanding and wise as you are.

You shall have charge over my house, and all my people shall be
governed according to your word . . . Only in matters of the throne
will I be greater than you are.   GENESIS 41:39–40

A pit is a ditch, a trap, or a snare. It refers to destruction. Satan always wants to bring us into the pit.

Joseph was sold into slavery by his brothers. They actually threw him into a pit and intended to leave him there to die, but God had other plans. Joseph ended up being sold into slavery in Egypt, where he was thrown in prison for refusing to compromise his integrity. Yet everywhere Joseph went, God gave him favor. Ultimately, Joseph was promoted to the palace, second in command to Pharaoh.

How did Joseph get from the pit to the palace? I believe it was by remaining positive, refusing to be bitter, and choosing to boldly trust God. Even though it looked like he was defeated on many occasions, he refused to give up on trusting God.

Joseph had a right attitude. He knew God was in control even when it looked like the circumstances of his life were spinning out of control. The same is true in your life. If you'll keep a positive attitude, knowing that God is in control, He can take you from the pit to the palace in ways you never imagined.

No matter where you started, you can have a great finish!

Refuse to Be Bitter

But Jesus said to him, Judas! Would you betray and deliver up the
Son of Man with a kiss?   LUKE 22:48

Jesus bore our sins so we do not have to bear them. But there are
other things He endured on His way to the cross that serve as an
example for us, things that we will have to go through and ways
we will have to follow in His footsteps. Jesus faced the betrayal of
Judas at the worst moment of His life but did not let it hinder Him.

Betrayal is especially painful when we are hurt by someone we
love, respect, and trust. We may become defensive and bitter in an
effort to never be hurt again. But with God's help, betrayal is something we can recover from and not let hinder us, no matter how we
feel.

In Matthew 24:10–13, Jesus warns us that in the last days betray-
als will increase. As believers, how we respond to disappointment
in people is more important than what they did to us. If you are
betrayed or wounded by someone you trusted, refuse to get bitter.
Instead, follow the example of Jesus and forgive them. We can't
choose what other people do, but we can choose to have a right
response.

We must determine that with God's help, we can allow
our pain to make us better, not bitter.

A Divine Attitude Adjustment

And be constantly renewed in the spirit of your mind [having a
fresh mental and spiritual attitude].   EPHESIANS 4:23

God wants us to always maintain a good attitude for two reasons.
First, it glorifies Him and encourages other people to remain positive
when they have problems; and second, it allows Him to work in our
lives, bringing help and deliverance from our struggles.

Always having a good attitude is difficult unless we receive God's
grace to do so. Jesus said that apart from Him, we could do nothing
(John 15:5), but through Him we can do all things (Philippians 4:13).

Don't wait until you are tempted to have a bad attitude, but pray
daily that no matter what comes your way, you can endure it with
a good attitude. We will always be tempted, but we can pray not to
give in to the temptation.

A good attitude is one of our greatest assets. It keeps us hopeful
no matter what is happening in our lives.

———————

**Ask God to fill your attitude with His Holy Spirit at
all times!**

Putting Others First

For by the grace (unmerited favor of God) given to me I warn
everyone among you not to estimate and think of himself more
highly than he ought [not to have an exaggerated opinion of his
own importance] . . .　　　ROMANS 12:3

Humility that is manifested in not thinking we are better than other
people always helps us treat people with respect and kindness. In
Matthew 7:12 Jesus gave us instruction that affects the way we deal
with every person we come across over the course of a day—friends,
family, coworkers, and even those people who are unkind to us.

Jesus said, "Whatever you desire that others would do to and for
you, even so do also to and for them, for this (sums up) the Law and
the Prophets." It's a pretty simple concept and a great way to live life.
In order to experience God's best for our lives, we are to treat people
the way we would like to be treated. We should look for the needs of
others first and see what we can do to serve them.

Our lives are going to be less than God's best if we are consumed
with "self." Self-centeredness keeps us from seeing the needs of others and causes us to miss the blessings that come when we serve. We
don't have to totally forget about our own needs. But we can chase
selfishness away by not *always* thinking about our needs first.

If you'll begin to treat the people around you with love,
kindness, and respect, you'll be surprised at how much it
will impact the way they treat you in return.

The Joy of Believing

Where there is no vision . . . the people perish . . .

PROVERBS 29:18

The book of Proverbs says that where there is no vision, people perish. A vision is something we see in our minds, "a mental sight" as one definition puts it. It may be something God puts in our hearts or it may be something we want to see happen and have prayerfully submitted to God. A vision for our lives involves the way we think about ourselves and our future.

I've noticed that some people are afraid to believe for something good. They think they may be setting themselves up for disappointment. They have not realized they will be constantly disappointed if they don't believe. I feel that if I believe for a lot and just get half of it, I am better off than I would be to believe for nothing and get all of it. I want to encourage you to start believing for good things. Believe you can do whatever you need to do in life through Christ. When you believe, it stirs up faith in your heart, and faith pleases God, bringing you closer to Him.

Avoid having an "It will never happen" attitude. Let your faith soar. If you're not sure how to do that, start by taking an inventory of your thoughts. What have you been thinking and believing lately? An honest answer may help you understand why you have not been receiving what you have wanted to receive.

God has invited us to pray boldly, with confidence in His goodness to us, and I suggest you start today!

Change Is a Process

*And so after waiting patiently, Abraham received what was
promised.*   HEBREWS 6:15 NIV

Change doesn't come easily. I'll never forget about the lady who
approached me one day after I finished teaching. In exasperation,
she put her hands on her hips and said, "I want my money back!" I
was pretty surprised by her declaration, and I replied, "What do you
mean you want your money back?" She said, "Joyce, I gave to your
ministry and I've been doing this stuff you say to do for *two whole
weeks* and nothing's changed!"

In hindsight, it's pretty comical, but in the moment I explained
to this woman that's not the way it works. Change takes time. And
patience is required to successfully work through the process of getting the result you want. She left disgusted because she wanted an
instant fix, and that is not what God offers us. When you were saved,
you stepped onto a road that led you to a lifetime journey of change.
And our lives are changed through God's Word (James 1:21–25).

In order to live in close, intimate fellowship with God, make the
decision to be a lifetime follower and learner. Read the Word. Listen
to teachings about the Word. There is nothing better than getting the
Word of God into your heart…it's the most important part of the
process.

**The Bible says we inherit the promises of God through
faith and patience (Hebrews 6:12), and faith comes
by hearing God's Word (Romans 10:17).**

Getting Untangled

No soldier when in service gets entangled in the enterprises of [civilian] life; his aim is to satisfy and please the one who enlisted him.   2 TIMOTHY 2:4

Do you ever find yourself not taking time to spend with God because you're so busy with other things? In 2 Timothy 2:4, Paul tells his protégé, Timothy, that a wise soldier avoids getting entangled in things that won't satisfy the person who enlisted him. In other words, a child of God who wants to please God keeps his priorities straight and refuses to do things that could distract him from what is really important.

In order to grow closer to God on a daily basis, you'll have to avoid some of the distractions and entanglements of the world. This may mean saying no to an opportunity you'd like to take but really don't have time for. It could mean exercising good boundaries and not getting too wrapped up in other people's problems. It's important to help people, but there is a difference between godly involvement and entanglement. It may even mean being less focused on the stresses and cares that come up over the course of each day, because they certainly can distract us from God's will and purpose for our lives.

God loves you and wants to be in relationship with you. Don't let the entanglements of the world keep you from enjoying daily fellowship with Him.

———————————

Don't let the less important things crowd out what is most important in your life.

Good Things to Come

Then I said to you, Dread not, neither be afraid of them. The Lord your God Who goes before you, He will fight for you just as He did for you in Egypt before your eyes.

DEUTERONOMY 1:29–30

Do you look forward to every day with a spirit of joy and expectation of good things to come, or do you awake each morning in a state of dread? One might dread going to work, driving in traffic, cleaning the house, or dealing with difficult people. Dread is a subtle form of fear that the devil uses to steal our joy and prevent us from enjoying life. It prevents us from walking in the will of God and moving forward in the plans of God to receive His blessings.

Dread comes after us aggressively and cannot be defeated passively. Allowing negative feelings and thoughts into your mind will steal your joy and peace. But you can trust God to help you with anything you need to do. And as He gives you grace, the thing you were dreading turns out not to be so bad after all. We can choose to believe that Jesus goes before us and makes a way for us. When a project seems difficult or unpleasant, don't start dreading it. If you are going to do it anyway, you might as well enjoy it!

As Christians, we can find joy even in unpleasant circumstances because the presence of God is with us. We can enjoy our life with Him in the midst of adverse and difficult conditions. Our joy comes from Who is inside us, not in what is around us.

If we set our minds to it, we can enjoy everything we do in life. Where God guides, He provides.

Avoid Comparisons

... When they measure themselves with themselves and compare themselves with one another, they are without understanding and behave unwisely.   2 CORINTHIANS 10:12

If you've dealt with insecurity in your life, an important key to overcoming that insecurity is this: *Never compare yourself with anyone else because it invites feelings of inferiority.*

I really want to encourage you to stop comparing yourself with other people about how you look, what position you occupy, or how long you pray. Comparison puts the focus on self and thwarts God's plan for your life.

In the same way, we would be wise to avoid comparing our trials to those of other people. You may be going through something difficult, but don't look at somebody else and say, "Why is all this happening to me while you've got it so easy?"

Jesus revealed to Peter ahead of time some of the suffering he would go through. Peter immediately wanted to compare his suffering and his lot in life with somebody else's by saying, "What about this man?" Jesus answered by saying, "If I want him to stay (survive, live) until I come, what is that to you? [What concern is it of yours?] You follow Me!" (John 21:22).

That is His answer to us also. We are not called to compare, only to comply to His will for us.

God wants you to know that you are unique and He has an individualized, specialized plan for your life.

Starting with Prayer

Be unceasing in prayer [praying perseveringly].

1 THESSALONIANS 5:17

I have been walking with God most of my life, and I am still learning the importance of not doing anything without praying about it first. The Bible says we are to pray without ceasing. This doesn't mean we sit around all day, doing nothing except praying. It simply means that we include prayer in everything we do. I like to say, "Pray your way through the day."

Praying is probably the most important part of life preparation. It has been said that every failure happens because of a failure to pray! I suggest you don't do anything without first praying.

The Bible says that we should acknowledge God in all our ways and He will direct our steps and make them sure (Proverbs 3:6). It's encouraging to know that we can call on God and He will provide daily guidance and strength.

You become closer to God when you go to Him in prayer all throughout the day. It allows you to fellowship with God and it opens the door for Him to work in your life, your situation, and the lives of your loved ones.

God will enable you to do things that will frequently surprise you if you take Him as your partner in life. But it all begins with prayer.

Having a Willing Heart

And Nathan said to the king, Go, do all that is in your heart,
for the Lord is with you.　　　　　　　　　　　　2 SAMUEL 7:3

A willing heart is a heart that "wants to." If there is something we want to do strongly enough, somehow we will find a way to do it. With God's help and a willing heart, we can have a close relationship with Him, keep our house clean, save money, get out of debt, or reach any other goal in life we may have set for ourselves. Our victory or defeat has a lot to do with our "want to."

Many times we lay the blame for our failures on the devil, other people, the past, and on and on. But the bottom line may be that we just don't have enough of the right kind of "want to."

If you really want to be closer to God, I believe you will be. Your willing heart will cause you to seek Him with a new passion. You'll choose to spend time each day in prayer and studying the Word. God will see your heart and draw close to you even as you are drawing close to Him.

We don't always feel like doing what we want to do, but you don't have to make your decisions based on feelings.

What Is Grace?

... The [Holy] Spirit [Who imparts] grace (the unmerited favor and blessing of God).   HEBREWS 10:29

Grace is the power of the Holy Spirit available to you to do with ease what you cannot do by striving in your own strength. Grace is God's power coming into our lives, freely enabling us to do whatever we need to do. God's grace is always available, but we do need to receive it by faith and refuse to try to do things in our own strength without God.

The Holy Spirit ministers grace to us from God the Father. Grace is actually the Holy Spirit's power flowing out from the throne of God toward people to save them and enable them to live holy lives and accomplish the will of God.

We can rejoice and be full of peace, joy, and contentment each day because of God's grace in our lives. It is His grace that allows us to live in close fellowship with Him. With the grace of God, life can be enjoyed with an ease that produces rest and contentment.

We are saved by grace through faith, and we should learn to live the same way!

Change Your Thinking About Fear

Fear not [there is nothing to fear], for I am with you; do not look around you in terror and be dismayed, for I am your God. I will strengthen and harden you to difficulties, yes, I will help you; yes, I will hold you up and retain you with My [victorious] right hand of rightness and justice.   ISAIAH 41:10

With God's help, you can move from cowering in fear to overcoming fear by changing the way you think. The Bible refers to this as renewing your mind (Romans 12:2). Simply put, we can learn to think differently. Experiences or people from your past may have taught you to fear, but the Word of God can teach you to push past that fear. You can learn to be bold, courageous, and confident.

Don't let the fear of something prevent your success and joy in daily living. Fear has a large shadow, but fear itself is actually very small. Fear brings unnecessary torment in your life. When you feel afraid, you don't have to quit or turn back. God is with you, and because He is with you, you can feel the fear and do it anyway.

Instead of thinking you cannot do something when you are afraid, make up your mind that you will meet your goal and conquer the challenge before you. You may have thoughts of fear, but the Holy Spirit inside of you can change your thinking about fear. Fear seems like a monster, but it is one that will back down quickly when confronted with the truth from God's Word. Fear is like a school bully: It pushes everyone around until someone finally challenges it.

When we fear we will suffer, we already suffer the thing we fear.

Relationship, Not Rules

A new heart will I give you and a new spirit will I put within you,
and I will take away the stony heart out of your flesh and give you
a heart of flesh.   EZEKIEL 36:26

Many times when somebody is born again, the first things they are
told are: "You need to change your hairstyle, or dress differently. You
have a tattoo that needs to be covered up. You've got an earring in
the wrong place." Their introduction to Christianity is a list of rules,
things they must do, and things they must not do, according to what
people think is right and wrong.

Sadly, too many times no one talks to them at all about their
heart or their relationship with God. Instead it's about all these
things they have to do if they want to be part of a particular religious
organization. Although God will lead us to make positive changes
in our lives, He totally accepts us as we are, and we need to do the
same for new Christians. Give them time, and God will lead them by
giving them new desires.

Jesus died so we could have a deep, passionate, personal relationship with God. He didn't die to give us a list of rules. He gave
us something much deeper and much better—He gave us access
to God so that we could be in close personal relationship with our
heavenly Father.

The closer you get to God, the more He lovingly and
graciously changes you from the inside out.

Waiting on the Lord

*Our inner selves wait [earnestly] for the Lord; He is our Help and
our Shield.*   PSALM 33:20

In our instant and fast-paced society, the spiritual discipline of waiting on the Lord is often lacking. We want everything we want and we
want it right now! But if we are always in such a hurry, we will miss
out on the close fellowship with God that takes time to develop. God
wants to speak to our hearts if only we will be patient to listen.

Elijah was a man who knew the secret of being patient. After slaying the prophets of Baal, Elijah learned a valuable lesson on waiting
on God. The Lord told Elijah to go stand on a mountain and wait. A
great wind came; then came a great earthquake and a great fire, but
the Lord was in none of those. Consider what 1 Kings 19:12 says:
"After the fire [a sound of gentle stillness and] a still, small voice."
The Lord spoke in a still, small voice, *after* the wind, the earthquake,
and the fire. If Elijah had been impatient in prayer, he would not
have heard the Lord's voice.

David also learned to wait in the house of the Lord and "to meditate, consider, and inquire in His temple" (Psalm 27:4). In order for
us to pray effectively, we can choose to wait patiently and listen for
His Word. Waiting and listening takes our focus off of us and places
it on Him, Who is the answer to all our needs.

**It is often in silence when the power of God is moving
the most mightily. Allow the Holy Spirit to teach you how
to wait in His presence.**

Keep Trusting God

But He knows the way that I take [He has concern for it,
appreciates, and pays attention to it]. When He has tried me,
I shall come forth as refined gold [pure and luminous].

JOB 23:10

There will always be situations in life where we will be required to trust God no matter what happens or whether we understand everything. This is why we often find ourselves saying to God, "What is going on in my life? What are You doing? What is happening? I don't understand." Sometimes the things happening in us seem to be taking us in the exact opposite direction of what we feel God has previously revealed to us.

This is when many people give up and go back to something that will be quicker and easier for them. If you are in a place right now where nothing in your life makes any sense, keep trusting God. He is close to you. He hasn't abandoned you. He is going to see you through.

There is no such thing as trusting God without unanswered questions. As long as God is training us to trust, there are always going to be things in our life we just don't understand. When heaven is silent, continue doing the things you have learned and know to do, and keep trusting Him. God will make all the pieces in your life work together for His purpose.

Tomorrow's answers usually don't come until tomorrow.

Learn to Love Yourself

. . . I have loved you with an everlasting love; therefore with loving-kindness have I drawn you and continued My faithfulness to you.   JEREMIAH 31:3

Many people don't really like themselves. They are very self-critical; they reject themselves and may even hate themselves. The Bible teaches us not to be selfish and self-centered, but it never instructs us not to love ourselves in a balanced way. I always say, "Don't be in love with yourself, but love yourself." If you don't love yourself, you will be miserable because you are always with yourself. You are the one person you will never get away from, not even for one second of your life.

I once heard a young woman ask a pastor to pray for her because she hated herself. He looked at her and took a step backward in dismay. He said very clearly, "Who do you think you are to hate yourself after God sent His only Son to suffer so horribly and die in your place? If God loved you that much, surely you can love yourself."

His statement opened her eyes to the mistake she was making, and she began her journey of learning to love and accept herself. I encourage you to do the same. Take a step of faith and say, "I love myself with the love of God. I accept myself."

As you begin to see yourself as God sees you, your entire attitude and disposition will change. You will become a more positive, confident person, and you will begin to enjoy your life so much more.

Because God loves you, you can love yourself.

Pray About Everything and Fear Nothing

Be strong and let your heart take courage, all you who wait for
and hope for and expect the Lord!   PSALM 31:24

Some time ago I felt the Lord speaking these words to me: "Pray about everything and fear nothing." Over the next couple of weeks, He showed me different things about prayer versus fear. Many of them dealt with little areas in which fear would try to creep into my life and cause me problems. He showed me that in every case, no matter how great or important or how small or insignificant, the solution was to pray.

Sometimes we become afraid by focusing on our circumstances. The more we focus on the problem, the more fearful we become. Instead, we can choose to keep our focus on God. He is able to handle anything that we may ever have to face in this life.

God has promised to strengthen us, to harden us to difficulties, to hold us up and retain us with His victorious right hand (Isaiah 41:10). He also commands us not to be afraid. But remember, He is not commanding us never to feel fear, but rather not to let it control us.

The Lord is saying to us today, "Fear not, I will help you." But we never experience the help of God until we place everything on the line, until we are obedient enough to step out in faith.

Don't back down when you feel fear. Trust the Lord and keep moving.

Good from Bad

As for you, you thought evil against me, but God meant it for good, to bring about that many people should be kept alive, as they are this day.   GENESIS 50:20

God wants to restore your soul. The closer you get to Him, the more you experience His healing, strengthening, restoring power. He'll take you back to where your life got off track and make everything right from that moment forward.

Joseph is the classic biblical example of how God takes what was meant for evil against us and works it for our good. In that dramatic scene where Joseph is speaking in Genesis 50:20, he tells his brothers that the evil they meant to do to him (and it was truly evil), God had used for good to save them and their families and hundreds of thousands of others in a time of famine.

In my own life, I cannot truthfully say I am glad I was abused. But through the power of forgiveness and yielding my pain to God, He has healed me and made me a better, stronger, more spiritually powerful and sensitive person. He has restored my soul and driven out the fear and insecurity. I can trust, love, forgive, and live with simplicity in my approach to life because God has restored my soul, and He can do the same thing for you.

———————————

If bad things have happened in your life, remember this: Only God can restore your situation. He can bring good from bad.

The Power of Joy and Peace

Be well balanced (temperate, sober of mind), be vigilant and cautious at all times; for that enemy of yours, the devil, roams around like a lion roaring [in fierce hunger], seeking someone to seize upon and devour   1 PETER 5:8

When you find yourself in a troublesome situation, let your goal be to simply stay calm. Each time you begin to feel upset or frustrated, stop and ask yourself, "What is the enemy trying to do here?"

If the devil cannot drive you to be fearful and upset about a problem, he has no power over you. You stay in God's strength and power when you maintain a calm, peaceful, trusting attitude.

The Holy Spirit works in an atmosphere of joy and peace. He does not work in turmoil. In a time of trial, your strength is found in drawing close to God and entering into His rest. All of these biblical words—*abide, still, rest, stand*, and *in Christ*—say basically the same thing: *Do not lose your joy and peace.*

In Christ, you are called to be an overcomer. You have the assurance of always triumphing in Him. If you take each problem as it comes, it will work out all right. Jesus is always with you in each situation. Just remember to trust Him for enough joy and peace for today.

———————

There is tremendous power in choosing to walk in peace and joy, regardless of the circumstances around you.

When You Feel Worried

To grant [consolation and joy] to those who mourn in Zion—to
give them an ornament (a garland or diadem) of beauty instead of
ashes, the oil of joy instead of mourning, the garment [expressive]
of praise instead of a heavy, burdened, and failing spirit . . . that
He may be glorified.   ISAIAH 61:3

God wants to take care of us, but in order to let Him, it is important
that we choose to stop worrying. Many people say they want God
to take care of them, but they spend their days worrying or trying
to figure out all the answers instead of waiting for God's direction.
They are actually wallowing around in their "ashes," but they still
want God to give them beauty. In order for God to give us the beauty,
we have to give Him the "ashes."

We give God our cares by believing that He can and will take care
of us. Hebrews 4:3 says, "For we who have believed (adhered to and
trusted in and relied on God) do enter that rest . . ."

We enter into the Lord's rest through believing. Worry is the
opposite of faith. Worry steals our peace, physically wears us out,
and can even make us sick. If we are worrying, we are not trusting
God, and we are not entering His rest.

What a great trade God has provided. You give Him ashes, and
He gives you beauty. You give Him all your worries and concerns,
and He gives you protection, stability, a place of refuge, and fullness
of joy—the privilege of being cared for by Him.

———————

Jesus did not worry, and you do not have to worry either.

Stirred to Action

And Moses called Bezalel and Aholiab and every able and
wisehearted man in whose mind the Lord had put wisdom
and ability, everyone whose heart stirred him up to come to do
the work.   EXODUS 36:2

Something powerful happens in your life when your heart is stirred
up for action. It doesn't do us any good to say, "Oh, I wish I felt that
way." We can decide to do something about the way we feel by stirring up our own hearts to do what God has called us to do.

How do we stir up our faith? I have discovered that the Word
of God coming out of my own mouth in the form of prayer, praise,
preaching, or confessions is the best way that I can find to fan the
fire. It stirs up the gift within, keeps my faith and my hope active,
and prevents my spirit from sinking within me.

Passivity, procrastination, and laziness are tools the enemy uses
against God's people. A passive person waits to be moved by an
outside force before taking action. But we can be motivated and led
by the Holy Spirit within us, not by outside forces. The best way to
guard against passivity is to do whatever is before you with all of
your might.

Keep your God-given gift, that fire within you, stirred up.

The Spirit of Adoption

*For [the Spirit which] you have now received [is] not a spirit of
slavery to put you once more in bondage to fear, but you have
received the Spirit of adoption [the Spirit producing sonship] in
[the bliss of] which we cry, Abba (Father)! Father!*

ROMANS 8:15

The apostle Paul teaches us that the Holy Spirit is the Spirit of adoption. The word *adoption* means that we are brought into the family of God, even though we were previously outsiders, unrelated to God in any way. We were sinners and separated from God, but God in His great mercy redeemed us, purchased us, and brought us close to Him once again through the blood of His own Son.

We understand adoption in the natural sense. We know that some children without parents are adopted by people who purposely choose them and take them as their own. What an honor to be chosen on purpose by those who want to pour out their love on them.

This is exactly what God did for us as believers in Christ. Because of what Jesus did for us on the cross, we are now eternally part of His family, and His Spirit dwells in our spirit and cries out to the Father. God the Father decided before the foundation of the world was laid that anyone who loved Christ would be loved and accepted by Him as His child. He decided He would adopt all those who accepted Jesus as their Savior. We become heirs of God and joint heirs with His Son, Jesus Christ.

**It is the knowledge of our family relationship to God
that gives us boldness to go before His throne and let our
requests be made known.**

Seek the One Thing

One thing have I asked of the Lord, that will I seek, inquire for,
and [insistently] require: that I may dwell in the house of the Lord
[in His presence] all the days of my life, to behold and gaze upon
the beauty [the sweet attractiveness and the delightful loveliness]
of the Lord and to meditate, consider, and inquire in His temple.

PSALM 27:4

If you knew you could only ask for one thing, what would your request be? David said there was only one thing he sought after: to dwell in God's presence.

Being close to God is the number one priority we should have in life.

But we can get so distracted with the events of daily life that we neglect the most important thing—spending time with God, knowing Him, appreciating Him, seeking His direction.

There are many empty people in the world who are trying to satisfy the voids in their lives with a new car, a promotion, a relationship, or some other thing. But their efforts to find complete fulfillment in those things never work, because each of us has a God-shaped hole inside, and nothing can fill it except God Himself.

I encourage you to seek God first and put the other things in your life *after* Him. If you will put Him first in everything you do, you will be blessed beyond measure.

God is the "One Thing" who can give you great joy, peace, satisfaction, and contentment.

Secure Enough to Be Different

The sun is glorious in one way, the moon is glorious in another
way, and the stars are glorious in their own [distinctive] way;
for one star differs from and surpasses another in its beauty and
brilliance.   1 CORINTHIANS 15:41

We are all different. Like the sun, the moon, and the stars, God has
created us to be different from one another, and He has done it on
purpose. Each of us meets a need, and we are all part of God's overall plan. When we try to be just like someone else, we lose ourselves
and stray from who God created us to be. God designed us to fit into
His plan, not to feel pressured trying to fit into everyone else's plans.

Not only is it okay to be different, it is how you were created. We
are all born with different temperaments, different physical features,
different fingerprints, different gifts and abilities. Our goal should
be to find out what we individually are supposed to be, then succeed
at being that. That is why Romans 12 teaches us to give ourselves to
our gift. We are to find out what we are good at and then throw ourselves wholeheartedly into it.

You can be free to love and accept yourself and others around you
without feeling pressure to compare or compete. Secure people who
know God loves them and has a plan for them are not threatened by
the abilities of others. They enjoy what other people can do, and they
enjoy what they can do too.

God gave you gifts and desires for you to use. Focus on
your potential instead of your limitations.

Rejoicing Every Step of the Way

Rejoice in the Lord always [delight, gladden yourselves in Him];
again I say, Rejoice!   PHILIPPIANS 4:4

Paul felt rejoicing in the goodness of God was so important that he
tells us twice in this verse from Philippians to rejoice. He urges in
the following verses not to fret or have any anxiety about anything
but to pray and give thanks to God in everything—not *after* everything is over.

If we wait until everything is perfect before rejoicing and giving
thanks, we won't have much fun. Learning to enjoy life even in the
midst of trying circumstances is one way we grow closer to God.
Paul also writes that we "are constantly being transfigured into His
very own image in ever increasing splendor and from one degree of
glory to another" (2 Corinthians 3:18). That means we can enjoy the
glory we are experiencing at each level of our development, because
each new day is another step toward the person God is shaping us
to be.

When I first started my ministry, my happiness was dependent
on my circumstances. Finally the Lord showed me the doorway to
happiness. He gave me a breakthrough by teaching me that fullness of joy is found in His "presence"—not in His "presents" (Psalm
16:11).

True joy is discovered when we seek God's face.

Shake Off Rejection

He who hears and heeds you [disciples] hears and heeds Me; and
he who slights and rejects you slights and rejects Me; and he who
slights and rejects Me slights and rejects Him who sent Me.

LUKE 10:16

It is a fact of life that we will deal with rejection from time to time. David dealt with rejection. Paul dealt with rejection. Even Jesus was rejected. So when you suffer rejection for doing what God leads you to do—doing things that are different from what others around you are doing—don't despair; you are in good company.

When I first started preaching, I was insecure and took my share of criticism and rejection. There were times when I was very discouraged. Finally, the Lord spoke to me in my spirit and said: "I am the One Who called you. Don't worry what people think. If you do, you are going to be worrying all your life because the devil will never stop finding people who think something unkind about you."

In Acts 28:1–5, when the apostle Paul was bitten by a snake, he simply shook off the snake and suffered no evil effects. That is what we can do with rejection. When we are close to God and find our identity in Him, rather than in other people's opinion of us, we can shake off whatever is trying to discourage us. Whatever you are dealing with today—fear, rejection, discouragement, disappointment, loneliness—shake it off and go on.

Even when our rejection is from people who are close to us, we can be determined to keep pressing on toward fulfilling what God has called us to do.

God's Protection

He who dwells in the secret place of the Most High shall remain stable and fixed under the shadow of the Almighty [Whose power no foe can withstand].   PSALM 91:1

God's presence is a secret place where we can dwell in peace, feel safe, and enter God's rest. This secret place is not a physical location; it is a spiritual place where worry vanishes and peace reigns. It is the place of God's presence. When we spend time praying and seeking God and dwelling in His presence, we are in the secret place.

When you and I *dwell in Christ* or *dwell in the secret place*, we do not just visit there occasionally, we take up permanent residence in this place of refuge. It is the place we run to when we are hurting, overwhelmed, or feeling faint. It is the place we run to when we are being mistreated or persecuted, and when we are in great need. It is also the place where we offer thanksgiving and praise for the goodness of God in our lives. I like to say that God's presence is my first "go to" place when I have any kind of need.

It is important that we be firmly planted in God—to know the Source of our help in every situation and in every circumstance. With God's help, we can have our own secret place of peace and security by simply relying on God and trusting Him completely. We are never more than one thought away from God's presence!

God wants us to take refuge under the protective shadow of His wings. He wants us to run to Him.

A Blameless Heart

*For the eyes of the Lord run to and fro throughout the whole
earth to show Himself strong in behalf of those whose hearts are
blameless toward Him . . .*   2 CHRONICLES 16:9

What does it mean to have a blameless heart? It means you have
a heartfelt desire to do right and to please God. A person who has
a blameless heart truly loves God, though he himself may not be
blameless or perfect in all of his ways. He may still have weaknesses.
He may make mistakes or lose his temper. But when he does, he
is quick to repent and receive God's forgiveness. If he has offended
someone else, he will humble himself and apologize. Because his
heart is right toward God, it is easy for the Holy Spirit to teach him.

When God searches for those to work through, He doesn't look
for somebody with a perfect performance. If any one of us could have
perfect behavior, we would not need Jesus. We can, however, love
God with a perfect heart, and when we do, He shows Himself strong
on our behalf.

**The Lord strengthens those who have a right heart
attitude toward Him.**

He Won't Let You Sink

Now to Him Who is able to keep you without stumbling or
slipping or falling, and to present [you] unblemished (blameless
and faultless) before the presence of His glory in triumphant joy
and exultation [with unspeakable, ecstatic delight]—

JUDE 24

Many children who are just learning to swim feel afraid in a swimming pool. Unless they are being carried by a parent or another trusted adult, they feel insecure because they realize the water is over their heads.

At various points in our lives, all of us fear we're getting "in over our heads" or we feel we are "out of our depth." The reality is that without God we're always in over our heads. There are difficulties and challenges all around us in life. Some are small and inconvenient; others are large and intimidating. The car breaks down, a job is lost, a friend or family member dies, an argument occurs, a bad report comes from the doctor. When these things happen, it's easy to panic because we feel we're in over our heads.

But the truth is we've never really been in control when it comes to life's crucial elements. We've always been dependent on the grace of God to carry us through. God is never out of His depth. When we depend on Him, we can relax and be at peace, knowing He'll carry us through. He'll never let us go.

_____

You are safe in your Father's arms. Even when you feel
you're in over your head, He is holding you by His grace.

Let the "Umpire" Make the Call

And let the peace (soul harmony which comes) from Christ
rule (act as umpire continually) in your hearts [deciding and
settling with finality all questions that arise in your minds, in
that peaceful state] to which as [members of Christ's] one body
you were also called [to live]. And be thankful (appreciative),
[giving praise to God always].   COLOSSIANS 3:15

In Colossians 3:15, Paul tells us that peace is much like an umpire—it makes the call in our lives, settling every issue that needs a decision.

That simply means that if you don't feel peace about a decision or an action, don't go through with it. Let the "umpire" make the call. Some people make a career decision they didn't really have peace about, and then they wonder why they are stressed-out and unhappy in their jobs. A lot of people make expensive purchases even though they don't have peace about it, and then they continue to lose their peace every month when they have to make payments on those purchases.

But we can let the peace of Christ "rule (act as umpire continually)" in our hearts. The presence of peace will help us decide with confidence the questions that arise in our minds. If you spend time in prayer and in the Word of God regularly, you'll discover great insight and wisdom from the Lord. You won't have to wonder, *Should I or shouldn't I? Is this the right thing to do or is this a mistake?* As a child of God, living in close relationship with your heavenly Father, you will be able to follow the peace that He provides.

When you're not sure what to do, always follow peace!

To Live Like Christ

God said, Let Us [Father, Son, and Holy Spirit] make mankind
in Our image, after Our likeness, and let them have complete
authority over the fish of the sea, the birds of the air, the [tame]
beasts, and over all of the earth, and over everything that creeps
upon the earth.   GENESIS 1:26

In Genesis 1:26, when God said, "Let us…make mankind in Our
image," this image does not refer to a physical likeness, but to character likeness. We were created to take on His nature, His character,
as reflected in His Son, Jesus.

The greatest goal for every believer is Christlikeness. It is our
highest calling in life. It's exciting to know that we can be so close in
our relationship with the Lord that we begin to handle situations the
way Jesus would handle them and to treat people the way He would
treat them. Our aim is to want to do things the way Jesus would do
them.

Jesus is our example. In John 13:15, He told His disciples, after
washing their feet as a servant, "For I have given you this as an example, so that you should do [in your turn] what I have done to you."
Every day, and in every way, look to Jesus and follow the example He
set in the Word of God for your daily life.

**God will graciously keep working with each of us until
we get to the place where we act the way Jesus would act
in every situation in life.**

Developing Your Potential

Do you not know that in a race all the runners compete, but [only] one receives the prize? So run [your race] that you may lay hold [of the prize] and make it yours.   1 CORINTHIANS 9:24

When we draw close to God, choosing to shed fear and self-doubt, we are able to develop our potential and succeed at being all God intended us to be. But we cannot develop our potential if we fear failure. We will be so afraid of failing or making mistakes that it will prevent us from stepping out.

I often see people who have great potential, and yet when opportunities and promotions are offered them, they quickly turn them down. In many cases, they are insecure and unaware of how much they could accomplish if they would only step out in faith, knowing God is with them.

When we are insecure, frequently we will stay with what is safe and familiar rather than taking a chance on stepping out and failing. We avoid accepting greater responsibility because we feel we aren't ready—but the truth is that none of us is ever ready. However, God is always ready, and when He begins to move in your life, you can know that He will equip you with what you need at the time you need it.

Humbly leaning on God leads to success. When our faith is in Christ rather than ourselves, we are free to develop our potential, because we are free from the fear of failure.

Keep Life Interesting

Whatever may be your task, work at it heartily (from the soul), as
[something done] for the Lord and not for men.

COLOSSIANS 3:23

Life wasn't meant to be dull and boring. We are not created by God to merely do the same thing over and over until it has no meaning at all. God is creative. If you don't think so, just look around you. Many of the animals, bugs, plants, birds, trees, and other living things are unique, out of the ordinary, and totally amazing.

You were created to be unique, out of the ordinary and totally amazing too. That is why I think it is good to occasionally do something that seems outrageous to people and perhaps even to you. Do something that people won't expect. It will keep your life interesting and keep other people from thinking they have you tucked away nicely in a little box of their own design.

One great woman who was seventy-six years of age said that her goal was to do at least one outrageous thing per week. Isn't that a great idea? If you purposefully do something out of the norm on a regular basis, this will keep you from getting stuck in a rut, bored and unenthused about your life.

What outrageous thing will you do today?

––––––––––

Refuse to be bored and just limp along through life.
Be creative and add fun to whatever you do.

Praying Bold Prayers

Up to this time you have not asked a [single] thing in My Name...
but now ask and keep on asking and you will receive, so that your
joy (gladness, delight) may be full and complete.

JOHN 16:24

The most effective prayers are bold prayers. They are prayed by believers who are specific and have the boldness to come before God and really ask for the things they need in life, unashamed to make their requests known.

One of the major things that keeps people from praying boldly is they look at what they have done wrong instead of what Jesus has done right. The Bible teaches us plainly that God "...made Christ [virtually] to be sin Who knew no sin, so that in and through Him we might become...the righteousness of God" (2 Corinthians 5:21). Because we are righteous in Him, we can approach the throne of grace boldly with our needs (Hebrews 4:16).

John 16:23–24 tells us we can come boldly before the throne in Jesus' name. The name of Jesus is powerful. When we use Jesus' name in our prayers, it's not some formula or magic charm that we tack on to the end of everything we pray. When we go in the name of Jesus, we're saying, "Father, I come to You presenting today all that Jesus is—not what I am."

Don't be vague or timid—be bold! You'll be surprised at the answers you'll receive.

God is waiting to surprise you with amazing things—are you ready to receive them?

God Has a Fantastic Plan for Your Life

Surely or only goodness, mercy, and unfailing love shall follow me all the days of my life, and through the length of my days the house of the Lord [and His presence] shall be my dwelling place.

PSALM 23.6

Psalm 23 is a powerful chapter of the Bible that describes the condition God wants us to live in constantly. He wants us to be protected, guided, and comforted. He wants to set a table of blessings before us in the very face of our enemies. He wants to anoint us with the oil of joy instead of mourning. He wants our cup of blessings to overflow continually in thanksgiving and praise to Him for His goodness, mercy, and unfailing love toward us. And He wants us to live every day, every moment, secure in His presence.

All these "wants" are a part of God's good plan for each of us. Regardless of how far we may have fallen, He wants to restore us to a closeness with Him and to that right and perfect plan He has for our lives.

It would benefit every one of us if we would say to ourselves several times a day, "God has a fantastic plan for my life. I want all that He wants for me. I receive His love and His goodness in my life. I will walk and live in the presence of the Lord."

Remember that the most important thing in receiving God's blessings is not our great faith but His great faithfulness.

Being Consistently Confident

*For in the Gospel a righteousness which God ascribes is revealed,
both springing from faith and leading to faith . . . The man who
through faith is just and upright shall live . . . by faith.*

ROMANS 1:17

Confidence is rooted in faith in God. This is why it is important that
we choose to be consistently confident, not occasionally confident.

I had to learn to remain confident when I was told by friends
and family that a woman should not be teaching the Word of God. I
knew God had called me to teach His Word, but I was still affected
by the rejection of people. I had to grow in confidence to the place
where people's opinions and their acceptance or rejection did not
affect my confidence level. My confidence had to be in God, not in
people.

Romans 1:17 tells us that we can go from faith to faith. I spent
many years going from faith to doubt to unbelief and then back to
faith. Then I realized that when I lose my confidence, I leave a door
open for the devil. If I allow him to steal my confidence, I suddenly
have no faith to minister to people.

If you want to succeed, choose to be consistently confident. Be
confident about your gifts and calling, your ability in Christ. Believe
you hear from God and that you are led by the Holy Spirit. Be bold in
the Lord. See yourself as a winner in Him.

**Focusing on God's great love for you helps you have great
confidence to do great things!**

Overcoming

The wicked flee when no man pursues them, but the
[uncompromisingly] righteous are bold as a lion.

PROVERBS 28:1

Fear robs many people of their faith. Fear of failure, fear of man, and fear of rejection are some of the strongest fears employed by Satan to hinder us from making progress.

But no matter what kind of fear the enemy sends against us, the important thing is to overcome it. When we are faced with fear, we must not give in to it. It is imperative to our victory that we determine, "With God's help, I will overcome."

The normal reaction to fear is flight. The enemy wants us to run; God wants us to stand still and see His deliverance. Because of fear, many people do not confront issues; they spend their lives running. We must learn to stand our ground and face fear, secure in the knowledge that we are more than conquerors through Christ (Romans 8:37).

Fear of failure torments multitudes. We fear what people will think of us if we fail. If we step out and fail, some people may hear about it; but they quickly forget it if we forget it and go on. It is better to try something and fail than to try nothing and succeed.

Approach life with boldness. The Spirit of the Lord is in you—so make up your mind not to fear.

The Power of a Renewed Heart

... For the Lord sees not as man sees; for man looks on the
outward appearance, but the Lord looks on the heart.

1 SAMUEL 16:7

God is the God of hearts. He does not look only at the exterior of a person, or even the things a person does, and judge the individual by that criterion. Man judges the flesh, but God judges the heart.

It is possible to do good works and still have a wrong heart attitude. It is also possible to do some things wrong but still have a right heart on the inside. God is much more inclined to use a person with a good heart and a few problems than He is to use a person who seems to have it all together but who has a wicked heart.

It is very important that we get in touch with our inner life and our heart attitude, the way we feel and think about things (what the Bible calls the hidden man of the heart), if we want to hear from God and live in close relationship with Him.

When God seeks to promote someone, He chooses a person after His own heart.

Looking Forward

And He Who is seated on the throne said, See! I make all things new. Also He said, Record this, for these sayings are faithful (accurate, incorruptible, and trustworthy) and true (genuine).

REVELATION 21:5

So many people live miserable lives because they are conflicted and feel burdened about the mistakes of their past. If you have been unhappy or discouraged because of the things that have happened in your past, I encourage you to change your thinking and set your focus in a whole new direction. Determine to be what God wants you to be, to have what God wants you to have, and to receive what Jesus died to give you.

Your new life in Christ means that you have been completely forgiven of all your sins. God has wiped your slate clean and taken up residence in your heart. You can let the past go and begin to get excited about your future.

When you feel discouraged, say, "I am not going to live in bondage anymore. I cannot do anything about what I have done in the past, but I can do something about my future. I am going to enjoy my life and have what Jesus died for me to have. I am going to let go of the past and go on pursuing God from this day forth!"

Yesterday is history. Tomorrow is a mystery. Today is a gift from God.

When We Need Him the Most

Lean on, trust in, and be confident in the Lord with all your heart and mind and do not rely on your own insight or understanding. In all your ways know, recognize, and acknowledge Him, and He will direct and make straight and plain your paths.

PROVERBS 3:5–6

Many times we say that we trust God, but inside we still have deeply embedded fears that He won't really come through for us when we need Him the most. So we falsely assume that if we keep thinking about the problem and worrying about it enough, then somehow we can take care of it on our own—just in case God doesn't show up and do something according to our timetable.

The problem with this attitude is that it brings us closer to our problems, not closer to God. However, when we choose to believe that God is in control and that He is going to handle whatever situation we are in, we move closer to God and our problems don't seem so worrisome after all.

Trusting God will keep you from reasoning and trying to figure out the things you don't have answers for yet. When you are faced with an overwhelming situation, don't listen to that nagging voice inside, asking, *What are you gonna do? What are you gonna do?* Just remind yourself, *I'm going to trust God, and He will show me what to do . . . if I need to do anything.*

Hold your peace, remain at rest, and God will fight for you.

God's Timing Is the Right Timing

*Consider it wholly joyful, my brethren, whenever you are
enveloped in or encounter trials of any sort or fall into various
temptations. Be assured and understand that the trial and
proving of your faith bring out endurance and steadfastness and
patience. But let endurance and steadfastness and patience have
full play and do a thorough work, so that you may be [people]
perfectly and fully developed [with no defects], lacking in nothing.*

JAMES 1:2–4

We don't usually see it while it's happening, but God is working out
His perfect plan for our lives behind the scenes. Though we want
results right now, character development takes time and patience.

The Bible says that patience does a thorough work in our lives.
When we wait on God, He makes us fully developed and complete,
lacking nothing. I've discovered that patience is more than the ability to wait; it is the ability to keep a good attitude while waiting.
This practical fruit of the Spirit comes from a close relationship
with God—it manifests itself in a calm, positive attitude despite the
circumstances.

"God's timing is usually not our timing. We are in a hurry, but
God isn't. He takes time to do things right—He lays a solid foundation before He attempts to build a building. We are God's building
under construction. He is the Master Builder, and He knows what
He is doing.

**When you are feeling impatient, remember that God's
timing is always perfect!**

Fullness of Joy

You will show me the path of life; in Your presence is fullness of
joy, at Your right hand there are pleasures forevermore.

PSALM 16:11

The presence of the Lord is always with us, but we do not always recognize it or take time to be conscious of it. I think this is why there
seems to be a lack of joy in the lives of many believers. There are a
lot of unhappy people who are spending their lives chasing things,
when nothing can keep us satisfied except God Himself.

When people are not satisfied inwardly, they usually look for
some outward object to satisfy their hunger. Often they end up in
a fruitless search for that which cannot fill the emptiness within.
We've heard it said, many people spend their lives climbing the ladder of success, only to find when they reach the top that their ladder
is leaning against the wrong building.

When we keep our priorities straight, we discover that everything
we really need in life is found in the Lord. Seek to dwell in His presence. In Him is the path of life, the fullness of joy, and pleasures
forevermore.

The reason we can laugh and enjoy life in spite of our
current circumstances is because Jesus is our joy.

Open-Book Tests

The Lord tests and proves the [unyieldingly] righteous....

PSALM 11:5

Sometimes teachers let students take open-book tests. They are allowed to have their textbook open while answering the questions. We are all going to go through tests. There are no exceptions—everybody is tested at different times in life. But they are all open-book tests; the answers are found in the Book. No matter what we are going through, God has provided the answers in His Word.

Drawing close to God through His Word during difficulty gives us strength and answers that we need. God often allows us to go through a difficult place because He is testing, stretching, and strengthening us. During such times Satan attacks us in our minds, telling us lies such as, "God doesn't love you, and if He was going to help you, He would have already done it. You might as well give up on trusting God and develop your own plan of escape." This is a time to hold on, not to give up!

Life isn't always easy. There are going to be some days and seasons when we are faced with challenges. But if you choose to lean on the Lord in those times, you'll realize that you can still have joy even on trying days. Godly strength, wisdom and knowledge, spiritual maturity, and character are developed in us as we go through tests.

In order to grow in God and do what He has called you to do, choose to be faithful. His character will be revealed in your life over time.

Kingdom Living

*[After all] the kingdom of God is not a matter of [getting the] food
and drink [one likes], but instead it is righteousness (that state
which makes a person acceptable to God) and [heart] peace and
joy in the Holy Spirit.*   ROMANS 14:17

God's kingdom is made up of things far greater and more beneficial
than worldly possessions. God does bless us with material possessions, but the kingdom is much more than that: It is righteousness,
peace, and joy in the Holy Spirit.

Righteousness is not the result of what we do, but rather what Jesus
has done for us (1 Corinthians 1:30). He takes our sin and gives us
His righteousness (2 Corinthians 5:21). When we accept this truth
by faith and receive it personally, we are free to live and enjoy the life
Jesus died to give us.

Peace is so wonderful—it is definitely kingdom living. This is why
we pursue peace, crave it, and go after it (Psalm 34:14; 1 Peter 3:11).
The closer we get to God, the more we understand that Jesus is our
peace (Ephesians 2:14). God's will for you and me is to enjoy His
peace that goes beyond understanding (Philippians 4:7).

Joy can be anything from calm delight to extreme hilarity. Joy
improves our countenance, our health, and the quality of our lives.
It strengthens our witness to others and gives us a godly perspective
on life (Nehemiah 8:10).

It is clear in the Word of God: Seek God and His kingdom, and
He will take care of everything else (Matthew 6:33).

There is no better life than life in the kingdom of God.

When You Feel Insecure

May Christ through your faith [actually] dwell (settle down,
abide, make His permanent home) in your hearts! May you
be rooted deep in love and founded securely on love.

EPHESIANS 3:17

Many people have feelings of insecurity about themselves because they can't accept themselves for who they are. Are you tired of being under pressure, wearing masks, trying to be someone you aren't? Wouldn't you like the freedom just to be accepted as you are, without pressure to be someone you really don't know how to be?

With God's help, we can learn our value is not in what we do but in who we are in Him. He wants us to come to Him as we are and trust Him to help us be all that He wants us to be.

The devil's plan is to deceive us into basing our worth on our performance, and then keep us focused on all our faults and shortcomings. Satan wants us to have a low opinion of ourselves so we'll pull away from God, and be miserable and unreceptive to His blessings, because we don't think we deserve them.

It is so important to develop a positive sense of being valuable, and being secure in Christ. Make a decision to accept yourself because that is what Jesus has already done. He will never reject anyone who comes to Him. You are greatly loved and highly valued!

God knows your faults and He loves you anyway.
Nothing will ever change His love for you.

A Tender Conscience

Therefore I always exercise and discipline myself [mortifying my body, deadening my carnal affections, bodily appetites, and worldly desires, endeavoring in all respects] to have a clear (unshaken, blameless) conscience, void of offense toward God and toward men.   ACTS 24:16

One way to live closer to God is to keep your heart tender. Having a tender conscience enables us to live closer to God. We become sensitive to His touch and we can easily discern when our behavior is right and wrong. Then we can promptly repent and be completely restored to wonderful, refreshing fellowship with God.

Don't waste your time making excuses for disobedience. When God shows you that you have done something wrong, just say, "You're right, Lord, I'm wrong. I have no excuse, so please forgive me and help me not to do it again."

It is amazing how much that will help you maintain a tender conscience toward God. When we are tender toward God, it enables us to be tender in our dealings with people. The world is filled with bruised, wounded, and brokenhearted people who need kindness and a loving touch from God. Let God touch them through you.

When you have a tender heart toward God, you will hear His voice more clearly and obey His Word more readily.

His Grace Will Carry You Through

*If you are censured and suffer abuse [because you bear] the name
of Christ, blessed [are you—happy, fortunate, to be envied, with
life-joy, and satisfaction in God's favor and salvation, regardless
of your outward condition], because the Spirit of glory, the Spirit
of God, is resting upon you . . .*   1 PETER 4:14

Have you ever suffered for being a Christian—been made fun of, left
out, misunderstood, passed over for promotion or worse?

Some think it is awful when they are mistreated because they are
Christians, but God sees it in an entirely different light. God never
expects us to suffer for Him without His help. We can firmly believe
that any time we are reproached or mistreated in any way because of
our faith in Christ, God gives us an extra measure of grace to coun-
terbalance the attack. There is power to overcome!

When we recognize and depend on the presence of God in our
lives, we can go through difficult circumstances and keep our peace
and joy. Like Shadrach, Meshach, and Abednego in Daniel 3:21–27,
we can go into the fiery furnace, or into problems and struggles, and
come out without even the smell of smoke upon us.

If we remain stable, confidently trusting God in difficult times,
we can be assured that God's glory will be our reward.

— — —

**Welcome the presence of God in your life and get excited
about seeing His grace empower you for whatever you
may face.**

A Bigger Plan

But Jesus looked at them and said, With men this is impossible,
but all things are possible with God.   MATTHEW 19:26

It is important to ask God to give you dreams and visions for your life. We atrophy without something to reach for. God has created us to have goals. Ephesians 3:20 (KJV) tells us that God is "able to do exceeding abundantly above all that we ask or think." This is why, as Christians, we can think big thoughts, have big goals, and hope for big things.

Many times we look at a task and think there is no way we can do what needs to be done. This happens when we are looking at ourselves instead of looking at God, Who can do all things.

When the Lord called Joshua to take the place of Moses and lead the Israelites into the Promised Land, He said to him, "As I was with Moses, so I will be with you; I will not fail you or forsake you" (Joshua 1:5).

If God promises to be with us—and He does—that is really all we need. His strength is made perfect in our weakness (2 Corinthians 12:9). Whatever weaknesses you have, God's strength is available to do things in your life bigger than you ever thought possible.

**God is honored when you trust Him to do the big things
that seem truly impossible.**

No More Self-Doubt

David was greatly distressed, for the men spoke of stoning him
because the souls of them all were bitterly grieved, each man for
his sons and daughters. But David encouraged and strengthened
himself in the Lord his God.   1 SAMUEL 30:6

If we don't believe in ourselves—in the talents and abilities God
has given us—who is going to? God believes in us, and it's a good
thing too; otherwise, we might never make any progress. We cannot
always wait for someone else to come along and encourage us to be
all we can be.

When David and his men found themselves in a seemingly hopeless situation, which the men blamed on him, David encouraged and
strengthened himself in the Lord. Later on, that situation was totally
turned around (1 Samuel 30:1–20).

When David was just a boy, everyone around him discouraged
him concerning his ability to fight Goliath. They told him he was too
young and too inexperienced, and he didn't have the right armor or
the right weapons. But David was close to God and had confidence
in Him. David believed that God would be strong on his behalf and
give him the victory.

Self-doubt is absolutely tormenting, but we can rid ourselves of
it. Like David, we can learn to know our God—about His love, His
ways, and His Word—then ultimately we can trust that He will provide us with the strength we need.

The way to end the torment of self-doubt is to look to
God and have faith in His mighty power.

The Power of Declaration

Death and life are in the power of the tongue, and they who
indulge in it shall eat the fruit of it [for death or life].

PROVERBS 18:21

If we want to see our prayers answered, it is essential we learn to pray and then make positive, faith-filled declarations about our circumstances. Negative confessions and faith just don't mix.

Let's say a mother is praying for her son who's having trouble in school. So she prays the prayer of faith and believes God for a breakthrough. Then she goes to lunch with two neighbors and spends the next hour saying, "I'm tired of all these problems I'm having with my child. Things aren't ever going to get better. Why me?" This kind of negative confession works against your faith.

After you have prayed, make the decision to keep your conversation in agreement with your prayers. Declare the Word of God! Declare your faith! When the neighbors ask how your son is doing, say, "You know what? In the natural, things have not changed a whole lot, but I'm praying for him, and I have assurance in my heart that God is with him, doing a mighty work in his life."

When your faith, your thoughts, and your words all agree with God's promises, it's just a matter of time until you see positive change.

———

Pray and then let what you say be in agreement with
what you have prayed and you will surely see amazing
results.

An Atmosphere of Worship

Give to the Lord the glory due to His name; worship the Lord in
the beauty of holiness or in holy array.   PSALM 29:2

When we worship God, we are recognizing Him for Who He is, all
that He has done in our lives, and all that He has yet to do.

Worship is not about us—it is all about God. But even though
worship is not about you, worship transforms you. By starting to
worship God for the changes that He is already working in you, you
find that those changes start manifesting more and more, and you
experience new levels of God's glory. In other words, God is close
to the worshipper, and He will pour out His goodness on those who
choose to magnify Him.

There is a release that comes through worship. Sometimes we
need a mental or emotional release. As we worship the Lord, we
release our emotional or mental burden that is weighing us down. It
is swallowed up in the awesomeness and majesty of God.

I encourage you to begin to worship early in the morning. Worship while you are getting ready for your day, and when you are at
work or out running errands. And worship God at the end of the day
for all He has brought you through. You will be amazed to see how
things begin to change at home and on the job when you keep God
at the highest place in your life.

Worship creates an atmosphere where God can work.

You Are Never Alone

> *. . . And behold, I am with you all the days (perpetually, uniformly, and on every occasion), to the [very] close and consummation of the age. Amen (so let it be).*   MATTHEW 28:20

God wants you to know that you are never alone. Satan will try to make you believe you are all alone, but that is a lie. He will try to deceive you by telling you that no one understands how you feel, but that is not true. In addition to God being with you, many believers know how you feel, what you are going through, and they understand what you may be experiencing.

When you are following God and making spiritual progress, Satan often brings affliction to discourage you and make you feel alone. I remember a time many years ago when God called me to do a new thing and it required me to separate myself from many of the people and things that were dear to me. Very often we have to let go of old things and ways in order to take hold of the new that God has for us. I was often lonely while establishing my new life, but God was with me each step of the way.

If you are battling loneliness and pain, draw strength from God. Know that He is with you, and He will move you forward. He has the power to turn your mourning into joy and to comfort you in your sorrow. Trust God with all of your heart, and don't let Satan steal your destiny.

Hope in God's love and know that He is always with you.

Greatly Loved

This is love: not that we loved God, but that he loved us and sent his Son as an atoning sacrifice for our sins.   1 JOHN 4:10 NIV

Many of us believe that God loves the world, but we're not as certain about His love for us individually, or we may feel that God loves us when we are good, but not when we make mistakes and sin. God's love is based on Who He is, not on what we do. He never stops loving us, not even for one second of our lives!

God loves *you*! You are special to Him. He doesn't love you because you are a good person or do everything right. He loves you because He is love. Love is not something God does; it is Who He is.

God's love cannot be earned or deserved. It must be received by faith. He is the everlasting God, and He does not get weary. Many of us think we have worn God out with our failures and mistakes, but you cannot do that. He may not always love everything you do, but He does love you. Love is His unfailing nature.

No matter how hard you seek the things of God, if you have not received the fact that God loves you, you are not going to get far.

Let God love you. Receive His love for you. Meditate on it. Let it strengthen you and draw you into close relationship with Him. Then look for opportunities to share that love with others.

——— — ———

If you had been the only person on the earth, Jesus would have gone through all His suffering just for you.

Free from Anxiety

Therefore do not worry and be anxious, saying, What are we
going to have to eat? or, What are we going to have to drink?
or, What are we going to have to wear? . . . your heavenly Father
knows well that you need them all.   MATTHEW 6:31–32

Worry fills us with fear and anxiety, causing us to think: "What if we
don't have enough? How will I find another job? What if things don't
work out?" In other words, "What are we going to do if God doesn't
come through for us?"

Instead of proclaiming the promises of God when we feel unsure
about something, we often speak about our worries and frustrations,
which only amplifies them and makes our problems seem worse
than what they are.

Worry and anxiety are what people experience when they don't
know that they have a heavenly Father Who loves them unconditionally. But you and I do know we have a heavenly Father Who is close
to us and has promised to provide everything we need. It is important for us to remember this and to act in faith, trusting God every
day. Just because we are tempted to worry doesn't mean we have to
do it!

Jesus assures you that your heavenly Father knows all your needs
before you even ask Him. So why should you worry? Instead, thank
God in advance for His provision in your life.

Seek first the kingdom of God and His righteousness;
then all these other things we need will be added to us
(Matthew 6:33).

A Steadfast Heart

My heart is fixed, O God, my heart is steadfast and confident! I will sing and make melody. PSALM 57:7

In order to experience victory in our lives and achieve great things for God, it is crucial that we choose to be determined. The Bible says that Jesus "steadfastly and determinedly set His face to go to Jerusalem" (Luke 9:51), and we can do the same thing as we live for God. If we are going to accomplish anything worthwhile, it is important we "steadfastly and determinedly" set our face in that direction and not give up.

When you receive Christ as your Savior and Lord, Satan will oppose you at every turn. He wants you to give up! The devil is not going to roll out a red carpet for us just because we decide to receive Christ. But Jesus has already overcome the devil. Satan is a defeated foe. His opposition is not strong enough to stop you if you are close to God, walking in His strength and will for your life.

Don't fall into the trap of thinking that everything in life should be easy for us. Ask for God's help, receive His grace, and be determined to do the will of God, to stay positive and happy, and to walk in the peace of God no matter what.

Press on with holy determination, and God's plan will be fulfilled in your life.

Keep Moving Forward

*That is why I would remind you to stir up (rekindle the embers
of, fan the flame of, and keep burning) the [gracious] gift of God,
[the inner fire] that is in you by means of the laying on of my
hands [with those of the elders at your ordination].*

2 TIMOTHY 1:6

In our spiritual lives we are either aggressively going forward on purpose, or we are slipping backward. There is no such thing as stag-
nant Christianity. It is vital to keep pressing on. That is why Timothy
was instructed to fan the flame and rekindle the zeal that once filled
his heart. He had gotten weary, and the fire that once burned in him
had become a dim flicker.

Evidently Timothy had taken a step backward, perhaps because
of fear. It is certainly easy to understand why Timothy may have lost
his courage and confidence. It was a time of extreme persecution,
and his mentor Paul was in jail. Yet Paul strongly encouraged Timothy to stir himself up, get back on track, remember the call on his
life, resist fear, and remember that God had given him a spirit of
power and love and of a sound mind.

Any time we let fear dominate us, we begin to slip backward. Fear
prevents our progress and causes us to want to turn and run instead
of aggressively moving forward. If you are unsure, uncertain, or even
feeling afraid today, receive Paul's encouragement to Timothy. Stir
up your faith, be on fire for God, and never forget that He is with you.
With Him at your side, no matter how difficult things may look, you
can do whatever you need to do through Him.

———

Never, Never, Never . . . Give Up!

What Is Holding You Back?

Therefore then, since we are surrounded by so great a cloud of witnesses [who have borne testimony to the Truth], let us strip off and throw aside every encumbrance . . . and let us run with patient endurance . . .   HEBREWS 12:1

When the writer of the book of Hebrews wrote that we can *strip off and throw aside every encumbrance*, he was thinking of the runners in his day who would literally strip off their clothes, down to a simple loincloth. They made sure nothing could entangle them and prevent them from running as fast as they possibly could. They were running to win!

An important part of drawing closer to God is taking an inventory of our life and casting aside anything that entangles us or pulls us away from Him. Being in close relationship with Him requires us to get rid of the things that grieve Him and distract us, things keeping us from living out God's plan for our life.

We often need to take a look at our lives and cast aside things that are entangling us or pulling us away from God. It is impossible to grow spiritually without doing so. When God shows you something to cast aside, I encourage you to do it without hesitation. Don't argue with God or feel sorry for yourself. What He is asking you to do will benefit you in the end. Whether it's a destructive friendship, a harmful habit, being offended, or any other sin in your life, be bold enough to deal with it. Ask God to help you and then draw strength from Him and His Word.

Lay aside everything that hinders and run the race of holiness. The reward is God himself.

You Have Spiritual "Power of Attorney"

Nevertheless I tell you the truth. It is to your advantage that I go away; for if I do not go away, the Helper will not come to you; but if I depart, I will send Him to you.   JOHN 16:7 NKJV

Oh, how wonderful it would have been to have physically walked with Jesus. But He told His followers they would be better off when He went away, because then He would send His Spirit to dwell in every believer. He told them that even though they were sorrowful at the news of His departure, they would rejoice again just as a woman has sorrow during her labor but rejoices when the child is born.

Jesus knew they would change their minds when they saw the glory of His Spirit in them and the power available to each of them through the privilege of using His name in prayer. He was literally giving to them—and has given to all those who believe in Him—His "power of attorney," the legal right to use His name. His name takes His place; His name represents Him.

Jesus has already been perfect for us. He has already pleased the Father for us; therefore, there is no pressure on us to feel that we must have a perfect record of right behavior before we can pray. When we come before the Father in Jesus' name, we can confess our sin, receive His forgiveness, and boldly make our requests known to Him.

When the name of Jesus is spoken by a believer in faith, all of heaven comes to attention.

Entering the Rest of God

Blessed (happy, fortunate, to be envied) are the undefiled (the upright, truly sincere, and blameless) in the way [of the revealed will of God], who walk (order their conduct and conversation) in the law of the Lord (the whole of God's revealed will).

PSALM 119.1

There is a divine freedom and ease that comes when you truly love the Word of God—when you hear it, receive it and *obey* it. Even in tough circumstances, your life will be free from misery and frustration. Your joy is full when you draw close to God through His Word, believing His promises for your life and obeying His commands.

The key to overcoming the difficulties you face in life is to believe the Word and obey whatever God puts in your heart to do. Standing on His Word delivers you from struggling so that you rest in the promises of God. Hebrews 4:3 says: "For we who have believed (adhered to and trusted in and relied on God) do enter that rest."

If you feel defeated today—if you're overwhelmed by a problem— the best thing you can do is dedicate yourself to hearing, receiving, and obeying God's Word. That is where you will find words of life. As soon as you start believing the Word of God, your joy will return and you will be at ease again.

―――――――――

A life of rest in Him is where God wants you to be every day of your life.

Come as a Little Child

*And He called a little child to Himself and put him in the midst
of them, And said, Truly I say to you, unless you repent (change,
turn about) and become like little children [trusting, lowly, loving,
forgiving], you can never enter the kingdom of heaven [at all].*

MATTHEW 18:2–3

One of the beautiful things about children is that they are not complicated. They will always let you know what they need, they'll run
into your arms when they are frightened, and they'll give you a big
kiss, sometimes for no apparent reason. It is refreshing to communi-
cate with children, because they don't try to hide their fears or their
feelings.

I believe that's how God wants us to be when we talk with Him.
He is pleased when we approach Him with childlike simplicity and
faith. Just as children are naturally inclined to trust their parents
completely, we can also be pure and full of enthusiasm as we trust
God. Share your whole heart with God, and remember: You can
entrust everything in your life to Him and know that He cares.

The Lord is not looking for complicated relationships. He is looking for sincere hearts and childlike faith. You can let God know what
you want (Philippians 4:6), and you can run to Him when you feel
afraid (Psalm 91:1–7). God wants you to feel free to show your affection for Him and to share your heart openly with Him. The more you
learn to come to God with a childlike faith, the closer you'll grow in
your relationship with Him.

**We do not want to be childish in our relationships with
God; we want to be childlike.**

Faithful in the Wilderness

O God, You are my God, earnestly will I seek You; my inner self thirsts for You, my flesh longs and is faint for You, in a dry and weary land where no water is.   PSALM 63:1

Eventually, no matter how much we love the Lord and no matter how close we get to Him, all of us go through dry times...times when few things minister to us or water our soul. We go to church, but we feel no different when we leave than we did when we arrived. We experience times when our prayers seem dry, and times when we can't hear or feel anything from God.

I have gone through mountaintop times, and I have gone through valley times. I have had dry times in my prayer life and in my praise and worship. There have been times when I could hear from God so clearly, but there have been other times when I have not heard anything at all.

When you go through a season like this, don't let it get you down. God is with you, whether you *feel* His presence or not. The mature believer doesn't let how he feels determine his relationship with God. You can simply choose to believe God is with you today. You can make the choice to love and worship God in faith. You can pray, believe He hears you, and trust that He is going to provide everything you need. When you make these choices, you will find a new peace in your walk with the Lord, and you will be stable in every season of life.

God loves you and He is right here with you—whether you feel it or not. Be faithful in the wilderness as well as on the mountaintop.

Love Is Patient

Love endures long and is patient...   1 CORINTHIANS 13:4

The world today is filled with impatient people. It seems that everyone is in a hurry. Stress levels are very high, and the pressure we live under often provokes impatience. Christians deal with the same pressures as everyone else, and we are often just as impatient as the world, but we shouldn't be.

The Bible teaches us that love is patient. The more we learn to receive God's love, love Him in return, and love those around us, the more patient we become. This patience helps us live in peace. We are not always in a hurry. We take the time to wait on God and to fellowship with Him. Out of His love, God is patient with us and we can be the same way with other people.

When your life is marked by love, not only will you be patient with other people, you will be patient with yourself. When you make mistakes, instead of being angry with yourself over them, you'll repent and stay in peace. You'll understand that God is working to correct those things in your life, and you'll patiently trust Him to do His work.

Patience is a wonderful virtue that can be developed in your life, but the key is to draw closer to God through trusting Him each and every day. The closer you get to the Lord, the easier it will be to let go of the frustrations of the world. You'll find a new sense of calm and peaceful assurance because God is the center of your life.

When you learn to respond patiently in all kinds of trials, you will find yourself living a quality of life that is not just endured but enjoyed to the full.

Prime the Pump

. . . For the joy of the Lord is your strength and stronghold.

NEHEMIAH 8:10

When we are going through difficult times, we can take some action to release joy before we start slipping into despair. We can start to rejoice whether we feel like it or not. It is like priming a pump by repeatedly moving the handle up and down until the pump kicks in and the water begins to flow.

I remember my grandparents had an old-time pump. I can recall standing at the sink as a small child, moving the pump handle up and down and sometimes feeling as though it would never take hold and start to supply water. It actually felt as if it was connected to nothing, and I was just pumping air.

But if I didn't give up, moving the handle up and down would soon become more difficult. That was the sign that water would start flowing shortly.

This is the way it is with joy. We have a well of water on the inside of our spirit. The pump handle to bring it up is the choices we make—smiling, singing, laughing, and so forth. At first the physical expressions may not seem to be doing any good. And after a while it even gets harder, but if we keep it up, soon we will get a "gusher" of joy.

The joy of the Lord is your strength. You can choose to be strong by choosing to live in joy.

The Truth of God's Word

Though a host encamp against me, my heart shall not fear; though
war arise against me, [even then] in this will I be confident.

PSALM 27:3

I have discovered that being confident in who God created us to be
is a key to living the joy-filled, overcoming life Jesus died to give us.

The devil is constantly trying to introduce thoughts into our
heads to make us lose our confidence. The mind is the battlefield,
and the devil lies to us through wrong thinking. He tries to tell
us we aren't good enough, we've made too many mistakes, God is
angry with us—any thought that would make us doubt the love God
has for us. If we meditate on those wrong thoughts, our confidence
begins to fade.

The key to winning the battle of the mind is to fight against the
lies of the enemy with the truth of God's Word. You don't have to
dwell on wrong thoughts; instead you can believe the promises of
God and boldly declare those promises over your life.

I encourage you to confidently declare what the Word of God
says about you, such as: "I am more than a conqueror through Jesus
(Romans 8:37). I can do all things through Christ Who strengthens
me (Philippians 4:13). I am triumphant in every situation because
God always causes me to triumph (2 Corinthians 2:14)."

When the devil tries to lie to you, boldly declare the truth
of God's Word over your life.

Staying Positive

[For being as he is] a man of two minds (hesitating, dubious, irresolute), [he is] unstable and unreliable and uncertain about everything [he thinks, feels, decides].   JAMES 1:8

If we take our concerns to the Lord in prayer and then continue to worry about them, we are actually contradicting our faith. Prayer is a positive force, and worry is a negative force. If we add them together, we come up with zero. I don't know about you, but I don't want to have zero power, so with God's help, I choose not to mix prayer and worry.

Even though we want to live an effective, powerful life, many people operate with zero power because they are always mixing the positives and the negatives. They have a positive confession for a little while, then a negative confession for a little while. They pray for a little while, then they worry for a little while. They trust for a little while, then they doubt for a little while. As a result, they just go back and forth, never really making any progress.

Let's not magnify the bad—let's magnify the good! Let's elevate the good things God is doing by talking about them, by being positive in our thoughts, in our attitudes, in our outlook, in our words, and in our actions.

Why not make a decision to stay positive by trusting God and refusing to worry?

Practice being positive in each situation that arises. Even if whatever is taking place at the moment is not so good, expect God to bring good out of it.

Molded into His Image

And I am convinced and sure of this very thing, that He Who began a good work in you will continue until the day of Jesus Christ [right up to the time of His return], developing [that good work] and perfecting and bringing it to full completion in you.

PHILIPPIANS 1:6

According to the Bible, God is the Potter, and we are the clay (Romans 9:20–21). When we first come to the Lord, we are like a hard lump of clay that is not very pliable or easy to work with. But God puts us on His potter's wheel and begins to refashion and remake us so that we can discover the wonderful plan He has for our lives.

Sometimes that process of molding is uncomfortable at first. The reason it hurts is because God has to peel away the things in our lives that would keep us distant from Him. So out of His love for us, He keeps working and working on us, trimming away this bad attitude and that wrong mind-set, carefully reshaping us until gradually we are changed into the likeness of His Son Jesus.

Don't be discouraged with yourself because you have not yet arrived. The more God works in your life, the closer you are growing in relationship to Him. Enjoy your life each day, even as God is shaping you. Let the Potter do His work, and trust that He has your best interest at heart.

———————

You can always trust God that He has your best interest at heart, and all that He does in your life is for your benefit.

Drawing upon God's Strength

... Be strong in the Lord [be empowered through your union with Him]; draw your strength from Him [that strength which His boundless might provides].   EPHESIANS 6:10

An important secret to being successful in any task that is set before you is to draw on God's strength. Your strength will run out eventually, but God's strength never will.

Many times in my life I have been in situations not knowing what to do, but God always helped me and brought me through to a place of victory. Each time He met me with His strength that I desperately needed in order to be successful. You can expect God to do the same thing for you no matter what challenges you are facing right now. God is your strength!

In Ephesians 6:10, Paul assures us that God will pour strength into our lives as we live in close relationship with Him. And the prophet Isaiah says that those who have learned the secret of waiting on the Lord "shall mount up with wings as eagles" (Isaiah 40:31 KJV). These scriptures, and others like them, show us that we are strengthened as we go to God for what we are lacking.

God has promised to never leave us or forsake us. He is with us each step of our journey and He gives us the strength we need when we need it.

**God wants to do more than just give you strength—
He wants to be your strength.**

In Times of Crisis

And it shall be that whoever shall call upon the name of the
Lord [invoking, adoring, and worshiping the Lord—Christ]
shall be saved.   ACTS 2:21

Years ago, before seat belt laws, a friend of mine was driving with his young son through a busy intersection one day. The car door on the passenger side was not secured tightly, and he made a sharp turn. The car door flew open, and the little boy rolled out right into traffic! The last thing my friend saw was a set of car wheels just about on top of his son. All he knew to do was cry out, "Jesus!"

He stopped his car and ran to his son. To his amazement, his son was perfectly safe. But the man driving the car that had almost hit the child was hysterical.

"Don't be upset!" my friend said. "My son is okay. Just thank God you were able to stop!"

"You don't understand!" the man responded. "I never touched my brakes!"

Although there was nothing the man could do, the name of Jesus prevailed and the boy's life was spared.

In times of crisis, call upon the name of Jesus. The more you and I see how faithful He is in times of need and crises—the more we witness the power of His name over situations and circumstances—the more our faith is developed, our trust grows, and the closer we will be to Him.

———————

There is power in the name of Jesus for every crisis you will ever face.

Accepting Who You Are on the Way to Where You're Going

Fear not, for you shall not be ashamed; neither be confounded and depressed, for you shall not be put to shame. For you shall forget the shame of your youth, and you shall not [seriously] remember the reproach of your widowhood any more.   ISAIAH 54:4

It's important that we embrace and accept ourselves. Ask yourself if you like yourself. If you don't like yourself, you are going to have a hard time liking anyone else. If you're unhappy with yourself, you'll have trouble with others.

When we are in close relationship with the Lord, we can be relaxed and at ease, knowing that our acceptance is not based on our performance or perfect behavior, but on the work Christ has done for and in us. It is based on our personal relationship with Jesus.

To like ourselves simply means we accept ourselves as God's creation. We don't need to like everything we do in order to like and accept ourselves. God loves us unconditionally, and even when we make mistakes we are no less His child.

I encourage you to look at yourself in the mirror every morning and say, "I like myself. I am a child of God and He loves me. I have gifts and talents. I am a special person—and I like and accept myself." If you do that and really believe it, it will work wonders in helping you accept the person God created you to be.

You can be at peace with your past, content with your present, and sure about your future, knowing they are in God's loving hands.

Father Knows Best

... Be transformed (changed) by the [entire] renewal of your mind [by its new ideals and its new attitude], so that you may prove [for yourselves] what is the good and acceptable and perfect will of God, even the thing which is good and acceptable and perfect [in His sight for you].   ROMANS 12:2

There will be times in our lives when God asks us to do something we don't understand or particularly agree with. When He does this, it is because He has something good in mind for us. His ways are higher than our ways, and His will is always best.

When God asks us to do something contrary to our will, we can remember the words of Jesus: "... Not My will, but [always] Yours be done" (Luke 22:42). These words aren't easy to pray, but they always pay huge dividends in our lives. When we want something, we don't usually give it up easily. It takes a lot of trust and brokenness to bring us to the place where we are willing to say, like Jesus, *not my will, but always Yours be done.*

The bottom line is that God has a great plan for our life, but that plan requires that we follow Him unconditionally. He may ask you to give away things you don't want to part with. He may ask you to go places, do things, or deal with people that are difficult for you. He may ask you to be quiet in some situations and speak up in others. But whatever God asks of you, do it and take comfort in the knowledge that your obedience is bringing you closer to Him.

Make the choice to always put God's will ahead of your own.

Drop it, Leave It, and Let It Go

And whenever you stand praying, if you have anything against
anyone, forgive him and let it drop (leave it, let it go), in order that
your Father Who is in heaven may also forgive you your [own]
failings and shortcomings and let them drop.   MARK 11:25

"Drop it, leave it, and let it go," is what the Bible says we are to do
with offenses (Mark 11:25). It is important to forgive quickly. The
quicker we do it, the easier it becomes. A weed that has deep roots is
harder to pull out than one that has just sprung up.

Love forgives; it does not hold a grudge. It is not touchy, easily
offended, nor is it fretful or resentful (1 Corinthians 13:5). Knowing this, we can look at our own lives and easily understand if we
are walking in love. If you have anything against anyone, make the
choice right now to "drop it, leave it, and let it go."

We have many opportunities every day to get offended, and
each time we have a choice to make. If we choose to live by our feelings, we will constantly be offended and upset. But if we choose to
live in love, we will forgive people when they offend us and trust
God to defend us, rather than feeling like we always have to defend
ourselves.

God is love, and He forgives and forgets: "For I will forgive their
iniquity, and their sin I will remember no more" (Jeremiah 31:34
NASB). And He is glad to do so. The closer we get to Him, the more we
become like Him. With God's help, we can learn to live a life of love
and forgiveness.

When you decide to "drop it, leave it, and let it go,"
joy and contentment are the natural results.

A Merry Heart

A merry heart does good, like medicine, But a broken spirit dries the bones.

PROVERBS 17:22 NKJV

God is life, and every good thing He created is part of that life. We can get so caught up in doing and accomplishing, in working and earning, that if we are not careful, we will come to the end of our life and suddenly wake up and realize that we never really lived. God desires for us to enjoy life and live it to the full, till it overflows.

We have a choice in life. We can grumble our way through our troubles, or we can draw closer to God in difficult times, going through any trouble we face with a merry heart. Either way, we will all deal with troubles from time to time, so why not take the joy of the Lord as our strength and be filled with energy and vitality?

In John 15, Jesus talks about abiding in Him. In verse 11, He says, "I have told you these things, that My joy and delight may be in you, and that your joy and gladness may be of full measure and complete and overflowing." Jesus made it possible for us to have merry hearts. With His help, no matter what you go through, you can put a smile on your face and enjoy every day of your life in Him.

Don't spend your life waiting for things to change before you can become happy. Make the decision to be happy now.

Waiting Expectantly for God

*Why are you cast down, O my inner self? And why should you
moan over me and be disquieted within me? Hope in God and
wait expectantly for Him, for I shall yet praise Him, my Help
and my God.*   PSALM 42:5

If you've ever felt discouraged, you're not alone. David did too. But
David didn't allow discouragement to keep him down. When he
felt that way, David put his hope in God and waited for Him, praising Him as his Help and his God. We can do the same thing if we
choose to.

To overcome his downcast feelings and emotions, David put
his focus on God, praising Him for His wonderful acts and great
exploits. David chose to focus on God, not on his problems.

David knew that if he focused on the negative, it would be easy
to get depressed and lose hope. That is why he chose to regularly
encourage and strengthen himself in the Lord (1 Samuel 30:6).

When we find ourselves in a discouraging situation, we can follow David's example and wait expectantly for the Lord, praising Him
no matter what the circumstances look like around us. The closer we
are to God, the easier it is to take refuge in Him. Instead of giving in
to frustration and discouragement, we can put our trust in the Lord,
and trust Him to deliver us.

**The Lord makes a covering over us and defends us.
He fights our battles for us when we praise Him
(2 Chronicles 20:17, 20–21).**

The Truest Tests of Character

And endurance (fortitude) develops maturity of character (approved faith and tried integrity). And character [of this sort] produces [the habit of] joyful and confident hope of eternal salvation.   ROMANS 5:4

Our character is most accurately revealed by what we do when nobody is watching. An important key to living in close, intimate relationship with God is being a person of strong character, because when you realize that God is with you every minute of every day—you live to please Him regardless of whether others are watching or not.

Many people will do the right thing when somebody—a leader, an employer, a person with influence—is watching them, but they take the easy way out when nobody sees but God. As Christians, our thought process should be, "I am going to do the right thing simply because I want to please the Lord."

Character is also seen when we do the right thing to others even though the right thing is not yet happening to us. Jesus demonstrated this for us—when He was "reviled and insulted, He did not revile or offer insult in return" (1 Peter 2:23). We can follow the example of Jesus by treating somebody right who is not treating us right, by blessing someone who is not blessing us, by loving people who don't necessarily love us. These are the things that Jesus did, and if we want to be like Him, we will need to choose to do them.

Our character is seen in how much we choose to do the right thing even when we don't want to do it.

Everyday Gratitude

*Enter into His gates with thanksgiving and a thank offering and
into His courts with praise! Be thankful and say so to Him, bless
and affectionately praise His name!*   PSALM 100:4

Grateful people are a joy to be around. There are people who go
through life grumbling, complaining, and ungrateful, but there are
also those who go through life joyful, optimistic, and full of gratitude. I sure prefer to be around joyful, optimistic, and grateful
people—don't you?

Not only does our grateful attitude make us more enjoyable to be
around, but it shows new levels of spiritual maturity as we go deeper
with God. The closer we get to God, the more aware we become of
all He has done for us, and the more thankful we naturally become.

If someone is not grateful for the things God has already given
them, why would they think that God is going to give them more? A
thankful heart shows God that we are good stewards of what He has
given us and that we can handle even more blessings with the right
heart and attitude.

The next time you feel a sense of ingratitude, just stop and praise
God for what He has already done in your life. Even if you feel you
only have a little, praise God for the little you have. When you do,
you may be surprised how He'll reward your thankful heart.

**Look around you and find something to be thankful for—
a relationship, a provision, a past victory, an answer to
prayer. Nothing is too small to praise God for today!**

Doers of the Word

*But be doers of the Word [obey the message], and not merely
listeners to it, betraying yourselves [into deception by reasoning
contrary to the Truth].*   JAMES 1:22

An important part of living in close relationship with God is learning to become *doers* of the Word and not hearers only. If we read and
hear the Word, but neglect to follow the instructions it gives us, we
are going to live far short of God's best for our lives.

It is the truth of God's Word—and that truth alone—that will set
us free. In order for that truth to work in our lives, it is essential that
we put it into practice. Obedience to His Word is what brings peace,
joy, and a life that is blessed in many ways.

The bottom line is this: God is your Helper. He is your Healer. He
has a personalized plan for your life in His Word. The more you read,
study, and obey His Word, the more you can learn what that plan is
and then begin to walk it out one step at a time. Obeying the Word
requires decisive consistency and determination—it is a daily process. The more you study God's Word, the more you learn to love it.
Something wonderful happens when you discover the instructions
and promises of God found in His Word. You'll always want to go
back for more!

**You will walk in victory if you make the decision to do
what the Lord says.**

No More Insecurity

And they who know Your name [who have experience and
acquaintance with Your mercy] will lean on and confidently put
their trust in You, for You, Lord, have not forsaken those who seek
(inquire of and for) You [on the authority of God's Word and the
right of their necessity].   PSALM 9:10

Every one of us has experienced a measure of insecurity. At one
time or another, we all want to step out and do something, but at
the thought of it, insecurity freezes us in our tracks. But this is not
the plan of God for our lives. He wants us to step out in faith and
confidence.

Insecurity tries to torment us into being so doubtful and miserable we will be prevented from doing what God wants us to do and
receiving all God has for us.

We can live without insecurity by building our faith on what God
has said in His Word. When we open our mouth and confess what
the Lord says to us and about us, God's Word will give us the power
to overcome fear, insecurity, and uncertainty.

If you find yourself trying to avoid confronting some issue in your
life because of dread or insecurity, I encourage you to pray and ask
God to do for you what He has promised in His Word—to go before
you and pave the way.

Ask God to strengthen you in the inner man, that His
might and power may fill you, and that you may not be
overcome with the temptation to give in to fear.

The Key to Conquering Frustration

*[Therefore, I do not treat God's gracious gift as something of
minor importance and defeat its very purpose]; I do not set aside
and invalidate and frustrate and nullify the grace (unmerited
favor) of God . . .*   GALATIANS 2:21

I know what frustration is like because I spent many years living
a frustrated life. I knew who God was, but I knew very little of His
grace and how to live in close relationship to Him. I have since
learned that when I get frustrated, it's almost always because I am
trying to make something happen in my own strength instead of
waiting on the Lord to make it happen. If I am frustrated, it is a sign
that I am acting independently instead of relying on Him and receiving His grace.

Are you frustrated? In your relationships? In your career? In your
walk with the Lord? Are you wrestling with an area of your personality that is causing you problems, or is there a specific habit in your
life that you can't break?

Frustration comes from trying to do something you cannot do
on your own. God is the only One Who can make things happen for
you in your life. You will be frustrated if you try to do things without
Him. But the minute you say, "Lord, I can't do this on my own, so I
turn it over to You. I am willing to do anything You ask me to do, but
I will need Your grace (power) in order to do it"—when you sincerely
pray that prayer, you will begin to enjoy the rest of God.

**Let go and trust God to do what only He can do. Let God
be God in your life.**

Peace in Any Circumstance

Casting the whole of your care [all your anxieties, all your worries, all your concerns, once and for all] on Him, for He cares for you affectionately and cares about you watchfully.

1 PETER 5:7

The peace that passes all understanding is a great thing to experience (Philippians 4:7). When, according to all the circumstances, you should be upset, in a panic, in turmoil, and worried yet you have peace, that is unexplainable. The world is starving for this kind of peace. You cannot buy it; it is not for sale. It is a free gift from God that comes out of a deep, abiding closeness to Him, and it leads to unspeakable joy.

Peace comes when you turn over your burden to the Lord—when you choose to cast your care on Him instead of keeping it for yourself. The sooner you do this the better. Commit your problems to God the moment you have one. Don't even try to handle them on your own. The longer you wait, the harder it is to break free from worry and anxiety.

Because God has promised that He is always with us, we can have incredible peace and joy…even in the midst of tribulation. Only He can give us that. That is what it means to have a peace that passes all understanding.

The believer who is experiencing God's peace through his relationship with Jesus can have peace even in the midst of life's toughest storms.

Believe

But without faith it is impossible to please and be satisfactory to Him. For whoever would come near to God must [necessarily] believe that God exists and that He is the rewarder of those who earnestly and diligently seek Him [out].   HEBREWS 11:6

A positive, believing heart is one of the heart attitudes that is absolutely vital in our relationship with God. That may sound funny, since we are called believers. It's easy to assume that all believers believe, but I've noticed there are many well-intentioned but "unbelieving believers." I slip into that state myself from time to time.

In Matthew 8:13, Jesus says that it shall be done for you as you have believed. Isn't that a powerful thought? It is amazing how much God will do in our lives if we will simply believe He can...and He will. Believing is a choice we make, and anytime we stop believing we lose our peace and joy. Form a habit of getting up each new day saying over and over, "I believe, I believe, I believe. With God's help, I believe I can do whatever He sets before me."

When you are tempted to doubt, just remind yourself that you are a believer, and believers always believe! Believing pleases God and releases the fulfillment of His promises in your life.

When you lose your joy and peace, check your believing!

Letting Go of the Ashes

To grant [consolation and joy] to those who mourn in Zion—to give them an ornament (a garland or diadem) of beauty instead of ashes, the oil of joy instead of mourning, the garment [expressive] of praise instead of a heavy, burdened, and failing spirit . . .

ISAIAH 61:3

Part of any restoration process in our lives is that God gives us beauty for ashes. But for that to happen, we must be willing to give Him the ashes.

You may have been hurt in the past and kept the ashes of that hurt somewhere close at hand. Every once in a while, you may get them out and grieve over them once again. If so, I understand because there was a time in my life when I did the same thing.

But I want to encourage you to do what I did and let go of these ashes, allowing the wind of the Holy Spirit to blow them away to where they cannot be found again. This is a new day. There is no more time left for grieving over the ashes of the past. Your future has no room in it for your past.

God has the same good plan for you that He had the moment you arrived on this planet. He has never changed His mind, and He never will. From the very moment the enemy hurt you, God has had your restoration in His heart. Know that you are valuable, unique, loved, and special in His eyes. It is time to go forward!

Allow the Holy Spirit to blow away the ashes and replace those ashes with beauty.

Exceedingly, Abundantly Above and Beyond

Now to Him Who, by (in consequence of) the [action of His] power that is at work within us, is able to [carry out His purpose and] do superabundantly, far over and above all that we [dare] ask or think [infinitely beyond our highest prayers, desires, thoughts, hopes, or dreams].   EPHESIANS 3:20

Have you ever been praying about all the people who are hurting and had a strong desire to help them all? I know I certainly have. In times like this I feel that my desire is bigger than my ability, and it is—but it is not bigger than God's ability.

When the thing we are facing in our life looms so big in our eyes that our mind goes "tilt," we can remember to think with the mind of Christ. In the natural, many things seem impossible. But God wants us to believe for great things, make big plans, and expect Him to do things so amazing it leaves us with our mouths hanging open in awe.

God does not usually call people who are capable; if He did, He would not get the glory. He frequently chooses those who, in the natural, feel as if they are completely in over their heads but who are ready to stand up on the inside and take bold steps of faith. They have learned the secret of staying close to God and trusting that His "superabundant" power will work within them.

When your desires seem overwhelmingly big, and you don't see the way to accomplish them, remember that even though you don't know the way, you know the Waymaker!

Hanging Tough

*The Lord God is my Strength, my personal bravery, and my
invincible army; He makes my feet like hinds' feet and will make
me to walk [not to stand still in terror, but to walk] and make
[spiritual] progress upon my high places [of trouble, suffering,
or responsibility]!*   HABAKKUK 3:19

The Old Testament prophet Habakkuk spoke of hard times, calling
them "high places," and stating that God had given him *hinds' feet* to
scale those high places.

A "hind" refers to a certain kind of deer that is an agile mountain
climber. It can scale up what looks like a sheer cliff, leaping from
ledge to ledge with great ease. This is God's will for us, that when
hardship comes our way, we are not intimidated or frightened.

To be truly victorious, we can grow to the place where we are not
afraid of hard times but are actually challenged by them. In Habakkuk 3:19, these "high places" are referred to as "trouble, suffering, or
responsibility." This is because it is during these times that we grow.

If you look back over your life, you will see that most of your spiritual growth didn't occur during the easy times in life; you grow during difficulty. Then during the easy times that come, you are able to
enjoy what you have gained during the hard times. Life is filled with
a mixture of abasing and abounding (Philippians 4:12), and both are
valuable and necessary.

**God often does His deepest work in some of the most
difficult circumstances.**

Recounting God's Victories

*David said, The Lord Who delivered me out of the paw of the lion
and out of the paw of the bear, He will deliver me out of the hand
of this Philistine. And Saul said to David, Go, and the Lord be
with you!*   1 SAMUEL 17:37

When David volunteered to go and fight Goliath, no one really
encouraged him. Everyone, including the king, told him he was too
young, too inexperienced, too small, and he didn't have the right
armor. But David encouraged himself by recounting the victories
God had given him in the past. Finally, Saul told him to go, but he
still didn't believe David could win.

There will be many times in life when you are left with no one to
encourage you, and during those times, you will need to rely on God
alone. The enemy never ceases trying to discourage us. He wants to
prevent us from being faithful to do what God wants us to do. Today,
I want to encourage you that with God, you can do anything you
need to do.

When you have to wait a long time for something, or when it
seems that everything and everybody is against you, instead of getting negative and downcast, say to God, "Lord, I will be faithful to
You. I remember what You've done in my life in the past. I know You
will deliver me again. I trust You to see me through." God is closer to
you than you may realize, and He will never fail you.

**God is your strength, and all things are possible
with Him.**

The Greatest Thing in the World

Beloved, if God loved us so [very much], we also ought to love
one another.   1 JOHN 4:11

Loving and being loved are what make life worth living. To love and
be loved is the way God created us—it gives life purpose and meaning. Love is the greatest thing in the world.

It is also the most fiercely attacked area in our lives. The devil's
goal is to separate us from God's love, and he will use anything he
can to complicate our understanding of God's love or make it confusing. His primary means of deception is to get us to believe that
God's love for us depends on our worthiness.

Here's how it worked in my life: Whenever I failed, I would stop
allowing myself to receive God's love and start punishing myself by
feeling condemned and guilty. I lived this way for many years of my
life, dutifully carrying my heavy sack of guilt on my back everywhere
I went. I made mistakes regularly, and I felt guilty about each one.
Then I would try to win God's favor with good works.

Thankfully, the day of freedom finally came for me. God graciously
revealed to me, through the Holy Spirit, His love for me personally.
That single revelation changed my entire life and walk with Him. The
same can be true for you. When you realize God loves you unconditionally, everything changes. You are loved, not because of what you
have done or haven't done, but because of who God is.

**God's love for you is perfect and unconditional. When
you fail, He keeps on loving you because His love is not
based on you but on Him.**

Focus on Potential, Not Limitations

Having gifts (faculties, talents, qualities) that differ according to the grace given us, let us use them . . .

ROMANS 12:6

Believing in the potential God has placed inside of you is an important part of building confidence and overcoming insecurity. When you focus on your potential rather than your weaknesses, you are giving God room to work, because you are trusting that He has a plan for your life.

Though people may say, "You can do anything you set your mind to do," you and I cannot really do *anything* . . . in our own strength. And we cannot do anything or everything that we see other people doing. But we can do everything God has called us to do. And we can be anything God says we can be.

Each of us is full of gifts and talents, potential and ability. If we really begin to cooperate with God, identifying our strengths and being content with what He has given us, we will realize our full potential. Gifts and talents are distributed by the Holy Spirit according to the grace that is on each person to handle them. If you are going to go higher in life, if you are going to make the most of what God has given you, learn to focus on your potential—what God has created you to be—not on your limitations.

If God has called you to do something, you will find yourself loving it despite any adversity you may face.

Seeing People as God Sees Them

Let each of you esteem and look upon and be concerned for
not [merely] his own interests, but also each for the interests
of others.   PHILIPPIANS 2:4

A big problem among believers today is selfishness and self-
centeredness. If we're not careful, we can get so self-absorbed that
we never know the real joy of forgetting about self and serving God
by helping others. When we reach out to others, God reaches out to
us and takes care of our needs. What we make happen for someone
else, God will make happen for us.

It is easy to judge and criticize other people, but God wants us
to love them instead. He wants us to show them the same mercy
that He has shown to us. Mercy triumphs over judgment according
to God's Word, so let's get busy being a blessing and our joy will
increase.

It is impossible to be selfish and happy at the same time. Joy only
comes through reaching out to others with the love of God. The more
self-absorbed we are, the more miserable we will be. I spent many
years being unhappy simply because I wasn't doing anything for
anyone else. I finally learned that God didn't create us for "in-reach"
but for "out-reach." When you reach out, then God will reach in and
meet all of your needs.

Ask God to show you who you can help and bless today.

Priorities

*Depart from evil and do good; seek, inquire for, and crave peace
and pursue (go after) it!*   PSALM 34:14

Being at peace should always be a priority in our lives. In Psalm
34:14, David instructs us to pursue peace, to crave and go after it.
That's how important peace is.

Frustration and stress are natural enemies of peace. Many times,
to combat these peace destroyers, it is necessary for us to reorganize
our priorities and let go of things that are not bearing fruit.

If you want to live in the peace of God, make the choice not to
exceed your limits. While many of the things in your life are important, are they all absolutely necessary? Think about it for a moment.
Start looking at your life, figure out the commitments that are not
bearing any fruit, and start pruning those things back. You are
the one who set your schedule, and you are the only one who can
change it.

It is so important not to overcommit yourself. Ask God for wisdom and follow His leading as to what you are to be involved in and
where you are to use your energy. When you do, you will find that
time with Him is always the priority—everything else is secondary.
When you make God your number one priority, and when you seek
His direction for how to spend your time and energy after that, you'll
be amazed at the peace that will come into your life.

———————————

**You can rest in the assurance that God is with you in all
that you face. He doesn't just give you peace—He is your
peace.**

Begun by Faith, Finished by Faith

Are you so foolish and so senseless and so silly? Having begun [your new life spiritually] with the [Holy] Spirit, are you now reaching perfection [by dependence] on the flesh?

GALATIANS 3:3

Paul asked the Galatians a question I think it is important we ask ourselves today: Having begun our new lives in Christ by dependence on the Spirit, are we now trying to live them in the flesh?

Just as we are saved by grace (God's unmerited favor) through faith, and not by works of the flesh (Ephesians 2:8–9), we draw close to God each day through faith. We can begin each day by saying, "Lord, today I depend on You once again. It's not about what I can do in my own strength; it's about what You call me to do in Your strength."

When we were saved, we were in no condition to help ourselves. Only pride, or a lack of proper knowledge, could make us feel differently today—we are still in no condition to help ourselves. But thankfully, we are in perfect condition to depend on God to be everything we need. As long as we look to Him, trusting His perfect work in our lives, we can relax and really enjoy the life Jesus died to give us.

Living in the flesh—doing things in our own effort—leads to frustration. But living in the Spirit—obeying, trusting, and depending on God—brings joy unspeakable. The next time you feel frustrated you might stop and ask yourself what you are trying to do without leaning on God, and you will probably find the source of your frustration.

It is the power of the Holy Spirit that enables you to live your new life in Christ.

The Power of "I AM"

And God said to Moses, I Am Who I Am and What I Am, and
I Will Be What I Will Be; and He said, You shall say this to the
Israelites: I Am has sent me to you!

EXODUS 3:14

Jesus replied, I assure you, most solemnly I tell you, before
Abraham was born, I AM.

JOHN 8:58

When God said to Moses—and when Jesus told His disciples—
"I AM," He was saying something quite incredible. It is something
that can change the way we live our daily lives if we will really
believe it.

God is so great, there is no word that can adequately describe
Him. How can we describe, with one name, Someone Who is inde-
scribable? God is not just one thing—He is everything. That is why
God was saying to Moses, *I AM can take care of anything you encounter. Whatever you need, I AM it. There is nothing I can't handle. I have
everything covered, not only now, but for all time. You can relax, because I
AM. I AM with you and I AM able to do whatever needs to be done!*

The same is true for you today. Whatever you need, God is I AM.
In Him, you will find provision, joy, peace, healing, restoration, and
strength. Even before you know what you need, I AM knows, and He
is always there to provide every good thing.

There is nothing to fear in life when you know you have
access to the limitless goodness, grace, and power of I AM.

The Servant Test

Each of you should use whatever gift you have received to serve others, as faithful stewards of God's grace in its various forms.

1 PETER 4:10 NIV

The closer we get to God, the more opportunities He gives us to serve others. I say "opportunities" because that is the way we need to view serving others. Every time we serve others, it not only blesses them, but it also brings tremendous joy to our lives. Jesus gave us an example of being a servant by washing the feet of the disciples and then saying, "You should do [in your turn] what I have done to you" (John 13:15).

Some people fail to live as servants because they don't know who they are in Christ. They feel they must be doing something they consider "important" to find a sense of self-worth. They fail to understand that their identity comes from who they are in Christ, not how prestigious their career or platform is. When you are secure in your place in Christ, and when you find your strength and confidence in God, you take great joy in helping others every chance you get.

The "servant test" is simply how we respond to the opportunities God gives us to be a blessing to others. It reveals whether we really and truly want to be like Jesus. God has blessed and made us a blessing! God's blessings are never meant to be consumed solely on ourselves, but always to be shared with those around us.

———————

Look for ways to serve others today, including those in your own home. This will be a great experience for you and for them.

Going over the Mountain

When you pass through the waters, I will be with you, and through the rivers, they will not overwhelm you. When you walk through the fire, you will not be burned or scorched, nor will the flame kindle upon you.   ISAIAH 43:2

When we know that God is with us, we know that we can overcome any difficulty with Him. We never have to avoid our problems. We can meet them head-on in the power and wisdom of God. Anything we hide or run from still has power over us.

Sometimes we go around and around the same mountain, and we end up like the Israelites in the wilderness who wandered around for forty years (Deuteronomy 2:1–3). But the closer we get to God, the more determined we are to face our mountains and confidently go all the way through with God. That is the only path to victory. David didn't run from Goliath, he ran toward him in the name of the Lord.

I encourage you to refuse to give up no matter how difficult your circumstance may seem. Trust that God has a plan for your life, and pray that God will give you the strength to keep climbing no matter how high the mountain seems.

Most importantly, I encourage you to be determined to enjoy the journey. Enjoying life is an attitude of the heart, a decision to enjoy everything because God can use everything—even the seemingly difficult things—to bring about His perfect plan.

The power and presence of God in your life will lift you above the circumstances that others can't seem to overcome.

First Things First

But seek (aim at and strive after) first of all His kingdom and
His righteousness (His way of doing and being right), and then all
these things taken together will be given you besides.

MATTHEW 6:33

Too often we spend all of our time seeking God for possessions, for blessings, for answers to our problems, when all we really need to do is just seek God. The more we seek God because we simply want to be in relationship with Him, the more everything else in our lives falls into place.

In the early years of my ministry, I sought God about how I could get the ministry to grow. The result was that it stayed just the same as it was. It didn't grow as quickly as I had hoped, and sometimes it even went backward. What I didn't realize at the time was that all I needed to do was to seek the kingdom of God, and He would add the growth.

The truth is that we don't have to beg God to give us anything. If what we want is His will, He will give us what is best for us at the right time. All we need to do is love God and seek Him first and want to do things His way. As we do, we will develop a closeness with God that is vital in order to properly handle success, or the material blessings of God.

Always seek the "presence" of God, and not the "presents" of God. He will give you many good things, but He does require first place in our lives. We are to have no other gods before Him!

Seek God before anything else, abide in Him, and you will draw closer to Him than ever before.

Conscious of God's Love

And we know (understand, recognize, are conscious of, by observation and by experience) and believe (adhere to and put faith in and rely on) the love God cherishes for us. God is love, and he who dwells and continues in love dwells and continues in God, and God dwells and continues in him. 1 JOHN 4:16

In 1 John 4:16, the Bible instructs us to "understand, recognize" and be "conscious of" the love God has for us. To be in close, personal relationship with God is to be conscious of His love at all times and to be continually amazed at the fact that He shows His love for us even when we don't deserve it.

One way I would encourage you to do this is to keep a book of remembrance, a book in which you write down special things the Lord does for you. When you begin observing and making note of God's goodness in this way, you will be surprised at how often God's love manifests in practical ways (big and small) in your life.

God's love can change your life if you will allow it. It contains the power to heal your emotional wounds. His love strengthens you to press on in difficult times, and it softens your heart, enabling you to show more love to others. Can you imagine anything better to be "conscious" and aware of than this great love?

Perhaps the best thing you can do today is simply observe God's love, recognize and celebrate it with thanksgiving.

Preparing for the Best

Rejoice in the Lord, O you [uncompromisingly] righteous [you upright in right standing with God]; for praise is becoming and appropriate for those who are upright [in heart]. PSALM 33:1

How we approach each new day and each new situation makes a huge difference. If we decide ahead of time that we won't be happy or peaceful unless we get exactly what we want, then we will rarely be at peace.

I have heard people say things like, "If it rains tomorrow I am *not* going to be happy," or "If I don't get the job, I am going to be *so* upset." When we think thoughts such as this, we are setting ourselves up to be unhappy and to lose our peace and joy before we even have a problem.

Instead of preparing to be upset, we can prepare to be at peace. We can think and speak things like, "I really hope the weather is nice tomorrow, and I hope I get this new job. But my joy comes from my relationship with Jesus, so I choose to be happy and have rest in my soul no matter what I come up against tomorrow. Whether it's rainy or sunny, whether I get the job or not, I choose the joy of the Lord!"

The way we approach our lives makes all the difference in the quality of life we can have. When we can't fix life, let's remember that we can fix our approach toward it.

Make up your mind that you will be happy if you get your way today . . . and if you don't.

Free to Fly

The Spirit of the Lord God is upon me, because the Lord has anointed and qualified me to preach the Gospel of good tidings to the meek, the poor, and afflicted; He has sent me to bind up and heal the brokenhearted, to proclaim liberty to the [physical and spiritual] captives and the opening of the prison and of the eyes to those who are bound.   ISAIAH 61:1

Love offers people both roots and wings. It provides a sense of belonging (roots) and a sense of freedom (wings). Love does not try to control or manipulate others.

Jesus said that He was sent by God to proclaim liberty. As believers, that is what we are meant to do also—to free people to fulfill God's will for their lives, not to bring them under our control.

Have you ever seen parents push their children to do things they do not even want to do just to meet the frustrated desires of their parents? Have you ever seen a person who is clingy and emotionally smothering to a new friend, because he is afraid to lose that person? Both of these examples bind rather than set free.

That is not the way true love works. Love does not try to gain personal satisfaction at the expense of others. Love will always proclaim liberty. When we love God, and when we love others, we will excitedly allow the people in our lives to follow God's plan—not our plan—and see who they can be and what they can accomplish in Christ Jesus.

A caged bird cannot fly! Proclaim liberty. Set people free and see what they can do.

Finding the Courage to Be Unique

Not with eyeservice, as menpleasers; but as the servants of
Christ, doing the will of God from the heart.

EPHESIANS 6:6 KJV

In order to be the person you are called to be in Christ, choosing to live confidently in close relationship with God, it is essential you have the courage to be uniquely you. That means being content in how God created you, choosing not to be like everyone else.

One of the easiest traps we can fall into is the trap of being a "manpleaser." But trying to please others ultimately leads to frustration. At first, when we begin changing our personality to please other people, we hear comments that make us feel good about ourselves. But this won't last. People's opinions are fickle and superficial. It is only God's opinion that counts.

You are worth something because God sent His only Son to die for you. You are worth something because God loves you, not because of what anybody else thinks about you or says about you.

I encourage you to embrace the things that make you unique. If your hair is a little different, if your personality is unique, if your talent is uncommon—whatever it is, thank God that He created you in a special way and choose to use your gifts and talents and personality for His glory.

It is only when you embrace the person God made you to be that you will really enjoy the life Jesus died to give you.

Living with Purpose

This is the [Lord's] purpose that is purposed upon the whole
earth . . . For the Lord of hosts has purposed, and who can annul
it? And His hand is stretched out, and who can turn it back?

ISAIAH 14:26–27

God is a God of purpose—He moves strategically, and He implements His perfect plan. As His children, God desires for us to be people of purpose. The closer we are to Him, the more purpose we will live with.

Jesus knew His purpose. He said that He came into the world that we might have life and that He might destroy the works of the devil (John 10:10; 1 John 3:8).

As far as our specific purpose, that varies from person to person and from one season of life to the next, but God has a general purpose we can all choose to live in each day.

For example, we love others, not because we always feel like it, but because we purpose to love others. The same is true when we give, show mercy, display kindness, forgive, and so many other things. Love, joy, peace, patience, kindness, goodness, and all the other fruit of the Spirit are ours to enjoy and to release to others if we do it on purpose. We do these things, not because we always necessarily feel like it, but because it is what we are called to do.

Joy and peace don't happen by accident; they come when
you choose to live your life on purpose.

The Word of God Sets You Free

*. . . Welcome the Word which implanted and rooted [in your
hearts] contains the power to save your souls.*   JAMES 1:21

The most powerful and effective tool to bring about real and lasting
transformation in our lives is the Word of God. It is the Word of God
that draws us and keeps us close to God.

The devil will always try to deceive you, telling you things about
yourself and your situation that are contrary to God's Word. As long
as we believe the lies, we remain frustrated, miserable, and powerless. But when God's Word of truth uncovers those lies, the truth
sets us free.

Only the Word of God has this power, and only God can change
us. The Word exposes wrong motives, wrong thoughts, and wrong
words. Truth can set us free from guilt, self-rejection, condemnation,
self-hatred, the works of the flesh, and every lie that we have bought
into and brought into our lives. God is out to set us free so that we
can enjoy the life He has given us.

A sword in the sheath is of no value. It must be wielded and
appropriately used. Well, the Word of God is the believer's sword,
and we can learn by applying it daily, getting it down in our heart,
and speaking it out our mouth. The believer who does this is full of
power and can accomplish great things for the kingdom of God.

**Studying the Word is the number one way to draw close
to God.**

God Is Never Late

And let us not be weary in well doing: for in due season we shall reap, if we faint not.

GALATIANS 6:9 KJV

Many people think that they are being patient just because they have had to wait for something. But patience is more than waiting. Patience is having a good, positive, joyful attitude in the waiting process. It is fruit of the Spirit that manifests itself in a believer who is submitted to God, regardless of their circumstances. The patient person will always stay calm and point us to the provision of our heavenly Father.

We often want God's plan in our lives to happen right now. But God's perfect work takes time and requires us to be patient. God is not working on our timetable. Though we are rushed and hurried, God never is. He takes time to do things right—He works on His masterpiece with thought, care, and precision.

We are God's masterpiece (Ephesians 2:10 NLT). He is the Designer, and He is crafting something beautiful out of your life. God's timing seems to be His own little secret. The Bible promises us that He will never be late, but I have also discovered that He is usually not early. No matter what you do, you cannot rush God. So I encourage you to enjoy the wait.

Enjoy where you are on the way to where you are going!

Can You Laugh at Yourself?

Then were our mouths filled with laughter, and our tongues with
singing. Then they said among the nations, The Lord has done
great things for them.   PSALM 126:2

One of the beautiful things about being a Christian is that it's not
complicated—in fact, we are instructed to humble ourselves and
become as little children. While the Lord wants us to grow up in
our attitude, behavior, and acceptance of responsibility in Christ
(Ephesians 4:15), at the same time He wants us to be childlike in our
dependence upon Him and in our desire to be close to Him.

One characteristic of a child is that he has fun no matter what he
does. He manages to find a way to have a good time. God desires for
us to be the same way. We can learn how to enjoy everything we do,
and to enjoy Him at all times. We can and should love all aspects of
life, the secular as well as the sacred. You can enjoy being in a Bible
study with friends, and you can enjoy doing household chores.

It is healthy to learn to enjoy yourself and find humor in your
everyday life. We can even learn to laugh at ourselves. As Art Link-
letter used to say, "People are funny!" And that includes us.

Laugh as often as you possibly can, because a merry
heart does you much good.

Convincing God or Trusting God?

For who has known the mind of the Lord and who has understood His thoughts, or who has [ever] been His counselor?

ROMANS 11:34

Life would be so much easier if we would live in the realization that God is smarter than we are. No matter what you or I may think, God's way is always better than our way.

We are often tempted to think we know what is best, and then we throw all our energy into bringing it to pass. We experience a lot of disappointment, which hinders joy and enjoyment, due to deciding for ourselves that something has to be done a certain way or by a certain time. When we want something very strongly, we often try to convince God why it is important and why He should bring our will to pass, instead of simply trusting that He knows what is best for our life.

As Romans 11:34 reminds us, God has no need of a counselor to tell Him what He should do for us. His will is perfect, and He has good plans for us to become all that He intends us to be. The prophet Jeremiah says, "For I know the thoughts and plans that I have for you, says the Lord, thoughts and plans for welfare and peace and not for evil, to give you hope in your final outcome" (Jeremiah 29:11).

When you face puzzling situations, I encourage you to pray, "Well, Lord, this may not make sense to me right now, but I trust You. I believe You love me, You are with me, and You are doing what is best for me."

———————

God does not need your counsel in order to work; He just needs your faith.

A Truly Fervent Prayer

... The effective, fervent prayer of a righteous man avails much.

JAMES 5:16 NKJV

If you've been a believer for any period of time, you've probably heard it taught that for prayer to be effective it must be fervent. However, if we misunderstand the word *fervent*, we may feel that we have to work up some strong emotion before we pray; otherwise, our prayers will not be effective.

I know there were many years when I believed this way, and perhaps you have been likewise misled. But praying fervently just means that our prayers must come from our heart and be sincere.

I remember enjoying prayer times when I could feel God's presence, and then wondering what was wrong during the times when I didn't feel anything. I learned after a while that faith is not based on feelings or emotions but the knowledge of the heart.

At times I experience a great deal of emotion while I'm praying. But there are more times when I don't feel emotional. Prayer that brings us closer to God only happens when we pray in faith, regardless of what we *feel* at any particular moment.

———

Trust that your earnest, heartfelt prayers are effective because your faith is in God, not in your own ability to pray passionately or eloquently.

God Understands You

No one understands [no one intelligently discerns or
comprehends]; no one seeks out God.   ROMANS 3:11

Anyone who decides to follow God closely will have times of being misunderstood by people who have not made the same commitment. Faithless people do not understand faithful people!

There will always be those who won't quite know what to think of us when we are fully surrendered to God. People did not know what to think of Jesus either. Nobody really understood Him or the call on His life, not even His family.

When we don't say or do what other people are saying and doing because we have decided to follow God rather than the world, we may be misunderstood and rejected. It hurts when that happens, but always remember that Jesus never rejects you, and that is what really matters.

Your obedience to God may mean that you won't fit into the regular regimen of what is going on around you. You may feel out of place at times, but in those moments remember that God will reward your faithfulness. He loves you, and when other people are asking, "What is wrong with you?" God will be saying, "There is nothing wrong with you. You are mine and I am proud of you."

Make up your mind to stand with God and do what He says, even if nobody understands or supports you. Jesus understands you, and He is enough.

Bridges Instead of Walls

*For even to this were you called [it is inseparable from your
vocation]. For Christ also suffered for you, leaving you [His
personal] example, so that you should follow in His footsteps.*

1 PETER 2:21

Instead of the walls that I used to build around my life, I have
learned to build bridges. By the power of grace and God's forgiveness, all the difficult and unfair things that happened to me in life
have been turned into highways over which others can pass to find
the same liberty that I found.

God is no respecter of persons (Acts 10:34). What He has done
for me, He will do for you too. As you draw closer to God on a daily
basis, you can discover the same freedom that I have found, and you
can become a bridge for others to pass over, instead of a wall that
shuts them out.

Jesus pioneered a pathway to God for us. He became a highway
for us to pass over. He sacrificed Himself for us, and now that we are
benefiting from His sacrifice, He is giving us a chance to sacrifice for
others so they can reap the same benefits we enjoy.

Instead of shutting people out, I suggest that you ask God to
allow you to see them as He sees them. Love them, forgive them, and
point them to God so He can heal their wounds and fill them with
His peace and joy.

**There are people who are lost and need someone to go
before them and show them the way. Why not be that
person for them?**

Is It Worth It?

. . . Therefore love truth and peace.   ZECHARIAH 8:19 NKJV

It is God's sincere desire for you to live a life full of peace. The closer you get to the Lord—the more you depend on Him—the more peace you will have.

No position or possession is worthwhile if you don't have peace. Money, status, popularity—it's all meaningless if you don't have peace. You simply cannot put a price on the value of peace.

Many people spend their lives trying to climb the ladder of success, but every time they go up one more rung, they lose more of their peace, joy, and time to spend with their family. Their whole life is consumed with the pressure and stress of trying to keep what they've gained. But we are never truly successful unless we have peace.

Some even work several jobs to acquire what the world dangles in front of them, saying, "You must have this to be truly happy." They get those "things," but they still don't have any peace.

Romans 14:17 tells us, "The kingdom of God is not meat and drink"—it is not things that money or status can secure—but it is "righteousness, and peace, and joy in the Holy Ghost" (KJV). The kingdom of God is found in knowing who we are in Christ and having "the peace of God, which surpasses all understanding" (Philippians 4:7 NKJV).

God wants you to have your needs met abundantly and be in a position to bless others. Never doubt that God wants to bless you, but don't seek to have anything if you cannot have it peacefully.

Love Shows Respect

Let all men know and perceive and recognize your unselfishness
(your considerateness, your forbearing spirit.) The Lord is near
[He is coming soon].   PHILIPPIANS 4:5

Love is a generous, selfless act. A selfish person expects everyone to
be just the way he is and to like whatever he likes, but love respects
the differences in other people.

Respecting individual rights is very important. If God had
wanted us to all be alike, He would not have given each of us a different set of fingerprints. I think that one fact alone proves that we are
created equal, but different. We all have fingerprints, but they are all
different!

We all have different abilities, different likes and dislikes, different goals in life, different motivations, and the list goes on and on.
We look different, we come in all sizes and shapes, and each of us is
unique.

Love respectfully frees others to be who they were created to be.
Freedom is one of the greatest gifts we can give. It was what Jesus
came to give us, and it is what love allows us to give to others.

God's love for us is unconditional, and we should learn to love
others the same way. Be generous with mercy and always believe the
best.

Unconditional love unselfishly loves selfish people,
generously gives to stingy people, and continually
blesses unappreciative people.

No Matter Where You Go . . . You're There

. . . You shall love your neighbor as [you do] yourself.

MATTHEW 19:19

I believe one of the greatest problems people have today concerns the way they feel about themselves. Many people go through life carrying a poor self-image and a low opinion of themselves. Oftentimes, people have had these negative thoughts so long they don't even realize they have them.

What do you think of yourself? What kind of relationship do you have with yourself? I ask because no matter where you go, or what you do in this life, you are always going to have to deal with you. There is no escaping from you.

The Lord commanded us to love our neighbors as we love ourselves, but what happens if we don't love ourselves? We cannot give away what we do not have. God loves us, and that gives us permission to receive His love and love ourselves in a balanced way. Many of us think we have worn God out with our failures and sins, but that is impossible to do. God never gives up on us! The closer we come to God in our daily lives, the more we realize how dearly we are loved, and the easier it is to begin to love ourselves.

Receive God's love for you. Meditate on it. Let it change and strengthen you. Then give it away.

The True Source of Confidence

For we [Christians] are the true circumcision, who worship God in spirit and by the Spirit of God and exult and glory and pride ourselves in Jesus Christ, and put no confidence or dependence [on what we are] in the flesh and on outward privileges and physical advantages and external appearances.

PHILIPPIANS 3:3

The most important key to becoming spiritually stronger and more secure is to discover the true source of confidence.

In what do you place your confidence today? Is it your level of education, your social group, the amount of money you have, or the position you hold at work— or is it rooted in God? That question must be settled for every believer who desires to draw closer to God each day.

If we place all our confidence in our education, our looks, our position, our gifts, our talents, or in other people's opinions, we are going to end up disappointed and miserable due to being insecure. Our heavenly Father is saying to us, "Though people and things may eventually fail you, I never will. You can put your trust and confidence in Me."

I encourage you to come to the place where your confidence is not in the flesh or the things of this world, but in Christ Jesus. He is the only One Who will strengthen you, always stand by you, and never let you down.

Honestly evaluate what your confidence is in, and if it is anything other than God, repent (change your mind for the better), and be ready to do things differently.

The Wisdom in Waiting Quietly

But Mary was keeping within herself all these things (sayings),
weighing and pondering them in her heart.   LUKE 2:19

There is great wisdom in learning to quietly ponder what you feel the Lord has spoken to you, especially when you're not sure exactly how it will work out.

You may feel that God has promised something for your children, spoken a new direction for your career, instructed you to make some changes in your character—whatever it is, if you'll trust God, wait patiently, and ponder what the Lord has spoken, He will show you exactly how to cooperate with His plan.

Mary had some pretty amazing things happen in her life. She was just a teenage girl who loved God when an angel of the Lord appeared to her and told her she was going to be the mother of the Son of God. But whatever Mary may have thought or felt, she trusted God, saying, "May it be done to me according to your word" (Luke 1:38 NASB).

When God speaks something to us, many times we need to keep it to ourselves. If He tells us things we don't really understand, things that seem to make no sense, we can follow the example of Mary. We can do a little more pondering instead of running to others for advice. The doubt of others can ruin your faith. Sometimes the best thing you can do is quietly hold on to God's promise and ask Him to make it clearer to you in His perfect timing.

When God calls you to do something, He also gives you the faith to do it.

The Best Time You Can Spend

... Let everyone who is godly pray—pray to You in a time
when You may be found; surely when the great waters [of trial]
overflow, they shall not reach [the spirit in] him.   PSALM 32:6

It's simple. The more time you spend with God, the more you con-
nect yourself to His power. David tells us that it is in the secret place
of the presence of God that we are protected (Psalm 91:1). When we
spend time in God's presence, in prayer, and in His Word, we are in
the secret place. The secret place is a wonderful place of peace and
rest!

It's powerful to think that the awesomeness of God's presence
is available to us as believers. With this in mind, why in the world
would we not want to spend time with God? Even Jesus would get
up early in the morning to be alone with God. He knew the value of
being in the presence of God. We draw strength and wisdom merely
from being with God!

The best thing to do is dedicate a portion of your time to spend
with God. Try not to be legalistic about it, but do try to be as regular
with it as you can. Talk to God about anything and everything that is
on your heart—He is interested in everything that interests or concerns you. Sometimes you may want to listen to music and worship;
other times you may just want to sit still and enjoy silence. Set aside
time to be with God and let the Holy Spirit lead you in the amazing
journey of becoming closer to God!

**Spending time in the secret place of His presence
changes you from what you are to what only He can
make you.**

Love, Trust, and Faith

*For [if we are] in Christ Jesus, neither circumcision nor
uncircumcision counts for anything, but only faith activated and
energized and expressed and working through love.*

GALATIANS 5:6

Instead of trying so hard to work up faith, we would be wise to spend
that time and effort simply receiving God's love and loving Him in
return. We are only going to be able to walk in faith based on what
we believe about the Father's love.

Galatians 5:6 says that faith works by love. Faith will not work
without love. This scripture is telling us that if we don't know how
much God loves us, we have nothing to base our faith on.

Trusting God and walking in faith is leaning on Him and trusting
Him for everything. You can only do that with someone when you
know you are loved unconditionally. God's love is His free gift to us,
and we simply need to receive it, be thankful for it, and let it bring us
closer to Him.

The Bible says, "We love Him, because He first loved us" (1 John
4:19). When you are assured of the fact that God loved you first, you
are excited to love Him in return—you are excited to live your life
completely for Him.

Nobody in all the world will ever love you as God loves you.

———————

**Faith becomes stronger and works more powerfully by
letting God love you.**

Dedicated for His Use

I appeal to you therefore, brethren, and beg of you in view of
[all] the mercies of God, to make a decisive dedication of your
bodies [presenting all your members and faculties] as a living
sacrifice, holy (devoted, consecrated) and well pleasing to God,
which is your reasonable (rational, intelligent) service and
spiritual worship.   ROMANS 12:1

In order for God to use us, we must dedicate our lives to Him. When
we truly dedicate ourselves to the Lord, we relinquish the burden of
trying to run our own lives.

Dedicating your life to God must be sincere. It is quite easy to
sing along with everyone else a song such as "I Surrender All." We
may even feel moved emotionally, but the real test is found in daily
life when circumstances don't always go the way we thought they
would. Dedicating your spirit, soul, and body to the Lord is more
than a song—it's a daily decision.

An important part of drawing close to God is having a heart dedicated to Him. When we choose to live in obedience to the Word of
God, it pleases the Lord greatly. When you sincerely dedicate yourself to Him, you're drawn into a new and deeper level of relationship that increases your strength and adds excitement to every day
of your life.

Dedicate every part of your life to God and let the Holy
Spirit make you into a vessel fit for the Master's use.

Balancing Work and Rest

For God did not give us a spirit of timidity (of cowardice, of craven and cringing and fawning fear), but [He has given us a spirit] of power and of love and of calm and well-balanced mind and discipline and self-control.   2 TIMOTHY 1:7

We have all been given twenty-four hours in each day. It is important how we use that time—how we regulate the different areas of our lives to keep them in proper perspective. If we have too much work and not enough rest, we get out of balance. We become workaholics and end up weary and worn-out.

I get a lot of satisfaction out of accomplishments and work. I don't like a lot of wasted time or useless activities. But because of my nature, it is easy for me to get out of balance in the area of work. I have to regularly determine that I will not only work but also rest. It must be a priority in order for me to be healthy and close to God.

But it is also possible to have too much rest and not enough work. Solomon says that through "...idleness of the hands the house leaks" (Ecclesiastes 10:18). In other words, people who don't work enough end up in trouble. Their finances, spiritual life, possessions, bodies, and everything else suffer because they don't do the work necessary to keep things in order.

Ask God to help you have a healthy and proper balance of work and rest. Take time to accomplish the tasks before you, but be sure to seize your opportunities to be at peace and enjoy rest. Both are important. Balance is the key!

———————

Pray for God to show you how to bring balance to your life one step at a time!

Keep Your Heart Free

And forgive us our debts, as we also have forgiven (left, remitted,
and let go of the debts, and have given up resentment against)
our debtors.   MATTHEW 6:12

Jesus frequently spoke of the need to forgive others. If we are to live
in close relationship with God, it is important that we are quick to
forgive. The quicker we forgive, the easier it is to live in peace. It
allows us to deal with the problem before it gets rooted in our emotions. Bitterness will be much more difficult to pull out if it has long,
strong roots.

When we hold a grudge against someone, we're not hurting that
person—we're only hurting ourselves. Harboring unforgiveness
against other people does not change them, but it does change us. It
makes us sour, bitter, miserable, and difficult to be around. Think of
it this way: When you think you are holding a grudge, it is actually
the grudge that is holding you.

Unforgiveness is Satan's deceptive way of keeping us in bondage.
He wants us to think we are getting even, that we are protecting ourselves from being hurt again, but none of that is true. Unforgiveness
continues to hurt you and keeps you from drawing closer to God.

If someone has hurt you, I encourage you to ask God for grace to
forgive that person against whom you are holding a grudge. Determine from this point on to keep your heart and life free from this
negative, destructive emotion.

———————

**It is only possible to have good emotional health when
you let go of all bitterness and unforgiveness.**

When You Feel Discouraged

Be glad in the Lord and rejoice, you [uncompromisingly]
righteous . . . shout for joy, all you upright in heart!

PSALM 32:11

People from all walks of life have bouts with discouragement and despair. There are many underlying causes for despair and a variety of treatments offered to deal with it. Some are effective, but many offer only a temporary solution. The good news is that Jesus can heal us and deliver us from discouragement. He can restore our lives to one of joy and peace.

If you are a believer in Jesus Christ, the joy of the Lord is already inside you. Even when you don't seem to *feel* joyful, you can tap into that joy and release it by faith. You can experience what is yours as a result of your faith in Jesus Christ. *It is God's will for you to experience joy!*

I had problems with discouragement and despair myself a long time ago. But thank God, I learned I didn't have to allow negative feelings to rule me. I learned how to release the joy of the Lord in my life! When discouragement comes, don't accept and agree with it, but encourage yourself by looking at God's promises and letting them fill you with hope. No matter what you have gone through in life or are going through now, being discouraged won't change it. No matter what you have lost, you still have a lot left. Stop living in the past and ask God to show you the future He has planned for you!

When you are tempted to be discouraged, say "no" to the temptation and stay positive, expecting something good to happen to you!

Filled with the Holy Spirit

If you then, evil as you are, know how to give good gifts [gifts that are to their advantage] to your children, how much more will your heavenly Father give the Holy Spirit to those who ask and continue to ask Him!   LUKE 11:13

We all need to be continually filled with the Holy Spirit. As believers in Jesus, we have the Holy Spirit, but perhaps have not surrendered ourselves entirely to Him for His use. That was the case with me for many years until I reached a crisis point in my life where I was no longer willing to limp along day after day with no real victory.

I ask God to do "something," and I was open to whatever His plan was! I didn't even know what I needed, but God did. He is always faithful to meet us right where we are and help us get to where we need to be.

I needed to be filled with God's Spirit, and by His grace and mercy, I was. I still ask God regularly to fill me afresh with His presence and power and enable me to be all that He wants me to be. We need the power of the Holy Spirit in order to do God's will. Never depend on yourself, for apart from Him you can do nothing (John 15:5).

Ask for the fullness of God's Spirit daily and you will experience closeness with God that is wonderful. When the Holy Spirit comes upon you, then you receive power to be His witness. You will change in amazing ways as you trust God's power to enable and strengthen you.

Ask for and receive the Holy Spirit's power in your life.

Unconditional Love

And this command (charge, order, injunction) we have from Him:
that he who loves God shall love his brother [believer] also.

1 JOHN 4:21

According to God's Word, He loved us before the world was formed, before we loved Him or believed in Him or had ever done anything either right or wrong. Isn't that amazing? God's love for us was, is, and always will be unending and unconditional.

Because God does not require us to earn His love, we can follow His example, not requiring others to earn ours. Love is not something we do and then don't do. We should not turn it on and off, depending on who we want to give it to and how they are treating us.

As believers in Jesus Christ, the love we can demonstrate to the world is the unconditional *love of God* flowing through us to them. We cannot understand this God-kind of love with our minds. It far surpasses mere knowledge. It is a revelation that God gives to His children. It is something we feel as we draw closer to the Lord, and it is something we can't wait to share with those around us.

Unconditional love always believes the best of people. It sees what they can become if only someone will love them. That is what God did for us. He believed the best and saw that His unconditional love could conform us to the image of His Son.

If you'll freely receive God's love, you'll be able to freely give that same love away.

A Sacrifice of Praise

*Through Him, therefore, let us constantly and at all times offer
up to God a sacrifice of praise, which is the fruit of lips that
thankfully acknowledge and confess and glorify His name.*

HEBREWS 13:15

Praise is an opportunity to dwell on, be thankful for, and recount
the goodness of God in our lives. And praise is something we can do
continually. We can praise Him for His mighty works, the wonders
He has created, and even the works of grace He is yet to do in our
lives. We can also praise Him for His daily provision.

A sacrifice of praise means doing it even when we don't feel like
it. As believers, in the hard times as well as the good, we can praise
God for His goodness, mercy, loving-kindness, grace, and long-
suffering. While we are waiting to see the fulfillment of our prayers,
we can choose to continually acknowledge and confess and glorify
His name.

It is not our responsibility to worry and fret or try to do God's
part by taking into our own hands situations that should be left to
Him alone. Instead, it is our responsibility to simply cast our care
upon the Lord (1 Peter 5:7), trusting Him and praising Him for what
He has done, is doing, and what we believe by faith He is going to do.

Even on days when it's not easy—when we don't necessarily see
how everything is going to work out—we can offer a sacrifice of
praise. This pleases the Lord and boosts our faith as we trust Him
regardless of the circumstances around us.

**May a sacrifice of praise continually be in our mouths for
the marvelous works of grace He has done for us.**

Free

... If anyone should sin, we have an Advocate (One Who will intercede for us) with the Father—[it is] Jesus Christ [the all] righteous [upright, just, Who conforms to the Father's will in every purpose, thought, and action].

And He [that same Jesus Himself] is the propitiation (the atoning sacrifice) for our sins ...   1 JOHN 2:1–2

There was a time in my life when, if you asked me, "What was the last thing you did wrong?" I could have detailed the precise time I had done it and how long I had been paying for it by feeling guilty. I worried about every tiny error I made and desperately tried to keep myself from sinning. It was not until I came to comprehend God's forgiveness that I was free from the self-analysis that complicated my life to the extreme.

If you believe you must be perfect to be worthy of love and acceptance, then you will be frustrated in life because you will never be perfect as long as you are in an earthly body. The closer you draw to God, the more you realize that He loves you even in the midst of your imperfections. Out of love for God, we will naturally seek to please Him, but we can be assured that He understands our imperfections.

Don't condemn yourself. God sees your heart—in that your desire is to please Him in all things—but your performance will not perfectly match your heart's desire until you get to Heaven. You can improve all the time and keep pressing toward the mark of perfection, but you will always need the mercy and forgiveness of Jesus.

God's answer for our imperfection is forgiveness.

The Gift of Righteousness

*... [Righteousness, standing acceptable to God] will be granted
and credited to us also who believe in (trust in, adhere to, and rely
on) God, Who raised Jesus our Lord from the dead.*

ROMANS 4:24

One of the first revelations God gave me in the Word was on righteousness. By "revelation," I mean something you understand to the point that it becomes part of you. The knowledge isn't only in your mind, but it is in your heart. You are assured of a truth.

Righteousness is God's gift to us. It is "granted and credited" to us by virtue of our believing in what God did for us through His Son, Jesus Christ Jesus, Who knew no sin, became sin so that we might be made the righteousness of God in Him (2 Corinthians 5:21).

Above all else, the devil does not want us to walk in the reality that we are in right standing with God. He wants us to feel insecure, ashamed, guilty, and condemned so that we shrink from God instead of enjoying closeness with Him.

Jesus wants us to know that we are right with God because of what He has done for us. He wants us to enjoy Him and enjoy living in relationship with Him. Receive the gift of God's forgiveness, mercy, and right standing today and embark on a journey of freedom and joy.

You can have a revelation of the gift of righteousness by meditating on God's Word and believing what it says about who you are in Christ.

A Living Message in Your Heart

This Book of the Law shall not depart out of your mouth, but you shall meditate on it day and night, that you may observe and do according to all that is written in it. For then you shall make your way prosperous, and then you shall deal wisely and have good success.   JOSHUA 1:8

The Word of God reveals His very thoughts written down on paper for our study and consideration. His Word is how He thinks about every situation and subject.

In order to be close to God, it is essential that you allow His Word to be a living message in your heart. This is accomplished by meditating on the Word of God, allowing His thoughts to become your thoughts. When you do this, you begin to develop the mind of Christ. I strongly encourage you to love God's Word and let it be the guiding light in your life.

Joshua 1:8 tells us that we can put the Word into practice mentally in order to experience good success physically. Meditating on or pondering the Word of God has the power to affect every part of our lives. Proverbs 4:20–22 even tells us that the words of the Lord are a source of health and healing to our bodies.

Remember the principle of sowing and reaping. The greater the amount of time you and I personally put into thinking about and studying the Word, the more we will get out of it.

The Lord reveals His thoughts to those who are diligent about reading the Word.

Awesome Containers for Power

[The Servant of God says] The Lord God has given Me the tongue of a disciple and of one who is taught, that I should know how to speak a word in season to him who is weary . . .   ISAIAH 50:4

Words are awesome containers for power. God created the earth with His words (Hebrews 11:3). The Holy Spirit changes lives with words. Jesus said that His words are spirit and life (John 6:63).

The power of words can either be used to lift people up or tear them down—it just depends on how we choose to use that power on a daily basis. People are encouraged or defeated by the words we speak. God's desire is for us to display His love to people through our encouraging, positive, life-giving words. Speaking the right word to a person at the right time can turn their whole life around.

The same is true in our own lives. When we speak the Word of God over our situation, things begin to change. Words are that powerful.

This is why knowing the Word of God is so important. We can study it, learn it, and then speak it out according to our situations. For instance, if you feel discouraged, don't say, "I'll never make it out of this situation." Instead, say, "Why are you so downcast, O my soul? Put your hope in God" (Psalm 42:5). You will be absolutely amazed at how your life will change when you change the way you talk.

Make the decision that your words will encourage, edify, and build up your life and the lives of those around you.

Rejoice in Each Day

*This is the day which the Lord has brought about; we will rejoice
and be glad in it.*   PSALM 118:24

One of my greatest desires in ministry is to see people thoroughly
enjoy the quality of life Jesus died to give us—not just to read about
it or talk about it, but to walk in it and experience it as a daily reality.

Many people, myself included, are extremely goal oriented. We
are so focused on tomorrow that we often fail to appreciate and enjoy
today because we are always thinking ahead, looking to the next
event, working to complete the next assignment, and seeing what we
can check off of our to-do lists.

Our fast-paced, high-pressure society urges us to accomplish as
much as we can as quickly as we can—so we can then accomplish
even more. Over the years, I have learned that the intense pursuit of
one goal after another can cause us to miss out on some of the enjoyment life offers us. God does have purposes and plans He wants us
to fulfill during the course of our earthly lives, but He also wants
us to enjoy and make the most of every day we live. God frequently
reminds me to live in the moment!

The closer you draw to God the more you will realize it is okay
to actually slow down and enjoy your life in Him. God's desire is for
you to experience His love, His peace, and His joy on a daily basis.

**Today is the day God has given you; choose to rejoice and
be glad in it.**

Freely You Have Received, Freely Give

Then Peter came up to Him and said, Lord, how many times may my brother sin against me and I forgive him and let it go? [As many as] up to seven times?

Jesus answered him, I tell you, not up to seven times, but seventy times seven!   MATTHEW 18:21–22

I don't know about you, but I am glad that God does not put a limit on how many times He will forgive us. Regardless of how many times we fail and fall short, He continues to demonstrate His love for us by forgiving us and welcoming us back time and time again.

But isn't it amazing how we are willing to keep receiving forgiveness from God, yet how little we want to give forgiveness to others? We freely accept mercy, yet it is surprising how rigid, legalistic, and merciless we can be toward others.

The bottom line is this: As people who have been forgiven much, it is important we learn to share that same forgiveness with others. We can't live in close relationship with God while we harbor bitterness, resentment, and unforgiveness toward another person. These are chains that will keep us spiritually bound up and far from God's best in our lives.

If there are people who have hurt you and you are finding it difficult to forgive them, just remember all the things God has forgiven you for. When you look at it that way, forgiveness becomes something much easier to give to others.

God's grace helps us do things easily that would otherwise be hard.

Experiencing the Love of God

*In this the love of God was made manifest (displayed) where we
are concerned: in that God sent His Son, the only begotten or
unique [Son], into the world so that we might live through Him.*

1 JOHN 4:9

For many people, if they were asked, "Are you lovable?"—they would
truthfully think to themselves, *No, I'm really not.*

I know this is true because I thought I was unlovable before I
came to understand the true nature of God's love and His reason
for loving me. This improper understanding of my value as a child of
God affected the way I treated others. I was impatient with people,
legalistic and harsh, judgmental, rude, selfish, and unforgiving.

A breakthrough came in my life when God began to show me that
I wasn't loving others because I had never received His love for me.
Yes, I had acknowledged the Bible teaching that God loved me, but I
had not embraced it and received it as a reality in my heart.

The truth is it pleases God to love us. Once you realize that you
are loved by God, not because of anything you have or haven't done,
then you can quit trying to deserve His love or earn His love and
simply receive it and enjoy it. This is an essential step to living in
close relationship with the Father.

Say out loud ten times every day, "GOD LOVES ME!"

Pray

Do not fret or have any anxiety about anything, but in every circumstance and in everything, by prayer and petition (definite requests), with thanksgiving, continue to make your wants known to God.   PHILIPPIANS 4:6

Far too many times we treat prayer as a last-ditch effort. The reasons vary—we try to fix a problem on our own, we assume God is too busy with other things, or we feel God is mad at us and won't listen to our prayers. But when we fail to pray the result is the same: We carry burdens we do not need to bear.

For many believers, life is much harder than it has to be because we do not realize how powerful prayer is. If we did, we would pray about everything, not as a last resort, but as a first response.

In James 5:13, the apostle James offers a simple, three-word solution to some of life's challenges: "He should pray." The message to us in this verse is that no matter what happens over the course of a day, we can go to God in prayer. There is a great benefit in this decision—the more you pray, the closer to God you will be.

Anytime you have a problem, make prayer your first response. If you have a need, don't hesitate to tell God what it is. When you are discouraged or feel like giving up, let God be the first person you talk to about how you are feeling. He loves you, and when you go to Him in prayer, you will be amazed at what a difference it will make in your life.

Whatever situation you find yourself in, make prayer your first response not your last resort.

Confident of God's Presence in Your Life

For in the Gospel a righteousness which God ascribes is revealed,
both springing from faith and leading to faith [disclosed through
the way of faith that arouses to more faith]. As it is written, The
man who through faith is just and upright shall live and shall live
by faith.   ROMANS 1:17

Years ago, as I was learning about confidence and trying to live a confident life, I still worried about making mistakes or "missing" God. I remember He spoke to my heart very clearly, saying, "Joyce, don't worry about it. If you miss Me, I'll find you." This reassurance helped me learn to live my life in confidence and trust rather than fear.

When I speak about faith, I often use the word *confidence*, because faith really is an attitude of complete confidence in God. It is an assurance that brings us into the rest of God.

I believe the closer we draw to God, the more confident we will become. Not confident in ourselves, but confident of His goodness and presence in our lives. We can be confident when we pray, confident in our relationships, confident when we make decisions, and confident as we carry out our daily responsibilities.

Today, I encourage you to take a bold stance and say: "I will live with complete confidence in my relationship with God. I believe He will lead me. I believe I can make good decisions. I believe my prayers are powerful. I believe God loves me and has a good plan for my life."

You don't have to "feel" confident in order to "be" confident!

Taking the Pressure off Other People

First of all, then, I admonish and urge that petitions, prayers,
intercessions, and thanksgivings be offered on behalf of all men.

1 TIMOTHY 2:1

Love and acceptance are universal needs people have. This includes
the people in our lives. If we demand that people change to be more
like us or to suit our liking, we are putting a tremendous strain on
those relationships.

I remember the years I furiously tried to change my husband,
Dave, and each of our children in different ways. Those were frustrating years, because no matter what I tried, it didn't work. My
efforts to change the people I loved weren't helping matters. In fact, I
often just made things worse.

As humans, all of us require space, or freedom, to be who we
were created to be. We want to be accepted as we are. We don't want
people giving us the message, even subtly, that we must change in
order to be approved or loved.

This doesn't mean we accept sin in other people and merely put
up with it. It just means that *the way to change is prayer, not pressure.* If
we love people and pray for them, God will work. For change to last,
it must come from the inside out. Only God can cause that type of
heart change.

Nagging is not an effective tool for change. Only prayer
and God's love will do the job.

Taking Care of Yourself

Do you not know that your body is the temple (the very sanctuary)
of the Holy Spirit Who lives within you, Whom you have received
[as a Gift] from God? You are not your own, you were bought with
a price [purchased with a preciousness and paid for, made His
own]. So then, honor God and bring glory to Him in your body.

1 CORINTHIANS 6:19–20

God calls each of us to do something special in this life. But to do that, it is important we determine to take care of our body—the house He has given us to live in. To fulfill our God-given purpose, we can choose to find balance in what we eat and drink, get enough rest and exercise, and maintain a healthy lifestyle.

There is nothing worse than going through life feeling bad all the time. As a person who struggled for years with nutritional choices and weight concerns, I know the feeling all too well. When we are unhealthy and out of balance, we just don't feel right. It's hard to do what God has called us to do when our bodies are sluggish because we haven't take care of them properly.

I believe it's actually a spiritual matter to know your body, what it needs, and what is really best for it. When you live in close relationship with God, your whole life is affected—spirit, soul, *and* body. I encourage you today to ask the Lord to help you determine to make healthy, wise choices that will benefit the body He has given you.

Ask God to help you follow the positive, healthy leading of the Holy Spirit and reject the negative, destructive promptings of the flesh.

What God Says About You

To the praise of the glory of his grace, wherein he hath made us accepted in the beloved.   EPHESIANS 1:6 KJV

It is not God's desire for us to feel frustrated and condemned in our lives. He wants us to realize that we are His children, and we are pleasing to Him.

There are plenty of voices trying to tell us who and what we aren't, but the closer we get to God, the more we hear Him telling us who we are—righteous in Christ, loved and well-pleasing to our heavenly Father.

The devil tells us we cannot possibly be acceptable to God because of our faults and sins, but God tells us that we are accepted in the beloved because of what His Son, Jesus, has already done for us.

If you have dealt or are dealing with any guilt or condemnation today, remember that God never reminds us of how far we have fallen. He always reminds us of how far we can rise. He reminds us of how much we have overcome, how precious we are in His sight, and how much He loves us.

The more you walk with God, the better you feel about the person He created you to be.

A Heart of Obedience

But thank God, though you were once slaves of sin, you have become obedient with all your heart to the standard of teaching in which you were instructed and to which you were committed.

ROMANS 6:17

Paul wrote that the believers in Rome were obedient with all their heart. This was important because it is possible to have halfhearted obedience—to be reluctantly obedient in behavior, but not be joyfully obedient with all your heart.

Obeying what God says is not just a matter of putting on a show, but a matter of having the right attitude. When you really want to please the Lord, you can't wait to follow His direction and instructions for your life.

I want to encourage you to come up higher in your obedience. Be quick to obey, radical and joyful in your obedience. Don't be the kind of person God has to deal with for weeks just to get you to do the simplest little thing. Gladly do what God asks of you.

Obedience is more than a spiritual obligation—it is a spiritual opportunity! Your obedience to God will ultimately be rewarded. Obedience sows the seed necessary to bring another blessing into your life. You can never outgive God; He will always reward your seeds of obedience.

———————

A heart of obedience results in the blessing of God on your life.

The Fruit in Your Life

A good (healthy) tree cannot bear bad (worthless) fruit, nor can a
bad (diseased) tree bear excellent fruit [worthy of admiration].

MATTHEW 7:18

During my first few years of ministry, I spent a lot of my prayer time asking God for powerful and dynamic gifts that would help me be an effective minister. I focused on the gifts I needed, but I didn't give much thought to the fruit of the Spirit. I must admit I was more concerned about power than godly character.

Then one day the Lord impressed upon me, "Joyce, if you would have put even half as much energy and time into praying about and trying to develop the fruit of the Spirit as you have the gifts, you'd already have both."

As Christians, many of us pray that God will give us great spiritual power, but our first priority really should be developing the fruit of the Spirit—love, joy, peace, patience, kindness, goodness, faithfulness, gentleness, and self-control. The closer we get to God, the more fruit we will naturally produce.

We are known by our fruit, not by our gifts. When people see the fruit of God's Spirit in your life, they can see what God is doing in your heart. I encourage you today to ask God to cultivate the fruit of the Holy Spirit in your life on a daily basis. If you'll focus on the fruit, the power will follow.

———————

People want to see if what you have is real before they listen to what you say.

How to Cultivate the Fruit of the Spirit

If we live by the [Holy] Spirit, let us also walk by the Spirit. [If by the Holy Spirit we have our life in God, let us go forward walking in line, our conduct controlled by the Spirit.]   GALATIANS 5:25

When the Holy Spirit lives inside us, we have everything He has. His fruit is in our spirit. The seed has been planted. The closer we are to God, the more we allow the seed of the fruit to grow up and mature in us by cultivating it.

We can cultivate all the fruit of the Spirit in a very practical way—by focusing on love and self-control, the first and last in the list. All of the fruit are based in love and actually are a form of love, but they are kept in place by self-control.

If you are concentrating on developing the fruit of love, you won't become impatient or unkind with people. You will be good to them, supportive, and faithful. You'll determine to live your life in a way that blesses others, rather than looking out for your needs first. This is a result of love.

Self-control helps us to make those little choices throughout the day to respond with the fruit of the Spirit. As we respond with those little choices, we begin to form good, healthy, God-pleasing habits. If you continue to cultivate these habits, you will grow the fruit into an exceptional life in the Spirit.

When our fruit is "squeezed," and we get caught off guard, we discover how developed or undeveloped our fruit is.

Take Time to Listen

*In the morning You hear my voice, O Lord; in the morning
I prepare [a prayer, a sacrifice] for You and watch and wait
[for You to speak to my heart].*   PSALM 5:3

In order to hear the voice of God, it is necessary to find times just to be still. This is an important part of living in close fellowship with God. It is how you recognize God's leading in your life. A busy, hurried, frantic, stressful lifestyle makes it very challenging to hear the Lord.

If you are hungry to perceive God's voice, find a place to get quiet before Him. Get alone with Him and tell Him that you need Him and want Him to teach you how to receive His guidance and direction. Ask Him to tell you what He has for your life and what He wants you to do that day.

And then I encourage you to do this: Take time to listen.

Even if you don't feel an immediate prompting in your spirit, God promises that if you seek Him, you *will* find Him (Jeremiah 29:13). You *will* get a word from God. He will lead you by an inner knowing, by common sense, by wisdom, or by peace. And each time, however He leads you, His leading will always line up with His Word.

I have found that God doesn't always speak to us right away or necessarily during our prayer time. He may end up speaking to you two days later while you are in the middle of doing something completely unrelated. Though it may not be in our timing, God will speak to us and let us know the way we should go.

Listening is a vital part of your daily time with God.

There Is Nothing Too Hard for God

Alas, Lord God! Behold, You have made the heavens and the earth by Your great power and by Your outstretched arm! There is nothing too hard or too wonderful for You.   JEREMIAH 32:17

In our own strength, there are many things that are impossible for us to accomplish. But with God—in His strength—all things are possible. There is nothing too hard for our God!

God desires for us to believe for great things. He wants our expectations and our plans in Him to be so great they leave us breathless. We can dream big when we are close to God, because there is nothing He can't do. James 4:2 tells us we have not because we ask not. We can (and should) be bold in our asking.

You may think, *Well, I don't have the gifts or talents to do great things in my life.* The truth is God doesn't call the qualified; He qualifies those He calls. If you will simply be available, God will use your life in ways you could have never imagined.

Don't limit God in your life today. Take a bold step of faith and trust that He can do something bigger than you ever thought possible. His plan for your life is exceedingly and abundantly more than you could ask or think. So simply say, "Lord, I am open to whatever You have for my life. I trust that You will give me everything I need to accomplish the great plans You have for me. In Jesus' name!"

When you don't feel capable or qualified, lean on the Lord and receive His strength. He will give you what you need to accomplish more than you ever imagined.

The One Thing That Never Fails

Love bears up under anything and everything that comes, is ever
ready to believe the best of every person, its hopes are fadeless
under all circumstances, and it endures everything [without
weakening]. Love never fails [never fades out or becomes obsolete
or comes to an end] . . .   1 CORINTHIANS 13:7–8

The love of God bears up under anything that comes. It endures everything without weakening. It is determined not to give up no matter what. Even the hard-core individual who persists in being rebellious can be eventually melted by love. The Bible says, ". . . God's kindness is intended to lead you to repentance" (Romans 2:4 NIV). It is God's love—His goodness, His kindness—that can change a heart.

I understand it is hard to keep showing love to someone who never seems to appreciate it or even respond to it. It is difficult to keep showing love to those individuals who take from us all we are willing to give, but who never give anything back. But we are not responsible for how others act, only how we act.

We have experienced the love of God by His mercy, and now He instructs us to show that same kind of love to the world. Our reward does not come from man, but from God. Even when our good deeds seem to go unnoticed, God notices and promises to reward us openly for them (Matthew 6:4). If you'll determine to demonstrate the love of God to all those around you, not only will they be blessed, but God will see to it that you are as well.

God is love, and love never quits on anyone.

Sometimes You Just Need to Take a Step

And Nathan said to the king, Go, do all that is in your heart, for the Lord is with you.   2 SAMUEL 7:3

Is there something you desire to do, but you have been waiting? Has God placed something on your heart, but you've been hesitant to take a step?

I believe God's timing is very important, and I certainly don't think we should rush into anything without praying about it and getting good godly counsel. However, I've noticed some people spend their lives stuck in "waiting mode." They're waiting when they could be taking a step in faith.

There is nothing more stressful than going through the motions each day only to get to the end of the day, week, month, or year and feel you are no closer to reaching your dream or goal. God doesn't want you to live in that frustration. He wants you to seek His will, then take an action step. If you miss God—if you take a step in the wrong direction—God will get you back on course.

It's your heart attitude that matters. God is pleased when He sees that you are stepping out in faith, trying to please Him and accomplish His will for your life. So don't be afraid today. Take a step, and watch God begin to work in your life.

———————

God will put the desire in your heart, and He will help you accomplish it. Your job is to simply use your faith to take a step toward that goal.

No Excuses

*Be not afraid of them [their faces], for I am with you to deliver
you, says the Lord.*   JEREMIAH 1:8

Whether it's a challenge, an obstacle, or an opportunity, when we
know God is with us, we can face the things before us. Running
away is not an option. Whatever you run from will always be waiting for you somewhere else. Our strength to conquer is found in
staying close to God and pressing forward with Him.

Jeremiah was a very young man who was given a very big job. God
told him that he had been called as a prophet to the nations. He was
to be a mouthpiece for God. The thought of it frightened Jeremiah,
and he began to make all kinds of excuses about why he could not
do what God was asking.

Jeremiah was making the initial mistake you and I often make—
he was looking at himself and his own abilities. All Jeremiah needed
to do was to look at God. He was also looking at people and wondering what they would think and do if he took the bold step God was
encouraging him to take. God told Jeremiah to just remember that
He was with him and that is all Jeremiah needed.

In the final verse of chapter one, the Lord told Jeremiah that the
people would oppose him, but they would not prevail for one simple
reason: "I am with you."

Whatever you're facing today, be encouraged. God is facing it
with you.

**When you take your eyes off your circumstances and put
them on the Lord, you are sure to overcome.**

Believe and Receive from God

*For out of His fullness (abundance) we have all received [all had a
share and we were all supplied with] one grace after another and
spiritual blessing upon spiritual blessing and even favor upon
favor and gift [heaped] upon gift.*   JOHN 1:16

Again and again, the Bible speaks of receiving from God. He is
always pouring out His favor and His blessing. In order to experience that favor and blessing—and in order to live in close fellowship
with God—it is important that we choose to freely receive all that
He offers us.

One of our biggest challenges is that we do not trust the word
free. We quickly find out in the world's system that things really are
not free. Even when we are told they are free, there is usually a hidden cost somewhere.

But God's kingdom of grace and love is not like the world's. God's
wondrous love is a gift He freely gives us. All we need to do is open
our hearts, believe His Word, and receive it with thankfulness.

No matter what the situation around you looks like today, stand
on the Word of God and trust that His goodness and grace are being
poured out over your life. Believe it and receive it today.

The world's system says, "I'll believe it when I see it."
God's kingdom says, "I'll believe it before I receive it."

The Power of Rejoicing

Rejoice in the Lord always [delight, gladden yourselves in Him];
again I say, Rejoice!   PHILIPPIANS 4:4

One of the best instructions God gives us in His Word is to be filled with joy and rejoice. What a great idea! This is a command that pleases God and brings direct and tangible physical, emotional, and spiritual benefit to us as we do it.

The apostle Paul, inspired by the Holy Spirit, told the Philippians twice to rejoice. Any time the Lord tells us twice to do something, we would be wise to pay careful attention to what He is saying.

Many times people see or hear the word *rejoice* and say, "That sounds nice, but how do I do that?" They would like to rejoice but don't know how! Paul and Silas, who had been beaten, thrown into prison, and their feet put in stocks, rejoiced by simply singing praises to God. They chose to rejoice, despite their circumstances. They looked to the things they believed and not just to what they could see.

The same power that opened the doors and broke the shackles off Paul and Silas, and those imprisoned with them, is available to you today. No matter what you're dealing with, no matter what your coworkers say about you, no matter how much the kids are driving you crazy—take a moment right in the middle of the chaos to rejoice. It will make all the difference!

Rejoicing is not something that happens accidentally.
It is a conscious decision that says, "I will praise God
today, regardless of the circumstances around me."

The Mind of Christ

. . . We have the mind of Christ (the Messiah) and do hold
the thoughts (feelings and purposes) of His heart.

1 CORINTHIANS 2:16

You and I have been given the mind of Christ—this is a promise straight from the Word of God. To begin to understand what that means, consider what Jesus' mind was like when He lived on the earth. He was confident in Who He was. He didn't let the negativity of others distract Him. He was fully aware that He was loved by God. And He was focused on accomplishing God's plan for His life.

Now take a moment to consider what thoughts occupy your mind. If you're distracted by the opinions of others, if you get upset easily, or if your mind is full of doubt and unbelief, you are not yet experiencing all that God desires for your life. But things can change. God can renew your mind and bring you to a place of victory!

The renewal of the mind is a process that requires time, and it's a process that the enemy aggressively fights against. It is important we purposely choose right thinking. When we feel the battle for our mind is difficult, we can determine that, with God's help, we are going to purposely choose life-generating thoughts.

The renewing of the mind takes place little by little, so don't be discouraged if progress seems slow. Take a stand and say, "I will never give up! God is on my side. He loves me, and He is helping me!"

Our thoughts affect our inner man, our health, our joy,
and our attitude.

A Simple Faith-Filled Prayer

Then you will call upon Me, and you will come and pray to Me,
and I will hear and heed you.   JEREMIAH 29:12

Sometimes when we pray a simple prayer, simply presenting to God our need or the need of another person, we think that we should do or say more. But I have found that when I pray what the Holy Spirit has put on my heart, without adding to it out of my own flesh, the prayer is very simple and not necessarily exceedingly long.

When we take a moment to thank God for something or ask Him for something, our mind tells us, "Well, that's not long enough, or that is not eloquent enough. You should pray louder and harder if you really want God to hear you."

Many times we think we have to impress God or other people with our prayers, and that's when we are robbed of the enjoyment that each simple prayer of faith is supposed to bring. When we live in close fellowship with God, we can say what is on our heart and believe that He has heard us, and that He will take care of it His way, in His timing.

Children are always good examples to follow when searching for simplicity. Listen to a child pray, and it will radically change your prayer life.

———— —

Keep prayer simple, and you'll enjoy it more.

Get Some Rest

Come to Me, all you who labor and are heavy-laden and overburdened, and I will cause you to rest. [I will ease and relieve and refresh your souls.]   MATTHEW 11:28

In 1 Kings 19, the prophet Elijah is terrified by the threats of Jezebel and is so discouraged he wants to die. Why in the world would Elijah, who on the previous day had triumphed over 450 prophets of Baal, suddenly allow himself to be so fearful and in such despair?

If you study the story closely, it's clear that he was totally worn out from pushing himself so hard for so long. Elijah's mind and body were completely exhausted, and his emotions had fallen apart. He was afraid, depressed, discouraged, and hopeless.

Nothing in life looks good to us when we are exhausted. It seems to us that nobody loves us, nobody helps us, nobody is concerned about us. We feel misused, misunderstood, and mistreated. Many times when we feel we have deep problems, our biggest problem is that we are exhausted.

The Lord knew that Elijah was worn-out. So he provided a good night's rest and a couple of good meals. It was such a simple answer to an extreme problem. Perhaps your answer is the same. Get some good, well-needed rest, and take in some healthy nutrition. They could be the most spiritual things you do today!

————————

Strength, wisdom, and courage come from a place of rest.

God's Love Overcomes and Transforms

So he got up and came to his [own] father. But while he was still
a long way off, his father saw him and was moved with pity and
tenderness [for him]; and he ran and embraced him and kissed
him [fervently].   LUKE 15:20

Any person can be completely transformed by regular, persistent
doses of God's love. It doesn't matter what they have done in life or
how good or bad we might consider them, God's love can warm even
the coldest heart.

Religion often gives people rules to follow and laws to keep. It
leads them to believe they must earn God's love and favor through
good works. That is the exact opposite of true biblical teaching.

God's Word says that "mercy triumphs over judgment" (James
2:13 NKJV). It is the goodness of God that leads men to repentance
(Romans 2:4), not the keeping of laws and rules. Jesus came to give
us something better than religion—He came to give us a close, personal love relationship with the Father through Him.

God's unconditional love does not allow people to remain the
same; instead, it loves them while they are changing. Jesus said that
He did not come for the well, but for the sick (Matthew 9:12). Much
of our world today is sick, and there is no answer for what ails it
except Jesus Christ and all that He stands for.

**Unconditional love will overcome evil and transform
lives.**

Receiving Your Encouragement

... If I do not go away, the Comforter (Counselor, Helper, Advocate, Intercessor, Strengthener, Standby) will not come to you [into close fellowship with you]; but if I go away, I will send Him to you [to be in close fellowship with you].   JOHN 16:7

Do you sometimes find yourself wishing you had more encouragement, maybe from your family, friends, or coworkers? I think we all feel this way at one time or another. When you are feeling in need of encouragement and you don't seem to be getting that from other people, you can encourage yourself in the Lord (1 Samuel 30:6), and you can also receive encouragement from the Spirit of God.

Did you know that the Holy Spirit is called "The Encourager"? The Greek word for "Holy Spirit" is *parakletos* and includes comfort, edification, and encouragement as part of its definition.

Jesus sent a Helper, a Strengthener, an Edifier, and an Encourager when He sent the Holy Spirit—and He sent Him to be in close fellowship with us. He lives inside of those who are believers in Jesus Christ.

If you're in need of encouragement, look to God first. He will never tell you that you're not going to make it. He will never tell you that your case is hopeless. Instead, He will encourage you that all things are possible in Him. He'll remind you that He loves you, He is with you, and He gives you the strength you need to do all He has called you to do.

Open your heart to receive comfort, reassurance, and encouragement from the Holy Spirit today.

Letting Go of Past Mistakes

Therefore, [there is] now no condemnation (no adjudging guilty of wrong) for those who are in Christ Jesus, who live [and] walk not after the dictates of the flesh, but after the dictates of the Spirit.

ROMANS 8:1

It is so comforting to know that God's compassion and kindness are new every morning. Because of His great love, God has provided a way for your past to have zero power over you. You don't have to live in guilt and condemnation over your past failings; you can live with great hope for a bright future ahead.

God's part is to forgive us—our part is to receive His gracious gift of forgiveness, mercy, and a new beginning. Many people think, *How could God forgive me when I've done so many bad things?* But the truth is that God is able to overcome and do far more than we could ever imagine that He could do for us (Ephesians 3:20).

When we ask God to forgive us, He is faithful and just to do it. He continuously cleanses us from all unrighteousness (1 John 1:9). We are said to be new creatures when we enter into a relationship with Christ (2 Corinthians 5:17). Old things pass away and we have an opportunity for a new beginning. We become new spiritual clay for God to work with. He arranges for each of us to have a fresh start—we simply must be willing to let go of the past and move forward with God.

Don't allow mistakes in your past to hold you back and threaten your future.

The Greatest Blessing

But if anyone has this world's goods (resources for sustaining life) and sees his brother and fellow believer in need, yet closes his heart of compassion against him, how can the love of God live and remain in him? Little children, let us not love [merely] in theory or in speech but in deed and in truth (in practice and in sincerity).

1 JOHN 3:17–18

The quickest way to be blessed is to decide to be a blessing to others. When you choose to have a generous heart that reaches out to meet the needs of those around you, God pours His provision into your life. A person who is a river of blessing never runs dry.

Something deep in the heart of every believer wants to help others. However, selfishness can make us so aggressive about our own desires that we become oblivious to the needs around us.

People are hurting everywhere. Some are poor; others are sick or lonely. Still others are emotionally wounded or have spiritual needs. A simple act of kindness to a hurting person can make that individual feel loved and valuable.

People can get caught in the trap of striving to have more and more. The struggle often produces little or no results. With God's help, we can strive to excel in giving to others. If we do so, we will find that God makes sure we have enough to meet our own needs plus plenty to give away.

There is no greater blessing than giving to others in need.

When You Feel Afraid

*Fear not [there is nothing to fear], for I am with you; do not look
around you in terror and be dismayed, for I am your God. I will
strengthen and harden you to difficulties, yes, I will help you; yes,
I will hold you up and retain you with My [victorious] right hand
of rightness and justice.*   ISAIAH 41:10

One of the benefits available to us as believers is the freedom from
fear. If fear has had power over you in the past, you can be free of it.
With God's help, you can learn how to overcome fear and begin to
experience the abundant life God has planned for you.

Even when we do *feel* afraid, we don't have to give in to that
feeling. We can go ahead and act on what God is calling us to do,
because God will be with us to protect us and see us through. He
will help us, go before us to fight the battle on our behalf, and bring
us through victoriously as we obey Him.

The message of "fear not for I am with you" is expressed all
throughout the Bible. God does not want us to fear, because fear
prevents us from moving forward and doing all He has planned for
us. He loves us and wants to bless us, but fear tries to keep us from
experiencing God's best.

The best attitude that a Christian can have toward fear is this:
"Fear is not from God, and I will not let it control my life! I will confront fear. I won't give in to fear. When I feel afraid, I will keep moving forward because I know God is with me."

**Jesus is your Deliverer. As you draw closer to Him, He
will deliver you from fear.**

Thinking Positive Thoughts

... Whatever is true, whatever is worthy of reverence and is honorable and seemly, whatever is just, whatever is pure, whatever is lovely and lovable, whatever is kind and winsome and gracious, if there is any virtue and excellence, if there is anything worthy of praise, think on and weigh and take account of these things [fix your minds on them].   PHILIPPIANS 4:8

If you want to improve your life, one of the first things you can do is improve your thoughts. There is tremendous power that comes when we choose to be positive people. God is positive, and in order to grow closer to Him, it is important to agree with Him (Amos 3:3) and think positively.

Having a positive mind-set and attitude does not mean you are not facing reality or ignoring real problems. It simply means that you are agreeing with the Word of God and dwelling on God's promises rather than the negative, depressing things of the world.

Notice that throughout His life Jesus endured tremendous difficulties, including personal attacks, and yet He remained positive. He always had an uplifting comment, an encouraging word. He always gave hope to those He came near. We can follow that example today. When we choose a positive outlook, maintain positive expectations, and engage in positive conversations, we are following the example Jesus gave us, and we are drawing closer to our heavenly Father.

Your life will follow the direction of your thoughts.

A Life That Pleases God

Therefore, since these [great] promises are ours, beloved, let us cleanse ourselves from everything that contaminates and defiles body and spirit, and bring [our] consecration to completeness in the [reverential] fear of God. 2 CORINTHIANS 7:1

In order to live in close relationship with God, there are some decisions we have to make on a daily basis. There will be times we need to say no to some things to which we would rather say yes, and yes to some things to which we would rather say no. This requires wisdom and self-control, but thankfully, the Holy Spirit gives us both these things.

It is important to teach people to live holy lives because it is an important part of living in close relationship with God. It doesn't mean we never make a mistake—it just means that our heart's desire is to live in a manner that pleases the Lord. This is accomplished by seeking to please God in our thoughts, conversations, companionship, music, entertainment, and so forth.

If our flesh desires to walk one way but God's Word teaches us to go another way, we can receive God's grace to obey what He is saying. The good news is that there is tremendous reward when we do.

When we choose to live our lives for God, rather than for self, we will experience righteousness, peace, and joy in the Holy Spirit. We will live in victory no matter what comes against us. That's a wonderful life—that is the abundant, overcoming, joy-filled life Jesus died to give us.

Invest in your future: Choose to live an uncompromised life for God.

Coming Boldly Before God

For we do not have a High Priest who cannot sympathize with our
weaknesses, but was in all points tempted as we are, yet without
sin. Let us therefore come boldly to the throne of grace, that we
may obtain mercy and find grace to help in time of need.

HEBREWS 4:15–16 NKJV

Jesus understands our human frailty because He was tempted in every way that we are, yet without sinning. Therefore, because Jesus is our High Priest, interceding before the Father for us, we can come boldly to God's throne to receive grace.

God has already made provision for every human mistake, weakness, and failure. Salvation and continual forgiveness of our sins are gifts bestowed on us by God because of our acceptance of His Son, Jesus Christ. In Him you can find forgiveness for every wrong thing you will ever do.

But the grace of God doesn't mean He doesn't deal with sin in our lives. Sin produces bondage and suffering. That is why God calls us to repent of our sin. Though God never condemns us, He does convict us of sin. He brings conviction so that we can repent, change our behavior, and find freedom in Christ.

Because of Jesus we can receive forgiveness, set aside sinful behaviors, and come boldly before God's throne of grace. All of these actions are essential components of living in close relationship with God.

Even at our very best, we make mistakes. To live under
condemnation will not help us live a holier life.

Don't Settle for Average

Now to Him Who, by (in consequence of) the [action of His] power that is at work within us, is able to [carry out His purpose and] do superabundantly, far over and above all that we [dare] ask or think [infinitely beyond our highest prayers, desires, thoughts, hopes, or dreams].   EPHESIANS 3:20

God loves to use common, ordinary, everyday people who have uncommon goals and visions.

That is what I am—just a common, ordinary person with a goal and vision that fuel my determination. But just because I am common and ordinary does not mean that I am content to be average. I don't like that word. I don't want to be average. I don't intend to be average. I don't serve an average God; therefore, I don't believe I have to be average—and neither do you.

The Word of God demonstrates that anyone can be used mightily by God. The closer we draw to God, the more it is possible for us to do great and mighty things, things that amaze even us. If we believe that God can use us, and if we will be daring enough to have uncommon goals and visions, God will do powerful things in us and through us.

An "uncommon goal" is something that is nearly impossible without God—it is beyond all that we could dare to hope, ask, or think, according to His great power that is at work in us. This is what God will do in our lives if we will determine to not settle for average.

Be determined to stretch your faith for something great. We can choose to be common people with uncommon goals.

Adapt and Adjust

Love one another with brotherly affection [as members of one family], giving precedence and showing honor to one another.

ROMANS 12:10

Demonstrating the love of God is a daily exercise in giving preference to others. The natural reaction of our human flesh is not to prefer someone else above ourselves. We tend to look to our own needs first, but love requires us to adapt and adjust ourselves to the needs of others.

To allow someone else to go first, or to insist another person have the best of something, takes a mental adjustment on our part. We were planning to be first, or to have the best, but love adapts and adjusts—love chooses to be second instead. We were in a hurry to get where we wanted to go, but love chooses to wait on someone else who seems to have a greater need.

The closer we are to God, the more we are actually rooted and grounded in love (Ephesians 3:17). Showing preference to someone else is a by-product of receiving God's love. The more we know we are loved, the more we want to share that love with others.

We have multiple opportunities to adapt and adjust almost every day. But if we are locked into our own plans, it will be difficult to do so. I encourage you to ask God to help you adapt and adjust with a joyful heart and a positive attitude. Ask Him to help you experience the joy and peace that come with loving others.

Only the love of God can change us from self-centered individuals into humble servants of God and others.

God Does Not Reject You

Although my father and my mother have forsaken me, yet the
Lord will take me up [adopt me as His child].   PSALM 27:10

We were created for acceptance, not rejection. To be rejected is to be thrown away as having no value or as being unwanted, but God does the opposite. He draws you to Himself, and He considers you to be of extreme value. The fact that God sent Jesus to die for you demonstrates that you are loved and valued by God.

If you have struggled with self-image issues in your life, it may be due to a root of rejection. The emotional pain of rejection is one of the deepest kinds known. Especially if the rejection comes from someone we love or expect to love us, like parents or a spouse. Overcoming rejection is certainly not easy, but we can overcome it through the love of Jesus Christ.

In Ephesians 3:18, Paul prayed for the church that they would know "the breadth and length and height and depth" of the love that God had for them. He said this experience far surpasses mere knowledge.

Watch for all the ways that God shows His love for you, and it will overcome the rejection you may have experienced from other people. Every time God gives you favor, He is showing you that He loves you. There are many ways He shows His love for you all the time. I encourage you to begin watching for those today.

A deep revelation of God's love for you will destroy any root of rejection.

Being God-Minded

You will guard him and keep him in perfect and constant peace whose mind [both its inclination and its character] is stayed on You, because he commits himself to You, leans on You, and hopes confidently in You.   ISAIAH 26:3

Jesus had a continual fellowship with His heavenly Father because He was focused on God. It is only possible to have full fellowship with someone when your mind is on that individual. This is a lesson we can learn as believers. In order to live in close relationship with God, it is important for us to live "God-minded."

It is tremendously uplifting to think on the goodness of God and all the marvelous works He has done. If you want to experience victory, take time to regularly meditate on God's unsurpassed greatness. Giving thanks to God and being aware of His goodness are two sure ways to begin enjoying life.

Jesus said that the Holy Spirit would bring us into close fellowship with Him (John 16:7). If we choose to think about the Lord, it will bring Him to the forefront of our lives, and we will begin to enjoy a fellowship with Him that brings joy, peace, and victory to our everyday life.

God is always with us, but it is important that we think about Him and be aware of His presence.

Showing Mercy

Blessed (happy, to be envied, and spiritually prosperous—with life-joy and satisfaction in God's favor and salvation, regardless of their outward conditions) are the merciful, for they shall obtain mercy!   MATTHEW 5:7

Being merciful can be defined as giving goodness that is undeserved. Anyone can give people what they deserve. It takes someone who desires to be close to God to give goodness to people when they do *not* deserve it.

Revenge says, "You mistreated me, so I'm going to mistreat you." Mercy says, "You mistreated me, but I'm going to forgive you, restore you, and treat you as if you never hurt me." What a blessing to be able to give and receive mercy.

Mercy is an attribute of God's character that is seen in how He deals with His people. Mercy is good to us when we deserve punishment. Mercy accepts and blesses us when we deserve to be totally rejected. Mercy understands our weaknesses and infirmities and does not judge and criticize us.

Do you ever need God or man to show you mercy? Of course, we all do on a regular basis. The best way to get mercy is to be busy giving it away. If you give judgment, you will receive judgment. If you give mercy, you will receive mercy. Remember, the Word of God teaches us that we reap what we sow. Be merciful! Be blessed!

Receive God's mercy and love. You cannot give away something you don't have.

Are You Willing to Be Trained?

For you see your calling, brethren, that not many wise according to the flesh, not many mighty, not many noble, are called. But God has chosen the foolish things of the world to put to shame the wise, and God has chosen the weak things of the world to put to shame the things which are mighty.

1 CORINTHIANS 1:26–27 NKJV

A quick look at the disciples Jesus chose shows us that God does not always choose those who seem to be qualified. It doesn't matter what gifts, talents, experiences you feel like you lack—God will provide all the teaching and training you need to do what He has called you to.

It is not always conventional, but God will prepare you in whatever way He chooses. Sometimes it is formal training, but often it is not. God will use everything in your life to train you if you are willing to be trained. It's sad to say that many people have great callings on their lives, but they are too impatient to go through the preparation that is necessary to equip them for the job.

Esther had to have a year of preparation before she was allowed to go before the king. For twelve months, she patiently went through the purifying process, and God used her to save her people from wicked Haman's evil plot.

If you're feeling under-qualified for something you believe God is calling you to do, don't let that stop you. He will be your trainer. Learn what He is teaching you during this season, and be ready to step out when the opportunity arises.

God will equip you for the vision He has given you.

It's Not That Complicated

Truly I tell you, whoever says to this mountain, Be lifted up and thrown into the sea! and does not doubt at all in his heart but believes that what he says will take place, it will be done for him.

MARK 11:23

People think that life is complicated, but oftentimes we are the ones who make things more complicated than they need to be. Living for God really isn't that complicated at all.

Think about the simple, uncomplicated approach a child has to life. Children are going to have fun and enjoy themselves no matter what. They are joyful, carefree, and completely without concern. And children believe what they are told. It is their nature to trust completely and enjoy their life on a daily basis.

The closer we grow to God, the more childlike we can become. Of course, God wants us to be mature in our behavior, but He also desires for us to have an attitude of trust and dependence toward Him that is simple and childlike in nature. When God speaks to your heart or when you read something in the Bible, you can simply say, "I trust God and I believe it's true!" It's that simple.

If God says He will prosper me, I trust God and believe it's true! If God says He will heal me, I trust God and believe it's true! If God says He will help me forgive those who hurt me, I trust God and believe it's true. If God says He is with me and I'm never alone, I trust God and believe it's true!

The simplest thing you can do is decide to trust God and obey His Word in every area of your life.

Standing on What You Know to Be True

To you it was shown, that you might realize and have personal
knowledge that the Lord is God; there is no other besides Him.
DEUTERONOMY 4:35

A lack of knowledge causes fear, but confident and certain knowledge removes fear and brings strength and courage. Let me give you an example:

One night years ago I was lying in bed and heard strange noises coming from somewhere in the house. The longer I listened to it the more frightened I became. Finally shaking in fear, I journeyed out of the bedroom to see what it was. I had to laugh when I discovered it was ice cubes falling in the ice tray from the icemaker. For some reason, they were making a noise they did not normally make. Because I had no knowledge of what was making that noise, I was needlessly afraid.

This is how people often feel in their lives. They don't know that God loves them, He is with them, and He has provided everything they need, so they are terrified by many things. When they hear of economic woes, they are fearful. When they hear that someone doesn't like them, they panic. When they hear a negative report on the evening news, they are terrified.

If you have the knowledge of Who God is *and* who you are in Christ, fear will have no place in your life. No matter what the situation looks like on the outside, you will have a peace in your heart, a confident assurance that fills every area of your life.

**When the unfamiliar sounds of the world try to fill you
with fear, be confident God is with you.**

The Beginning, the Middle, and the End

*Better is the end of a thing than the beginning of it, and the
patient in spirit is better than the proud in spirit.*

ECCLESIASTES 7:8

The most important thing is not necessarily how we start something.
The beginning is important, but so is the middle, and so is the end.
In fact, seeing something through is more important than just start-
ing it, especially when it's something God has called us to do.

Some people get started with a bang, but they never finish. Others
are slow starters, but they finish strong. Regardless of how we start,
God wants us to stay faithful every step of the way—beginning, middle, and end. God's desire is for you to finish well.

God has a good plan for each of us. But it is a possibility, not a
"positively." It won't "positively" happen if we don't cooperate with
God. We have a part to play in seeing the plan come true. God won't
do anything in our lives without our cooperation.

I challenge you to cooperate with God every single day of your life
to develop your potential and see His plan come to pass. Every day
you can learn something new. Every day you can grow. Every day
you can be a bit further along than you were the day before. This is
how you turn a great start into an even better finish.

**Cooperate with God to develop your gifts, talents, and
capabilities to their fullest extent. Be all you can be for
the glory of God!**

Living in the Now

Beloved, we are [even here and] now God's children; it is not yet disclosed (made clear) what we shall be [hereafter], but we know that when He comes and is manifested, we shall [as God's children] resemble and be like Him, for we shall see Him just as He [really] is.   1 JOHN 3:2

The choices we make today will determine whether we will enjoy the moment or waste it by worrying. Sometimes we end up missing the moment of today because we are too concerned about tomorrow. We are wise when we keep our mind focused on what God wants us to be doing now.

It's important to understand that God wants us to learn how to be *now* people. For example, 2 Corinthians 6:2 says, "Behold, now is the day of salvation" (KJV) and Hebrews 4:7 says, "Today, if you would hear His voice and when you hear it, do not harden your hearts."

We will be more fruitful for the kingdom of God, and happier in our lives, if we will determine to live in the moment. Often we spend our mental time in the past or the future. When we don't really give ourselves to what we are doing at the moment, we become prone to worry and anxiety. However, if we will live in the now, we will find the Lord there with us. Regardless of what situations life brings our way, we will know that today—right now—is a part of God's plan, and He will bring us through it if we will trust in Him.

The time you have now is valuable. Don't waste your "now" worrying about tomorrow.

Finding the Wisdom in Balance

If any of you is deficient in wisdom, let him ask of the giving God [Who gives] to everyone liberally and ungrudgingly, without reproaching or faultfinding, and it will be given him.

JAMES 1:5

If the tires on your vehicle get out of balance, you're in for a bumpy ride. I think the same thing can happen in our lives. If we get out of balance in one or more areas, what could be a smooth journey becomes bumpy and uncomfortable.

It's possible to go overboard and get out of balance in any area of life—even the best areas. A woman can damage her marriage by getting too focused on the children. If she spends every waking moment and all her energy doing for the kids but failing to pay attention to her husband's needs, her marriage will suffer.

Men (and many women too) get consumed in their careers. If a man spends all his time at work, neglecting his wife and his children, he may be a great provider, but he is lacking as a husband and a father. Balance is key.

This is true even in the small areas of life. Some people rarely talk, and some talk too much. Some people overplan, and some don't plan at all. Sometimes we think too highly of ourselves, and sometimes we think too lowly of ourselves. Even the littlest things can get out of balance.

Take an honest look at your life and see if there is any area where you are out of balance. Ask God for the wisdom to make the necessary correction so that you can live a balanced, healthy, joy-filled life.

When you ask God for wisdom, He gives it to you.

New Hope for Each Day

It is because of the Lord's mercy and loving-kindness that we are not consumed, because His [tender] compassions fail not. They are new every morning; great and abundant is Your stability and faithfulness.   LAMENTATIONS 3:22–23

I like the way God has divided up the days and nights. No matter how difficult or challenging a specific day may be, the breaking of dawn brings new hope. God wants us to regularly put the past behind and find a place of "new beginnings."

Perhaps you have felt trapped in some sin or addiction, and although you have repented, you still feel guilty. If that is the case, be assured that sincere repentance brings a fresh, new start because of God's promise of forgiveness.

Only when you understand the great mercy of God and begin receiving it are you more inclined to give mercy to others. You may be hurting from an emotional wound. The way to put the past behind is to forgive the person who hurt you. You do yourself a favor when you forgive.

God has new plans on the horizon of your life, and you can begin to realize them by choosing to live in the present rather than the past. Thinking and talking about the past keeps you trapped in it. Let go of what happened yesterday, make the choice to receive God's love and forgiveness today, so that you can get excited about His plan for tomorrow.

God's mercy is new every morning.

The Importance of Treating Others Well

And do not grieve the Holy Spirit of God [do not offend or vex or sadden Him], by Whom you were sealed (marked, branded as God's own, secured) for the day of redemption . . .

EPHESIANS 4:30

I take a verse such as Ephesians 4:30 very seriously—I certainly do not want to "grieve the Holy Spirit" and I know you don't either. But how do we avoid doing it?

Reading the verses surrounding verse 30 makes it clear that one thing that grieves the Holy Spirit is when people mistreat one another. Consider that:

- In verse 29 we are encouraged to edify others with the words or our mouth.
- Verse 31 exhorts us not to be bitter, angry, or contentious and to beware of slander, spite, and ill will.
- In verse 32 we are told to be kind to one another, forgiving readily and freely.

When we realize it grieves the Holy Spirit when we are sharp or hateful with someone, or when we stay angry with someone, we will look to change.

I encourage you to ask God to help you see others the way He sees them. Ask Him to give you the kindness and patience you need to deal gently and lovingly with the people in your life, especially those who are unkind or difficult to be around. God will be pleased when He sees you have a heart attitude that wants to love and bless others.

One of the most important secrets to being happy is to walk in love.

More Than Enough

For if our heart condemns us, God is greater than our heart, and
knows all things.   1 JOHN 3:20 NKJV

Guilt and condemnation are major problems for many believers. Satan's great delight is to make us feel bad about ourselves. He never tells us how far we have come, but rather, he constantly reminds us of how far we still have to go.

When the enemy attacks, you can say to him, "I'm not where I need to be, but thank God I'm not where I used to be. I'm okay, and I'm on my way."

Like David, we can learn to keep ourselves encouraged in the Lord (1 Samuel 30:6). None of us has arrived at the state of perfection and we cannot perfect ourselves. Sanctification is worked out in our lives by the Holy Spirit as a process, so learn to enjoy the process.

The Bible teaches that we can have total forgiveness of our sins (total freedom from condemnation) through the blood of Jesus Christ. We don't need to add our guilt to His sacrifice. He is more than enough.

Jesus has already done everything that needs to be done—the work is finished. He has made a way for you to be forgiven. All you have to do is receive it. Complete forgiveness is completely free!

Don't let the devil fill your head with thoughts of unworthiness as a sinner. Begin to see yourself as the righteousness of God in Christ Jesus.

The Most Important Time of the Day

O God, You are my God, earnestly will I seek You; my inner self
thirsts for You, my flesh longs and is faint for You, in a dry and
weary land where no water is.   PSALM 63:1

God loves it when you spend time with Him in fellowship and worship on a daily basis. It is this time with God that will change your
outlook on life, give you the strength you need to overcome, and
draw you closer to God.

It is often in our most private times with God that He does the
deepest work in our hearts. It is the intimate time you spend with
God, just loving Him and letting Him love you, that is going to cause
you to grow up and see real spiritual transformation take place.

Life is busy, and there will always be excuses not to spend time
with God. There will always be errands to run, phone calls to make,
messes to clean up, and so on and so forth. But if you will determine to put God first, seeking Him regardless of the distractions of
the day, you will be greatly rewarded.

The more time you spend with God, the more confidence, peace,
joy, strength, favor, and victory you will experience. He is the source
of all these things. When you commit to spending time with Him,
they will naturally flow into your life.

There is nothing more important in your life than your
personal relationship with Jesus Christ.

Being God-Loves-Me-Minded

*Beloved, let us love one another, for love is (springs) from God;
and he who loves [his fellowmen] is begotten (born) of God and is
coming [progressively] to know and understand God [to perceive
and recognize and get a better and clearer knowledge of Him].*

1 JOHN 4:7

The more we meditate on God's unconditional love for us, the more we begin to really experience it. I urge you to practice being conscious and aware of God's love for you. Paul prayed in Ephesians 3 that the people would experience the love of God for themselves. That's the life God wants us to live—a life where we truly know and experience His never-ending, unconditional love.

I became conscious of God's love for me through learning scriptures about His love. I meditated on them and confessed them out of my mouth. I did this over and over for months, and all the time the revelation of His unconditional love for me was becoming more and more of a reality for me. The same thing can happen for you. If you'll study God's Word, standing on every promise of the Father's love, you'll learn to live in the life-changing revelation that you are loved. Think of it like this: There is never one moment in your life when you are not loved.

———————

You are loved!

Led by the Spirit

*But I say, walk and live [habitually] in the [Holy] Spirit
[responsive to and controlled and guided by the Spirit]; then
you will certainly not gratify the cravings and desires of the flesh
(of human nature without God).*   GALATIANS 5:16

It's interesting that in Galatians 5:16 Paul did not say the cravings,
or the desires of the flesh, would no longer exist for the children of
God. He said that we can choose to be led by the Holy Spirit, and
by making that choice, we would not give in to the temptations that
would try to separate us from God.

There are many things that try to lead us—other people, the
devil, our own flesh (our body, mind, will, or emotions). There are
many voices in the world that are speaking to us, and often several
at the same time.

In order to live in close relationship with God, it is imperative
that we choose to be led by the Holy Spirit instead of those other
voices. He alone knows the will of God and is sent to dwell in each of
us, to aid us in being all God has designed us to be, and to have all
God wants us to have.

Being led by the Spirit means He leads us by peace and by wisdom, as well as by the Word of God. He speaks in a still, small voice
in our heart as we seek to live our lives for God. The more we follow
His leading, the more we will be victorious in life.

**I encourage you to begin each day by saying, "Holy Spirit,
I will listen for Your leading today. Give me wisdom and
peace so I can move in step with Your guidance."**

Love Is Not Envious or Jealous

. . . Love never is envious nor boils over with jealousy.

1 CORINTHIANS 13:4

The Bible tells us that love is not envious or jealous, but jealousy is a little thing that can easily sneak into our lives if we are not careful. I have discovered the best way to get over envy or jealousy is to admit it. When you begin to feel jealous, be honest with God and ask Him to help you live free from it.

I must admit, like most people, I have dealt with jealousy at times in my life. There were days when I heard about a blessing that someone had received and I thought, *When will that happen for me?* But I've learned that when thoughts like that enter my mind, I need to immediately open my mouth and say, "I am happy for that person, and I refuse to be jealous and envious."

A mark of spiritual maturity—of living in close fellowship with God—is choosing to bless others and not be afraid they will get ahead of us. We can choose not to envy anyone else's appearance, possessions, education, social standing, marital status, gifts and talents, job, or anything else, because it will only hinder our own blessing.

Be confident in the gifts and talents you have. God has given you everything you need to fulfill His call on your life.

You Can Be Honest with God

Then He was praying in a certain place; and when He stopped,
one of His disciples said to Him, Lord, teach us to pray, [just] as
John taught his disciples.   LUKE 11:1

A successful prayer life is not developed overnight nor can it be copied from someone else. God has a personal plan for each of us. We cannot always do what someone else is doing and expect it to work for us. Our prayer life is progressive—it progresses as we progress.

Often our prayers are too vague, meaning they are not clearly expressed. When we pray, we can be clear and honest with the Lord. The Bible teaches that we can pray boldly, expectantly, specifically. Your heavenly Father loves you, so you can come fearlessly, confidently, and boldly to the throne of grace (Hebrews 4:16).

If you need help with your prayer life, be honest with God. Tell Him your needs. He will help you if you ask Him to do so. Like the disciples, simply ask, "Lord, teach me to pray."

An essential key to prayer is more confidence in the name of Jesus and less confidence in ourselves or anyone else to solve our problems. There is power in the name of Jesus.

Look How Far You've Come

So that [the genuineness] of your faith may be tested, [your faith] which is infinitely more precious than the perishable gold which is tested and purified by fire. [This proving of your faith is intended] to redound to [your] praise and glory and honor when Jesus Christ (the Messiah, the Anointed One) is revealed.   1 PETER 1:7

There are many tests that come our way every day. For example, our boss tells us to do something we don't want to do. Or we're going to pull into a parking space and someone zooms in and takes it. Or someone speaks rudely to us when we've done them a favor.

In 1 Peter 4:12, Peter tells us not to be amazed and bewildered by the tests that we have to endure because by them God is testing our "quality," or our character. Peter knew the value of being tested in his own life. We all go through them, and we shouldn't be confused about why they come our way. Our hearts are being tested in order to prove our character.

Every time God gives us a test, we can tell how far we've come and how far we still have to go by how we react in that test. Attitudes of the heart that we didn't even know we had can come out when we are in tests and trials. This is a good thing because we can never get to where we need to be if we don't recognize where we are.

Everything that God permits in our lives is for our good, even if it doesn't feel good at the time.

Everyone Has Limitations

Moses' father-in-law said to him, The thing that you are doing is not good.

You will surely wear out both yourself and this people with you, for the thing is too heavy for you; you are not able to perform it all by yourself.   EXODUS 18:17–18

God used Moses' father-in-law to tell Moses that he was trying to do too much. This is a message God is still speaking to many in the body of Christ today. Sometimes we like to think we are invincible. We don't like anybody telling us that something is too much for us to handle, and we push on and on despite what we feel.

I was always the kind of person who thought I could do anything I set my mind to. I was thoroughly convinced I could accomplish the task before me. If someone told me differently, it just made me determined to prove them wrong. I found out that if we have an attitude that we must do everything, no matter how tough the task is, we can hurt ourselves. It took some health problems to prove it to me. We cannot push ourselves beyond reasonable limits without eventually falling apart.

Here's the truth: God does not give us power for anything He does not tell us to do, but He always gives us the power and ability to do joyfully and peacefully all that He is leading us to do. God wants you to enjoy your life, and you cannot do that if you live under constant stress.

Are there any adjustments you need to make in order to be healthy, peaceful, and in balance?

Speaking Love to Others

Pleasant words are as a honeycomb, sweet to the mind and healing to the body.

PROVERBS 16:24

An important part of learning to really love other people is learning to love them with our words. The strength and encouragement we share with our words make a difference! People everywhere need someone to believe in them. They have been wounded by wrong words, but right words can bring healing in their lives.

It's easy to point out the flaws, weaknesses, and failures in those around us. This is a natural reaction, one that comes from our flesh. But these words don't bring life—they magnify all that is wrong with people and situations. But the Bible says in Romans 12:21 that we are to overcome evil with good.

The closer we are to God, the more we will learn to speak positive, encouraging words of life. God is positive, and as we walk with Him, we will learn to be in agreement with Him (Amos 3:3).

It is easy to find something wrong with everyone, but love overlooks the faults of others. First Peter 4:8 says it this way: "Above all things have intense and unfailing love for one another, for love covers a multitude of sins [forgives and disregards the offenses of others]."

Believing the best about people and speaking words that build them up is an important way of loving them.

Dealing with Disappointment

*We are assured and know that [God being a partner in their
labor] all things work together and are [fitting into a plan] for
good to and for those who love God and are called according to
[His] design and purpose.* ROMANS 8:28

There are many causes of disappointment, ranging from minor let-
downs to major setbacks, and Satan wants to use the disappointments in our life to steal our joy. He wants to keep us discouraged so
that we won't receive all that Jesus died to give us.

No matter what the causes of disappointment—physical, emotional, mental, or spiritual—as soon as we feel disappointment coming on, we can choose to resist it immediately and take whatever
action the Lord leads us to take.

As soon as we start feeling disappointed (especially if it is a recur-
ring issue), it is important for us to say to ourselves, *I'm going to
focus on the goodness of God in my life today. Whatever I may have lost
is nothing compared to all I have gained in Christ.* When you have this
attitude, it will keep those disappointments from turning to discouragement and even depression.

Jesus gave us the "garment of praise for the spirit of heaviness"
(Isaiah 61:3 KJV). This is something we can choose to put on rather
than sinking into despair when things don't go our way. Resisting
the enemy and making a conscious, determined choice to joyfully
praise God even in the tough times will allow you to overcome disappointments and be a powerful Christian each and every day.

**When you're not sure what to do, stand on the Word of
God and declare His promises over your life.**

Always Choose Life

Now the mind of the flesh [which is sense and reason without
the Holy Spirit] is death [death that comprises all the miseries
arising from sin, both here and hereafter]. But the mind of the
[Holy] Spirit is life and [soul] peace [both now and forever].

ROMANS 8:6

The best condition for our minds is—as Paul described in Philippians 4:8—pure, lovely and lovable, kind and winsome and gracious, thinking on those things that are virtuous and excellent. This is what it means to have the mind of Christ. I like to remind people that it is important that we think about what we're thinking about.

Many people falsely think that the source of their misery or trouble is something other than what it really is. They are blaming an outside condition when it is their own inner thoughts that are causing them trouble. But if we'll choose to "watch over" our thoughts, we can begin to take every thought captive into the obedience to Jesus Christ (2 Corinthians 10:5).

A big part of drawing close to God is submitting our thoughts to Him. When we do this, the Holy Spirit is quick to remind us if our minds are beginning to take us in a negative direction. The decision then becomes ours—will we continue down that path or will we choose to think with the mind of Christ? One way of thinking leads to frustration, negativity, and despair, the other leads to life. Choose life today!

––––––––––––

**Your thoughts, your words, your attitudes, and your
actions are all results of the daily choices you make.**

A Discerning Heart

Lean on, trust in, and be confident in the Lord with all your heart
and mind and do not rely on your own insight or understanding.
In all your ways know, recognize, and acknowledge Him, and He
will direct and make straight and plain your paths.

PROVERBS 3:5–6

People who tend to overthink things have a difficult time with faith. When we overthink something, worrying and obsessing about how we can fix a problem or create an opportunity, we are usually trusting in ourselves instead of God.

I used to be a class A, chief over-thinker. I had to have everything figured out. I had to have a plan all worked out in order to be happy. I was continually asking, "Why, God, why? When, God, when?" Then one day the Lord spoke to my heart and said, "As long as you continue to live in reasoning, you will never have discernment."

Discernment starts in the heart and moves up and enlightens the mind. As long as my mind was so busy reasoning apart from the Holy Spirit and contrary to the truth in the Word of God, Jesus could not get through to me. He wants us to use our mind to reason, but He wants us to reason in a way that lines up with His Word and allows Him to be in control.

I have discovered that I can reason in my mind about an issue until it begins to confuse me, and when that happens, it is my signal to let it go and wait for God to reveal to me what only He can show me.

If we try to figure out why everything happens in life,
we will not have peace of mind and heart.

Watch and Pray

*All of you must keep awake (give strict attention, be cautious
and active) and watch and pray, that you may not come into
temptation. The spirit indeed is willing, but the flesh is weak.*

MATTHEW 26:41

Fear is Satan's way of trying to prevent us from going forward so we
cannot enjoy the life Jesus died to give us. And fear attacks everyone
at some time. But fears are not realities. Fears are False Evidence
Appearing Real.

Fear is a force that can weaken our lives if we give in to it, but God
desires to strengthen us as we fellowship with Him in prayer. Faith is
released through prayer, which makes tremendous power available
for our lives.

The Bible teaches us to "watch and pray." With God's help, we
can watch ourselves and the circumstances around us and be alert
to the attacks the enemy launches against our minds and emotions.
When these attacks are detected, we can go to God immediately in
prayer. He is our strong tower, and when we are in Him there is nothing to fear.

The best way to resist the devil is to pray. Our honest, sincere
prayers draw us closer to God. And the closer we are to God, the
easier it is to dismiss fear.

**Pray about everything and fear nothing. When fear
knocks at the door, let faith answer.**

Be Usable

I appeal to you therefore, brethren, and beg of you in view of [all] the mercies of God, to make a decisive dedication of your bodies [presenting all your members and faculties] as a living sacrifice, holy (devoted, consecrated) and well pleasing to God, which is your reasonable (rational, intelligent) service and spiritual worship.
ROMANS 12:1

If you are a believer, your life has been consecrated to God, set apart for His use. You don't belong to yourself; you're a part of something bigger now. It is amazing to think that our lives are not our own; we have been bought with a price (1 Corinthians 6:20). We belong to God and our lives have a great purpose in Him!

As we get closer to God, we discover that we belong to Him, and that we are partners with Him in life and we should make ourselves available daily for His use.

I spent many years praying for God to give me what I wanted. "God, if only You would give me this or that, then I'd be happy." But God showed me joy comes when I submit my plans to Him. Instead of asking Him to do what I wanted, I began to learn to ask what He wanted for my life.

God simply requires that we be available and usable. All of us can do that! We can submit our lives to God, trusting Him to work out His good plan for our future.

We may not get everything we want. But if we'll trust God, we'll realize that what He wants for our lives is greater than anything we could imagine.

Developing Trust

So trust in the Lord (commit yourself to Him, lean on Him, hope confidently in Him) forever; for the Lord God is an everlasting Rock [the Rock of Ages].   ISAIAH 26:4

How many times have we allowed trying situations that come our way to frustrate us and get us needlessly upset? How many years of our lives have we spent saying, "Oh, I'm believing God. I'm trusting God," when in reality, we are worrying, talking negatively, and trying to figure everything out on our own?

Sometimes we think we are trusting God just because we are saying the words, but inside we are anxious and panicky. It is good that we are taking the initial steps to trust God, but we must also realize we can still grow in trust. Trusting God is more than just words—it's words, attitudes, and actions.

Trust and confidence are built up over a period of time. It usually takes some time to overcome an ingrained habit of worry, anxiety, or fear. That is why it is so important to "hang in there" with God. Don't quit and give up, because you gain experience and spiritual strength as you go through situations. Each time you become a little stronger than you were the last time. Sooner or later, if you don't give up, you will find yourself in a place of complete rest, peace, and trust in God.

If you are in a time of trial, realize that worry is completely useless, and use the time to build your trust in God.

Do Your Best and Let God Do the Rest

Not that I am implying that I was in any personal want, for I have learned how to be content (satisfied to the point where I am not disturbed or disquieted) in whatever state I am.

PHILIPPIANS 4:11

We function best when we have a calm, well-balanced mind. When our mind is calm, it is without fear, worry, or torment. When our mind is well balanced, we are able to look the situation over and decide what to do or not to do about it.

Where many of us get in trouble is when we get out of balance. Either we move into a state of total passivity in which we do nothing, expecting God to do everything for us, or we become hyperactive, operating most of the time in the flesh. The closer we are to God, the more well balanced we become. We are able to face any situation of life and say, "I will do what God leads me to do, but I trust Him to do the rest."

It is useless to keep trying things that are not working. Wait on God and be obedient to Him, and realize that His timing is perfect in your life. Even if God seems to be doing nothing about your situation, don't panic. As long as you are trusting God, He is working, and you will see the results in due time.

Once we have done what God asks us to do, we can trust Him with the rest.

The Reward of Sharing Love

By this shall all [men] know that you are My disciples, if you love one another [if you keep on showing love among yourselves].

JOHN 13:35

One of the best ways to share Jesus with the world is to simply show love to others. Jesus Himself taught on love and walked in love, because that is what the world needs. The world needs to know that God is love and He loves each person unconditionally (1 John 4:8).

The Word of God teaches that God wants us to be committed to developing the character of Jesus Christ in our own lives and then go out as Christ's ambassadors to the world (2 Corinthians 5:20).

To be His ambassadors, it is crucial that we have our minds renewed to what love really is. Love is not merely a feeling we have; it is a decision to treat people the way Jesus would treat them.

When we truly commit to walking in love, it usually causes a huge shift in our lifestyle. Many of our ways—our thoughts, our conversation, our habits—need to change. Love is tangible; it is evident to everyone who comes in contact with it.

Loving others does not come easily or without personal sacrifice. Each time we choose to love someone, it will cost us something—time, money, or effort. But the reward of loving others is far greater than the cost ever is.

———————

Loving others does not depend on our feelings; it's a choice we make.

Understanding Your Forgiveness

In Him we have redemption (deliverance and salvation)
through His blood, the remission (forgiveness) of our offenses
(shortcomings and trespasses), in accordance with the riches and
the generosity of His gracious favor.   EPHESIANS 1:7

One of the biggest obstacles that keeps us from celebrating the life
that God has freely bestowed upon us is our own sin consciousness.
Sin is a problem for everyone, but it does not have to be the compli-
cating problem we tend to make it.

That we struggle with our sins is a huge understatement. When
we make a mistake, display a weakness, or fail in any way, we often
doubt that God loves us, wonder if He is angry with us, try to do all
kinds of good works to atone for our failure, and surrender our joy as
a sacrifice for our error.

God desires to give us the gift of forgiveness. When we confess
our sins to Him, He forgives us of our sins, puts them away from
Him as far as the East is from the West, and remembers them no
more (Psalm 103:12). But for us to benefit from that forgiveness, it is
essential we receive it by faith.

When I was a new believer, each night I would beg God's forgiveness for my past sins. One evening as I knelt beside my bed, the Lord
spoke to my heart, "I forgave you the first time you asked, but you
have not received My gift because you have not forgiven yourself."

**Jesus bore your sins on the cross, and He offers forgive-
ness. You don't have to condemn yourself anymore.**

Conscious of Your Righteousness

*For our sake He made Christ [virtually] to be sin Who knew
no sin, so that in and through Him we might become [endued
with, viewed as being in, and examples of] the righteousness
of God [what we ought to be, approved and acceptable and in
right relationship with Him, by His goodness].*

2 CORINTHIANS 5:21

Believers who are living in close fellowship with God are not going
to think about how terrible they are. They will have righteousness-
based thoughts that come through meditating regularly on who
they are "in Christ."

Yet a large number of Christians are tormented by negative
thoughts about how sinful they are, or how displeased God is with
them because of their weaknesses and failures. How much time is
wasted living under guilt and condemnation?

I encourage you to think about how you have been made the
righteousness of God in Christ Jesus. Remember: Thoughts turn
into actions. If you want to enjoy the life Jesus died to give you, it is
important to align your thinking with God's Word.

Every time a negative, condemning thought comes to your mind,
remind yourself that God loves you, and that you have been made
righteous in Christ.

**You are changing for the better all the time. Every day
you're growing spiritually. God has a glorious plan
for your life.**

God Hears and Understands

And this is the confidence (the assurance, the privilege of
boldness) which we have in Him: [we are sure] that if we ask
anything (make any request) according to His will (in agreement
with His own plan), He listens to and hears us.   1 JOHN 5:14

Prayer is one of the things that reflects our closeness to God and
our confidence in Him. If we pray about everything instead of worrying and trying to work it out ourselves, we say by our attitude and
actions, "Lord, I trust You in this situation."

I believe many of us pray and then wonder if God heard. We wonder if we prayed properly or long enough. We wonder if we used the
right phrases, enough Scripture, and so on. We cannot pray properly
with doubt and unbelief. Prayer requires faith.

God has been encouraging me to realize that simple faith-filled
prayer gets the job done. I don't have to repeat things over and over.
I don't need to get fancy in my wording. I can just be me and know
that He hears and understands me.

I encourage you to simply present your request and believe that
God has heard you and will answer at the right time. Have confidence when you pray. Know that God hears and is delighted by simple, childlike prayer coming from a sincere heart.

**Trust God to answer your prayers in His way and in
His perfect timing.**

Chosen by God

You have not chosen Me, but I have chosen you and I have
appointed you [I have planted you], that you might go and bear
fruit....   JOHN 15:16

When God chooses us for His divine plans and purposes, He uses different criteria than what the world uses. The world chooses people based upon their looks, their talent, education, or their accomplishments, but God doesn't do that. In fact, 1 Corinthians 1:26–29 tells us that God chooses what the world thinks is foolish to put the wise to shame, and what the world calls weak to put the strong to shame.

I am so glad to know God deliberately chooses us despite our weaknesses. When God got the idea for *Joyce Meyer Ministries*, He didn't look for the most qualified. He chose someone who loved Him, someone who would work hard, and someone who was determined. I had no special talent, except I communicated well, but even then, my voice was a bit unusual. I am sure the world would have rejected me as unqualified, but thankfully God didn't.

What was true for my life is true for yours too. People may look at the exterior, but God looks at the heart. There may be others more qualified or talented, but His choice is not based on appearance, education, possessions, or even talents. It is based on your heart attitude. If you have a good heart toward God and an available attitude, God can do more through your life than you ever thought possible.

If we continue being faithful to God, we will eventually get where God wants us to be.

Refuse to Give Up

Also [Jesus] told them a parable to the effect that they ought always to pray and not to turn coward (faint, lose heart, and give up).   LUKE 18:1

Many people drift backward when things get difficult, but with God's help we can press forward no matter how tough things seem. It's not always easy, but it's always worth it. Victory is on the other side if we will keep pressing ahead.

Jesus told us in John 16:33: "In this world you will have trouble. But take heart! I have overcome the world" (NIV). Just because we go through a difficulty, we don't have to despair and give up. We can believe that Jesus has overcome every trouble, and we can "take heart." We weren't created to turn back in the face of trouble; we were created to be strong in the Lord and in His mighty power. If we never had a challenge, we would not need faith.

There are numerous examples of people in the Bible who simply refused to give up. Zacchaeus could not be kept from Jesus, despite his shortcomings. The woman with the issue of blood pressed through the crowd and was rewarded for her determination. They reached their objectives because they boldly pressed ahead to receive all that God had for them.

When faced with an obstacle, instead of drifting back in fear, ask God to give you the strength and courage to go forward in Him.

When you feel like quitting, make the declaration: "I will not give up! God is with me, and He will help me move forward one step at a time!"

Letting Love Win the War

For though we walk (live) in the flesh, we are not carrying on our
warfare according to the flesh and using mere human weapons.
For the weapons of our warfare are not physical [weapons of flesh
and blood], but they are mighty before God for the overthrow and
destruction of strongholds.   2 CORINTHIANS 10:3–4

We are definitely in a war. The Bible teaches us that the weapons
of our warfare are not carnal, natural weapons, but ones that are
mighty through God for the pulling down of strongholds.

Part of growing closer to God is working with the Holy Spirit
in pulling down the strongholds of selfishness, pride, and self-
importance. Purposely taking the focus off of ourselves and doing
something for someone else while we are hurting is one of the most
important things we can do to overcome evil.

When Jesus was on the cross in intense suffering, He took time to
comfort the thief next to Him (Luke 23:39–43). When Stephen was
being stoned, he prayed for those stoning him, asking God not to lay
the sin to their charge (Acts 7:59–60).

If the church of Jesus Christ, His body here on earth, will wage
war against selfishness and walk in love, the world will begin to take
notice.

————————

**Walking in love is an important part of spiritual
warfare.**

From Glory to Glory

And all of us, as with unveiled face, [because we] continued to
behold [in the Word of God] as in a mirror the glory of the Lord,
are constantly being transfigured into His very own image in
ever increasing splendor and from one degree of glory to another;
[for this comes] from the Lord [Who is] the Spirit.

2 CORINTHIANS 3:18

How do you see yourself?

Are you able to honestly evaluate yourself and your behavior and not come under condemnation? Are you able to look honestly at how far you still have to go, but also at how far you have come?

In 2 Corinthians 3:18, Paul states that God changes us "from one degree of glory to another." In other words, the changes in us personally, as well as those in our circumstances, take place in degrees. Where you are now is not where you will end up.

If you are born again, then you are somewhere on the path of the righteous. You may not be as far along as you would like to be, but thank God you are on the path. Enjoy the glory you are in right now and don't get jealous of where others may be, or condemned about where you are. Perhaps we won't pass into the next degree of glory until we have learned to enjoy the one we are in at the moment.

Don't be too hard on yourself. God is changing you day by day and drawing you closer to Him.

Faith Is the Antidote

For God did not give us a spirit of timidity (of cowardice, of craven and cringing and fawning fear), but [He has given us a spirit] of power and of love and of calm and well-balanced mind and discipline and self-control.   2 TIMOTHY 1:7

If you're dealing with doubt, worry, anxiety, or fear in any area of your life today, faith is the antidote.

Think of it this way: If you or I ingested some kind of poison, we would need an antidote right away. The same is true when dealing with the toxic poisons of doubt, worry, anxiety, and fear. There must be an antidote received—and that antidote is faith.

When these joy-stealers come knocking at our door, we can answer with faith, knowing that our faith in God defeats the enemy and will draw us closer to Him and allow us to rest and find safety in Him.

James 1:5–7 tells us that when we find ourselves in need of something, we can pray in faith, and God will answer without faultfinding. This is simple, but very important. Even if we have not been perfect in our ways, all we have to do is ask God with faith, and He will help us!

———————

Put your faith in the Lord. He has the power to deliver you and set your life in a whole new direction.

Believing the Best

*... For out of the fullness (the overflow, the superabundance) of
the heart the mouth speaks.* MATTHEW 12:34

The person who is close to God thinks positive, uplifting, edifying
thoughts about other people as well as about himself and his own
circumstances.

You exhort others with your words only after you have first had
kind thoughts about that individual. Remember that whatever is in
your heart will come out of your mouth (Mathew 12:34). Thoughts
and words are containers or weapons for carrying creative or
destructive power (Proverbs 18:21). This is why it is so important to
do some "love thinking" on purpose.

I encourage you to send thoughts of love toward other people.
Speak words of encouragement. Come alongside others and urge
them to press forward in their spiritual life. Speak words that make
others feel better and that encourage and strengthen them.

Everyone has enough problems already. We don't need to add to
their troubles by tearing them down. We can build up one another in
love (1 Thessalonians 5:11). Love always believes the best of everyone (1 Corinthians 13:7).

**We are living in obedience to the Word of God when
our thoughts, actions, and attitudes line up with
what it says.**

Better Than Self-Confidence

I have strength for all things in Christ Who empowers me
[I am ready for anything and equal to anything through Him
Who infuses inner strength into me; I am self-sufficient in
Christ's sufficiency].   PHILIPPIANS 4:13

Confidence is generally referred to as "self-confidence" because we all know that we need to feel good about ourselves if we are ever to accomplish anything in life. We have been taught that all people have a basic need to believe in themselves. However, that is not the complete truth.

More than believing in ourselves—we need to believe in Jesus in us. We can't really think highly of ourselves apart from Him. We can do amazing things, but only through Christ!

If we believe the false assumption of "self-confidence," we will create many complicated problems. We will live in fear and insecurity, and we will settle for less than our full potential in Christ.

Don't be concerned about yourself, your weaknesses, or your strengths. Put your focus squarely on God. If you are weak, He can strengthen you. If you have any strength, it is because He gave it to you. Either way, focus on the Lord and place your confidence in Him.

We do not need self-confidence; we need God-confidence.

Two Powerful Words for Your Life

... Fear not; stand still (firm, confident, undismayed) and see the salvation of the Lord which He will work for you today ...

EXODUS 14:13

Jesus said that the devil is a liar and the father of all lies (John 8:44). The truth is not in him. He tries to use falsehood to deceive God's people into fear so they will not be bold enough to be obedient to the Lord and reap the blessings He has in store for them.

Often the fear of something is worse than the thing itself. If we will be courageous and determined to do whatever it is we fear, we will discover it is not nearly as bad as we thought it would be.

Throughout the Word of God we find the Lord saying to His people, "Fear not." I believe the reason He did that was to encourage them so they would not allow Satan to rob them of their blessing.

In the same way, because He knows we tend to be fearful, the Lord continues to exhort and encourage us to press through what lies before us to do His will. Why? Because He knows that great blessings await us.

The enemy wants to tell you that your current situation is evidence that your future will be a failure, but the Bible teaches us that no matter what our present circumstances, nothing is impossible with God (Mark 9:23).

There is victory in store for your life if you'll put these two words into practice: Fear not.

A Grateful Attitude

Enter into His gates with thanksgiving and a thank offering and into His courts with praise! Be thankful and say so to Him, bless and affectionately praise His name!   PSALM 100:4

A person flowing in the mind of Christ will find his thoughts filled with praise and thanksgiving. A powerful life cannot be lived without thanksgiving. The Bible instructs us over and over in the principle of thanksgiving. It is a life principle.

Many doors are opened to the enemy through complaining. Some people are physically ill and live weak, powerless lives due to this disease called complaining that attacks the thoughts and conversations of people.

We can offer thanksgiving at all times—in every situation, in all things—and by so doing, enter into the victorious life Jesus died to give us. It may require a sacrifice of praise or thanksgiving, but a person who consciously takes the time to be grateful is always happier than someone who does not.

You can choose to be filled with gratitude not only toward God but also toward people. Expressing appreciation blesses the people around you, but it is also good for you because it releases joy in your life.

Offer thanksgiving to God, and as you do, you will find your heart filling with life and light.

Grace Versus Works

*[Therefore, I do not treat God's gracious gift as something of
minor importance and defeat its very purpose]; I do not set aside
and invalidate and frustrate and nullify the grace (unmerited
favor) of God. For if justification (righteousness, acquittal from
guilt) comes through [observing the ritual of] the Law, then
Christ (the Messiah) died groundlessly and to no purpose...*

GALATIANS 2:21

It is curious that we come to God through Christ just as we are, relying on nothing but the blood of Jesus to cleanse us from our sins.
Our hearts are full of gratitude because we know we don't deserve it.
But from that moment on, for some reason, we tend to want to earn
everything else He gives us.

We assume God won't bless us because we think we don't deserve
it. We didn't read the Bible enough, didn't pray enough, or lost our
temper in traffic. We find a million ways to be disqualified from
God's love. God never stops loving us, but we often stop receiving it.

Despite all our emphasis on faith, we try to live a life that was
brought into being and designed by God to be lived by grace in
our own strength, by works. It's no wonder we feel frustrated and
confused—both are signs that we are out of grace and into works.

When you have a problem in your life that you do not know how
to handle, what you need is not more figuring and reasoning, but
more grace. If you can't find a solution to your problem, simply trust
God to reveal it to you. You don't have to earn God's help or qualify
for it—He wants to equip and empower you every single day through
His grace.

Where works fail, grace always succeeds.

Comfortable and Confident in Prayer

Be unceasing in prayer [praying perseveringly].

1 THESSALONIANS 5:17

The closer we are in our relationship with God, the more confident we become in prayer. The truth is that God wants us to be so confident and comfortable in prayer that it becomes like breathing, an effortless action that we do every moment we are alive. We don't work and struggle at breathing, and neither will we in prayer if we understand its simplicity.

To pray without ceasing like Paul talks about in 1 Thessalonians 5:17 does not mean that we must be offering some kind of formal prayer every moment twenty-four hours a day. It means that all throughout the day we can be in a prayerful attitude. As we encounter each situation or as things come to our minds that need attention, we can simply submit them to God in prayer. I often say, "Pray your way through the day."

Don't forget: It is not the length or loudness or eloquence of prayer that makes it powerful—prayer is made powerful by the sincerity of it and the faith behind it.

We can pray anywhere at anytime about anything. Our prayers can be verbal or silent, long or short, public or private—the most important thing is that we pray.

Closer to God Each Day

For this is My Father's will and His purpose, that everyone who sees the Son and believes in and cleaves to and trusts in and relies on Him should have eternal life, and I will raise him up [from the dead] at the last day.   JOHN 6:40

The life for a Christian was never meant to be all about following rules and meeting a list of requirements. Yes, God gives us directions and instructions for living, but these aren't meant to be religious duties; they are principles that will help us discover the joyful, abundant, overflowing life Jesus died to give us.

God desires for you to move past "religion" and live in a deep, close, intimate relationship with Him. This is what it means to be closer to God. He is not some distant deity who is legalistic, cold and out of reach. God is your heavenly Father Who loves you unconditionally and without fail.

No matter what happened in your past, no matter how many times you've failed, no matter what disadvantages you think you may have, you can live in close relationship to God. He will forgive you. He will comfort you. He will walk with you. And He will never leave you or forsake you.

God loves you more than you could ever imagine. All you have to do is receive His love today.

Living "closer to God each day" is simply a matter of receiving God's love and learning to love Him in return.

About the Author

Joyce Meyer is one of the world's leading practical Bible teachers. Her daily broadcast, *Enjoying Everyday Life*, airs on hundreds of television networks and radio stations worldwide.

Joyce has written more than 100 inspirational books. Her best sellers include *Power Thoughts*; *The Confident Woman*; *Look Great, Feel Great*; *Starting Your Day Right*; *Ending Your Day Right*; *Approval Addiction*; *How to Hear from God*; *Beauty for Ashes*; and *Battlefield of the Mind*.

Joyce travels extensively, holding conferences throughout the year and speaking to thousands around the world.

Other Books by Joyce Meyer

Devotionals

* Also available in Spanish

Joyce Meyer Ministries

P.O. Box 655
Fenton, MO 63026
USA
(636) 349-0303

Joyce Meyer Ministries—Canada

P.O. Box 7700
Vancouver, BC V6B 4E2
Canada
(800) 868-1002

Joyce Meyer Ministries—Australia

Locked Bag 77
Mansfield Delivery Centre
Queensland 4122
Australia
(07) 3349 1200

Joyce Meyer Ministries—England

P.O. Box 1549
Windsor SL4 1GT
United Kingdom
01753 831102

Joyce Meyer Ministries—South Africa

P.O. Box 5
Cape Town 8000
South Africa
(27) 21-701-1056